Identity, Politics and the Study of Islam

Culture on the Edge: Studies in Identity Formation
Series Editor: Steven W. Ramey, University of Alabama

Editorial Board:

Leslie Dorrough Smith, Avila University
Craig Martin, St Thomas Aquinas College
Russell T. McCutcheon, University of Alabama
K. Merinda Simmons, University of Alabama
Vaia Touna, University of Alabama

Culture on the Edge is devoted to studies – both monographs and collections of essays – that explore how social formation involves a series of strategies that present identity as static and uniform. Volumes in this series study identity formation as a sequence of interconnected historical practices, revealing ways that the image of stable selves and groups conceals the precarious and shifting nature of cultures.

Published:

Claiming Identity in the Study of Religion: Social and Rhetorical Techniques Examined
Edited by Monica R. Miller

Forthcoming:

Identifying Roots: Alex Haley and the Anthropology of Scriptures
Edited by Richard Newton

Strategic Acts in the Study of Identity: Towards a Dynamic Theory of People and Place
Edited by Vaia Touna

Identity, Politics and the Study of Islam

Current Dilemmas in the Study of Religions

Edited by
Matt Sheedy

SHEFFIELD UK   BRISTOL CT

Published by Equinox Publishing Ltd.

UK: Office 415, The Workstation, 15 Paternoster Row, Sheffield, South Yorkshire S1 2BX
USA: ISD, 70 Enterprise Drive, Bristol, CT 06010

www.equinoxpub.com

First published 2018

© Matt Sheedy and contributors 2018

All rights reserved. No part of this publication may be reproduced or transmitted in any form or by any means, electronic or mechanical, including photocopying, recording or any information storage or retrieval system, without prior permission in writing from the publishers.

British Library Cataloguing-in-Publication Data
A catalogue record for this book is available from the British Library.

ISBN-13 978 1 78179 488 3   (hardback)
         978 1 78179 489 0   (paperback)
         978 1 78179 713 6   (ePDF)

Library of Congress Cataloging-in-Publication Data
Names: Sheedy, Matt, editor.
Title: Identity, politics and the study of Islam : current dilemmas in the study of religions / edited by Matt Sheedy.
Description: Bristol, CT : Equinox Publishing Ltd., 2018. | Series: Culture on the edge | Includes bibliographical references and index.
Identifiers: LCCN 2018001726 (print) | LCCN 2018005867 (ebook) | ISBN 9781781797136 (ePDF) | ISBN 9781781794883 (hb) | ISBN 9781781794890 (pb)
Subjects: LCSH: Islam and politics. | Identity politics.
Classification: LCC BP173.7 (ebook) | LCC BP173.7 .I175 2018 (print) | DDC 297.07–dc23
LC record available at https://lccn.loc.gov/2018001726

Typeset by S.J.I. Services, New Delhi
Printed and bound by Lightning Source Inc. (La Vergne, TN), Lightning Source UK Ltd. (Milton Keynes), Lightning Source AU Pty. (Scoresby, Victoria).

Contents

Introduction
Identity, Apologetics and the Shapes of Critique in the
Study of Islam 1
Matt Sheedy

Part I: Theory and Identity Politics in the Study of Islam

1. The Modesty of Theory 19
   Ruth Mas

2. "I Want My Discipline Back" 43
   Salman Sayyid

Part II: Critique and Identity in Qur'anic Studies

3. Religion, History, Ethics: Rethinking the Crisis of
   Western Qur'anic Studies 69
   Alexandre Caeiro and Emmanuelle Stefanidis

4. Identity Politics and the Study of Islamic Origins: The
   Inscriptions of the Dome of the Rock as a Test Case 98
   Carlos A. Segovia

Part III: Comparative Views from Outside Islamic Studies

5. Jews, Jewish Studies and the Study of Islam 121
   Sarah Imhoff

6. The Quest for the Historical: Can Biblical Studies Lead
   Qur'anic Studies away from Theology? 138
   James Crossley

Part IV: A Critical Appraisal

7. A Modest Proposal for Islamic Studies   157
   Devin Stewart

   Afterword
   The Meaning and End of Scholarship on Religion   201
   Russell T. McCutcheon

   Index   224

Introduction

Identity, Apologetics and the Shapes of Critique in the Study of Islam

Matt Sheedy

The initial idea for this collection of essays came out of a post by Aaron W. Hughes that appeared on the *Bulletin for the Study of Religion* blog on February 3, 2014, "When Bad Scholarship Is Just Bad Scholarship: A Response to Omid Safi" (Hughes 2014). Hughes was writing in reply to a post by Safi dated January 31, 2014, "Reflections on the State of Islamic Studies" (Safi 2014), which appeared on the ezine *Jadaliyya*. If one searches their respective Wikipedia pages, the exchange is listed as a "public dispute," although this section has since been taken down from Safi's page. The section from Hughes's page reads as follows:

> In the 2012 book *Theorizing Islam*, Hughes had written critically about the scholarship of Omid Safi, a professor of Islamic studies at the University of North Carolina at Chapel Hill, and other scholars in the academic study of Islam. In January 2014, Safi published a piece on the ezine *Jadaliyya* presenting his "impressions about the state of Islamic studies in the North American academy." In the course of the article, in which he [Safi] expressed his concern regarding unreconstructed orthodox Muslim voices entering the American academy, he stated that Hughes and two other scholars had written "pieces attacking and critiquing the prominence of Muslim scholars in the Study of Islam Section." Specifically, he described Hughes' piece as "grossly polemical and simplistic." In response, Hughes characterized Safi as calling him a racist, and demanded that he "do what the Western tradition of scholarly discourse demands and

respond to my ideas in print as opposed to engaging in innuendo and identity politics." He further suggested that Safi may have been motivated by Hughes' Jewish background, adding sarcastically, "[w]e all know that Jews are the arch-enemy of Islam."
(Wikipedia)

It is not surprising to see Roland Barthes's "death of the author" on full display here, where this so-called "dispute" is reduced to identity politics, distorting what is at stake both for Safi and for Hughes. Although blogging as an academic form is distinct from traditional modes of scholarship, its immediacy and accessibility can have the effect of transforming what would otherwise be a limited conversation among specialists into a public conversation with the ability to reach a wider audience, and to even spur the creation of intellectual products like the one you are reading here.

One possible downside to blogging is that it can be more easily appropriated than traditional modes of scholarship since its aim is typically not to make an extended argument with footnotes, but rather to offer a brief commentary, most often in direct response to current affairs. Religions scholar Tim Murphy frames this problem in relation to the tension between practical and theoretical reason: whereas politics in the public realm (especially in the news and social media) is driven by practical questions that concern the "here and now," and often presents issues in a narrow and partisan fashion, the scholar aims to make careful distinctions with attention to theory and method as a guiding framework. In this sense, the scholar has (or at least should have) more room to "wait and see" where the data lead without the same kind of pressure to choose sides or stake a normative claim that we find in political disputes (Murphy 2000: 188). This is not, of course, to suggest that scholarship is disinterested, but rather to signal that the tangled webs of scholarly and political concerns – the "here and now" vs. the "wait and see" – are perennial sources of controversy that require ongoing attention, especially in an age of social media as the range of narratives and mediums expands into the ether.

One example of the political uses to which scholarly "disputes" can be reduced comes from a 2014 article entitled "New Wave or

Clever Ruse" that appeared on *Campus Watch*, a web-based project of the Middle East Forum that critics describe as a neo-conservative outlet dedicated to calling out scholars who are critical of the state of Israel. In this post, author Jay Schalin muses about whether Safi, in his role as director of Duke University's Islamic Studies Center (DISC), ignores "Islam's supremacist side" in favor of a progressive Muslim agenda, or, what is worse, if his work provides "cover for violent jihadists." Schalin goes on to note that Hughes describes Safi (in his book *Theorizing Islam*) as ignoring "Islam's supremacist side," writing:

> He [Hughes] says that Safi belongs to a new wave of American Muslim academics who are "interested in creating a liberal Islam that they believe is in keeping with Western, democratic values." Yet their rejection of Islam's troubling aspects only extends so far, and they tend to judge the Western world much more harshly. While Safi has indeed spoken out against terrorist organizations such as the Taliban, al-Qaeda, and Boko Haram, he does not explore their existence critically as a real part of Islam. (Schalin 2014)

A few things are worth noting here. While it is not surprising that an ideologically-driven web forum would caricature Safi's work and distort Hughes's critique,[1] Schalin's framing of these issues reveals a common trope in representations of Islam (and of religions in general) that is often found in political commentary and in much scholarship up to the present – namely, the ahistorical deployment of "religion" as a self-evident category that can be used to describe the identities and motivations of disparate peoples, both past and present. In this sense, the main issue for Hughes is not that creating a "liberal Islam" detracts from acknowledging its "troubling aspects" per se, as he has acknowledged the political value of such an endeavor in several

---

1 For example, he refers to Hughes as "a professor of Jewish Studies at the University of Rochester who writes about modern Islamic scholarship," thus implying that he has a sectarian bone to pick, and ignoring that he is also a scholar of Islam, and trained as such.

places,[2] but that such a move often confuses political aspirations with the wide range of variations found in any large social formation that the scholar is tasked with historicizing. This is a point that Hughes tries to make in a more recent work when he writes:

> Rather than judge the Islamic bona fides of groups such as Boko Haram and ISIS, why not attempt to explain such groups within the larger context of globalization, religious fundamentalism, the crisis of Islamic masculinities, and the intersection of politics and religion? ... If we did this, we might say that groups like Boko Haram and ISIS are engaged in acts of legitimation based on the manipulation of a set of finite symbols that the tradition of Islam considers normative (e.g., Qur'an, Sunna). In this, they are not any different than any other social group, including those that say such versions of Islam are inauthentic, that sits under the canopy we often label, monothetically and monovocally, as "Islam." (2015: xxi)

One of the aims of the *Culture on the Edge* book series is to reflect critically on various aspects of the identity formation of social groups, which does, admittedly, align more closely with certain aspects of Hughes's work than with Safi's. The aims of this series are described as follows:

> *Culture on the Edge* is devoted to studies – both monographs and collections of essays – that explore how social formation involves a series of strategies that present identity as static and uniform. Volumes in this series study identity formation as a sequence of interconnected historical practices, revealing ways that the image of stable selves and groups conceals the precarious and shifting nature of cultures.

It should be stressed, however, that the point of this collection of essays is not to choose sides in this "dispute," but to attempt to situate the ideas and concerns that it raises and place them within a broader framework of theoretical, methodological and political debates within

---

2   See, for example, Hughes (2013: 234–336; 2015: 18, 32, 63–4, 76, 82, 84, 89).

Introduction 5

the subfield of Islamic studies, and in the broader study of religions. Accordingly, the contributors are not limited to Islamic studies scholars, but also include a scholar of contemporary Judaism and a scholar of early Christianity, in order to highlight the interdisciplinary nature of these concerns.

Initial Provocations

Safi opens his remarks by noting how he had been asked to share his thoughts on *Jadaliyya* about the "state of Islamic studies in the North American academy," and proceeds to trace an arch from his graduate work in Islamic studies in the early 1990s, where he notes that most students were "converts" and jobs in Islam were few and far between, to the present-day state of the field, where he finds both drastic improvements as well as problems still in need of redress.

Safi's concern is both to remind a new generation of scholars of Islam of the many battles that have been fought over the last several decades, as well as to critique the current state of Islamic studies as he sees it. Accordingly, he reminds scholars of the shift that took place from the study of Islam within Middle and Near Eastern area studies toward a more integrated relationship with the American Academy of Religion (AAR), which he deems a positive step, where the latter's theoretical focus meant taking feminist, postcolonial and anthropological insights seriously, as well as "the work being done in different realms of 'theory', the Said and post-Said critique, and more."

In light of this history, Safi remarks that he is pained to see scholars of Islamic studies today, especially Muslim scholars, "who move through the discussions of normative/descriptive approaches to religion without an awareness of how much effort has gone into working out the uneasy compromises in the religion academy." Indeed, it is "Muslim" scholars in particular with whom he appears most concerned, especially those who "dismiss minority opinions in the Islamic traditions" in favor of a particular normative (theological) position. In this context, Safi also notes a backlash from other scholarly quarters, which is where his comment about Hughes appears.

> One indication of the rising prominence of Muslim scholars of Islamic studies is that over the last few years we have seen three separate pieces attacking and critiquing the prominence of Muslim scholars in the Study of Islam Section. These have ranged from friendly concern (Richard Martin's) to inaccurately outdated (David Freidenreich's) to grossly polemical and simplistic (Aaron Hughes'). Yet the increasing frequency of these attacks/responses from non-Muslim scholars is one indication that something fundamental has changed.

These lines are followed by remarks about the influx of women and scholars of color in the Islamic studies section at the AAR, which Safi lauds as "remarkable achievements," while also stressing the lack of theoretical knowledge among Muslim graduate students. Given the importance and prominence of the study of Islam within religious studies since 9/11, Safi cautions Muslim scholars to avoid proselytizing and adapt to the broader theoretical aims of religious studies at the risk of becoming marginalized or irrelevant. For Safi, scholars such as "Sherman Jackson, Amina Wadud, Jonathan Brown, Kecia Ali, [and] Ingrid Mattson" are all models of those who have been able to work effectively between the "academy" and the "community," which he upholds as a path for the future.

Aaron Hughes's response to Omid Safi takes aim at what he sees as a thinly veiled charge of Islamophobia against him and seeks to clarify that his concerns reside solely with examining the lines between good and bad scholarship, especially the preponderance of "particularistic and apologetical concerns" that he sees Safi and others putting forward in place of "non-apologetical Humanities scholarship."

Hughes notes how he has criticized Safi in print (see Hughes 2012b: 13, 16, 17, 20–3, 24, 34, 111–12, 120, 128) for his "historically inaccurate portrayal of Muhammad" and thus has provided evidence for his claim of Safi's "bad scholarship."

> It is based on a misreading of the sources, of wanting to find solid ground when all we possess is quicksand, of engaging in hermeneutical *legerdemain*. I counter his utopic vision with a dystopian universe. And I do so, moreover, with fact and with argumentation, not with insinuation. I don't care whether he is

a Muslim, a Christian, a Jew, a Buddhist, or a member of the Seneca First Nation. I care about scholarship. I do so because, as a scholar, my first commitment is to uncovering truth. Not to apologetics; not to wishful thinking.

Hughes takes issue with Safi calling out scholars of Islam who also hold positions in Jewish studies, such as himself and David Freidenreich, and wonders whether he is trading in innuendo and identity politics and thereby reinforcing a line in the sand between insiders and outsiders (i.e., Muslims and non-Muslims) within the study of Islam? Moreover, he asks for evidence as to why Safi feels that his work is "grossly polemical and simplistic" and challenges him to back up his claim with argumentation.

In his recent book *Islam and the Tyranny of Authenticity* (2015), Hughes revisits his debate with Safi and adds some follow-up remarks that are worth mentioning here. To the best of my knowledge, Safi has not revisited this debate at the time of this writing. In a chapter titled "Business as Usual," Hughes considers Safi's comment, quoted above, regarding Muslim scholars of Islamic studies "who move through the discussions of normative/descriptive approaches to religion without an awareness of how much effort has gone into working out the uneasy compromises in the religion academy." As Hughes reads it, by "normative/descriptive" Safi is referring to the exclusion of, in his own words, "Shi'a, Sufis, philosophers, or feminists" in the face of more orthodox varieties of Islam, leading Hughes to conclude that the main problem for Safi is less "about intellectual or historical integrity and more about theological turf wars between rival Islams" (76). While Safi is encouraged, as also quoted above, that scholars of Islamic studies have begun to embrace feminist, postcolonial and anthropological insights, as well as "the work being done in different realms of 'theory', the Said and post-Said critique," Hughes reads this statement as placing a limit on what constitutes "theory." He elaborates:

> It thus dawned on me that what counts for "theory" for one person or group might not count as "theory" for another. For those in Islamic religious studies, the AAR provides the ideal forum in which to discuss issues of gender and post-colonial

theory inspired by the writings of Edward Said. ... Others, however, myself included, have real difficulties with what passes as theorizing at the AAR. Rather than [to] engage in reifying or essentializing gender, race or religion when it suits us, the goal of theory ought to be to undermine such claims and show their investment in a host of political and ideological processes. (77)

What is ultimately at stake here for Hughes is in determining Islamic religious study's "theoretical first principles" (78). Such principles, he argues, should hold that theory is "about dismantling what we hold dear" and not, as he reads Safi, in serving to buttress "truth claims." One further problem for Hughes, which he spends the rest of the chapter critiquing, is that the scholars Safi holds up as role models for Islamic religious studies – Sherman Jackson, Amina Wadud, Jonathan Brown, Kecia Ali and Ingrid Mattson – are all "Muslim scholar activists," which he argues may leave "the non-Muslim who wants to engage in historical or literary scholarship" in a predicament if they are not willing or able to assent to these preferred terms of activism and apologetics to guide their work.

While this short, informal exchange between two contemporary scholars of Islam does not by itself tell us much about their work as a whole or resolve the issues that they raise, it does offer a glimpse into some of the overarching concerns that have troubled the institutional study of religion since its formal beginnings in late 19th-century Europe, including the lines between insiders and outsiders, between critique and identity politics, theology and *Wissenschaft*, along with the search for historical-critical and comparative theories and methods that can offer a model for the study of religions as a whole. The contributions here do not, of course, resolve these debates, but rather contribute to an ongoing conversation.

Expanding the Conversation

This volume is part of a broader conversation that began on the *Bulletin for the Study of Religion* blog, and culminated in a special issue of the *Bulletin*'s journal. Beginning in February 2014, Carl Stoneham, Ruth Mas, Vernon Schubel, James Crossley, Sarah Imhoff,

Introduction 9

Edward E. Curtis, Juliane Hammer and Eleanor Finnegan all weighed in on the "dispute" between Safi and Hughes in a blog series titled "Reflections on Islamic Studies." The purpose of this series was to get scholars from a range of disciplinary backgrounds and perspectives to help clarify some of the faultlines and subject positions that characterize the field, as well as to provide, as per Hughes's critique of Safi, a response to "ideas in print." In this vein, Vernon Schubel criticizes Hughes with specific reference to his work, as does Devin Stewart in the present volume, thus providing a concrete basis for claims and refutations that readers are encouraged to take up. Edward Curtis holds a more optimistic view of the state of Islamic studies than either Safi or Hughes in this blog series, while Juliane Hammer provides a defense of normative commitments among scholars in the field. Although the remainder of contributions are more critical of normative commitments in the study of religions, and are thus more in line with the stated aims of both the *Bulletin for the Study of Religion* and the *Culture on the Edge* book series, each provides a specific instance for exploring how and why scholarly positions are justified and on what grounds.

In the November 2014 issue of the *Bulletin*'s journal, Ruth Mas, Vernon Schubel, Edward Curtis, Sarah Imhoff and James Crossley expand their blog posts into more developed essays, which Philip Tite describes in his editorial introduction to the issue as follows:

> Since 9/11, scholars of Islam (especially within the North American context) have been called upon by the general public, especially via the media, to speak about Islam, religious violence, and East/West relations. ... Undoubtedly we have been witnessing a new phase in the history of Islamic studies within religious studies. While this transformation of Islamic studies has brought about many benefits, it has also resulted in the charge of apologetics. Hughes is not alone in his concern that Islamic scholars have been actively constructing a progressive, liberal, and benign image of Islam as normative (as a defense of Islam vis-à-vis those "fringe" or "sectarian" groups who do violence in the name of Islam). This charge of "caretaking" a religious tradition feeds into a dichotomous discourse of insider vs. outsider, along with the question of whether Muslim or

non-Muslim (i.e., Western) scholars should be studying Islam within the academy? Does insider status obscure or enhance the academic endeavor?

The present volume continues along this line of questioning, and parallels an earlier debate in a special issue of *Method & Theory in the Study of Religion* (*MTSR*) journal, where scholars Herbert Berg, John Kelsay, Richard C. Martin, Ruth Mas and Andrew Rippen reply to Aaron Hughes's assessment (2012a) of the state of Islamic studies within the study of religions. Here we find questions of postcolonial studies and Orientalism, the lines between normative, descriptive and explanatory analysis, Islamic origins, the study of ethics, and the historical Muhammad being discussed and debated. Readers are encouraged to think about the present volume in relation to these particular debates, as they reflect some of the contemporary challenges and occasional breakthroughs in the attempt to work out questions of identity in light of epistemological hegemony, contemporary politics and the functions of theory and method in the academic study of religion.

Plan of the Book

This volume features expanded versions of essays from Ruth Mas, Sarah Imhoff and James Crossley that appeared in the *Bulletin for the Study of Religion* (2014), along with new contributions from Salman Sayyid, Alexandre Caeiro and Emmanuelle Stefanidis, Carlos A. Segovia and Devin Stewart. It is worth noting that the majority of these scholars work in institutions outside of North America (including Germany, the UK, Spain, France and Qatar), and thus offer a more global perspective than what Safi and Hughes initially had in mind.

The first two essays grapple with the question of what constitutes knowledge in light of the historical dominance of Euro-centric models of epistemology, and explore some of the ways that politics and scholarship may be approached differently. In Chapter 1, Ruth Mas builds on insights from a previous essay that appeared in the above-mentioned special issue of *MTSR*, "Why Critique" (2012), where she calls attention to how the entanglements of secularism, Christianity and Enlightenment belie modernist claims to objectivity in the humanities, and in the study of Islam in particular. With an eye to the Hughes-Safi "dispute," her aim here is to lay out some of the current impasses that she sees between theory and politics, with specific reference to scholars of Islam within religious studies. Borrowing the title of her essay from a phrase by Stuart Hall on the "necessary modesty of theory," Mas looks to foreground the tension between politics and thought as a necessary and productive one, especially in the post-9/11 era. Salman Sayyid's contribution in Chapter 2 turns to the legacies of Orientalism, the question of identity politics and the underlying structures of power that frame it. Centering his concern on how geopolitics has shaped our view of what constitutes knowledge, Sayyid wants to provoke his readers into thinking through the role of scholarship on Islam in the West, especially in spaces such as the UK and the US, which he characterizes as "the heart of Empire." For Sayyid, neither Safi nor Hughes focuses on the politics of Muslim subjectivity, which he argues is less of a disciplinary issue and more an epistemological one, and how the production of knowledge is tied to this history in inextricable ways.

The next two essays come from scholars of Qur'anic studies, which is a subdiscipline that some see as a central component to critical historical analysis in the field as a whole, for it is here that we find the most enduring sites of authority (i.e., sacred texts) butting-up against redaction criticism and revisionist histories that call into question any facile links between the past and the present. Alexandre Caeiro and Emmanuelle Stefanidis kick off Chapter 3 by situating their essay "Religion, History, Ethics: Rethinking the Crisis of Western Qur'anic Studies" in the post-9/11 era, where increased public attention to all things "Islam" has seen a resurgence in the study of the Qur'an. Zeroing-in on debates about Orientalism, the "revisionist challenge" (i.e., the challenge to traditionalist scholars on the reliability of "Muslim" sources), along with posing certain ethical questions (e.g., on representation, subjectivity, "Islamic Reformation," and bridge-building), they urge a more critical engagement between Western, non-Muslim Qur'anic scholars and Muslim scholars of the Qur'an, noting how the latters' epistemological positions vary widely and should be engaged with rather than ignored. In Chapter 4, Carlos Segovia begins his essay "Identity Politics and Scholarship in the Study of Islamic Origins" by arguing that most scholars of the Qur'an fail to engage with intertextual analysis (e.g., the influence of previous writings). Siding largely with Hughes's position, Segovia finds that there is a type of "conspiratorial silence" (albeit an unconscious one) amongst scholars of the Qur'an in confronting these issues, at least when compared to some of the critical-historical work that can be found in the study of Christian origins. In the second half of his essay, Segovia turns to a case study on "Identity Politics and the Ambivalent Confessional Rhetoric of the Dome of the Rock Inscriptions," where he traces previous historical continuities and ambivalences between inscriptions related to the Prophet Muhammad.

The final pairing of essays in this volume features two scholars outside of Islamic studies, from contemporary Jewish studies and early Christianity respectively. Given the perennial challenges of constituting "religious studies" as a unified field, turning to look at analogous contests and controversies in related subdisciplines, and how they have played out over time, provides useful points for comparison with the study of Islam within the study of religion. Sarah Imhoff offers a view from Jewish studies in Chapter 5. On one level, she notices that these two areas of study (broadly speaking) seem to face opposite problems: whereas Jewish studies is "too Jewish" in that it comprises a history of scholarship that has been largely populated by insiders, Islamic studies in the Western academy has historically been the domain of outsiders (i.e., non-Muslims), hence the long-standing and ongoing concern with the legacies of Orientalism. Imhoff traces a history of the development of Jewish studies in the (mostly) American academy, dating back to when 19th-century German Jewish scholars applied "scientific" methods to the study of Judaism (*Wissenschaft des Judentums*). As Islamic studies continues to develop, Imhoff hopes that insights from the history of Jewish studies offer a useful point of comparison (and caution), especially when it comes to tensions between the identity of scholars, the "scientific" imperatives of *Wissenschaft* and the influences of donors and organizations, whose confessional and political interests reflect an ongoing challenge. James Crossley's essay rounding out Chapter 6,

"The Quest for the Historical: Can Biblical Studies Lead Qur'anic Studies away from Theology?" takes the Safi-Hughes debate as a jump-off point to revisit emic and etic tensions in the study of religion. At stake for Crossley is whether scholars of religion should be "critics" or "caretakers," and, perhaps equally important, whether the field should accommodate both? Crossley frames his essay around a comment made by Carl J. Stoneham (2014) on the importance of the study of Islam making a similar turn toward the "historical Mohammed" as the study of Christianity has done with the "historical Jesus." While siding with Hughes's concerns, the main lesson from biblical studies that Crossley wants to stress is that historical Jesus studies have largely remained the province of theology. In addition to cautioning Islamic studies about the potential pitfalls of this line of inquiry, Crossley stresses the value of engaging these questions more in terms of their economic, social and political contexts, and concludes with some theses for the "critical historian" of religions.

The final essay in Chapter 7 by Devin Stewart is the longest in this book, and presents a critique of Hughes's work that is markedly different in tone than the other essays. Given that the aims of the *Culture on the Edge* series align more closely with Hughes's work, and given Hughes's own challenge to Safi to "to respond to my ideas in print as opposed to engaging in innuendo and identity politics," Stewart's provocation is an attempt to do just that, regardless of whether or not one agrees with his analysis. Part of Stewart's concern is with what he takes to be Hughes's narrow focus on scholars in religion departments in North America since 2002, and members of the Study of Islam Section at the AAR. Stewart goes on to distinguish between what he considers soft vs. solid scholars in the field of Islamic studies, along with works that fall somewhere in between, and concludes with twenty-seven theses for the improvement of Islamic studies.

The Afterword by Russell T. McCutcheon addresses two models for how we talk about religion in relation to popular media. The first is a hybrid model, which considers those things classified as religious as inextricably caught up in other categories (e.g., culture, history, gender, etc.), while the second is a binary model, which considers religion as a distinct and separate category unto itself. This essay sets out to highlight the ways in which public discourse about religion and scholarly analysis often fall into the same traps by failing to redescribe the claims of self-described religious actors in the language of theory. The Afterword also weighs in on the question of normativity in the study of Islam with particular reference to a roundtable discussion on the study of Islam that appeared in the *Journal of the American Academy of Religion* in 2016 (see Hammer 2016). Here McCutcheon stakes a particular claim on the question of normativity in the study of religions by suggesting that the study of history should be viewed as a process of social groups re-imaging what is normative or authentic based on contingency and not on some essence that is always present, waiting to be uncovered. Ultimately siding with Hughes, the Afterword urges scholars to avoid linear and continuous constructions of religion toward "a more meandering historical trail of debate, disagreement, compromise, unanticipated result, etc."

References

Hammer, Juliane. 2016. "Roundtable on Normativity in Islamic Studies: Introduction." *Journal of the American Academy of Religion* 84(1): 25–7. https://doi.org/10.1093/jaarel/lfv123

Hughes, Aaron W. 2012a. "The Study of Islam Before and After September 11: A Provocation." *Method & Theory in the Study of Religion* 24(4/5): 314–36. https://doi.org/10.1163/15700682-12341234

— 2012b. *Theorizing Islam: Disciplinary Deconstruction and Reconstruction*. Sheffield, UK: Equinox.

— 2013. *Muslim Identities: An Introduction to Islam*. New York: Columbia University Press.

— 2014. "When Bad Scholarship Is Just Bad Scholarship: A Response to Omid Safi." *Bulletin for the Study of Religion* blog. http://bulletin.equinoxpub.com/2014/02/when-bad-scholarship-is-just-bad-scholarship-a-response-to-omid-safi/ (accessed August 1, 2017).

— 2015. *Islam and the Tyranny of Authenticity: An Inquiry into Disciplinary Apologetics and Self-Deception*. Sheffield, UK: Equinox.

Murphy, Tim. 2000. "On Speaking Different Languages: Religion and the Study of Religion." *Secular Theories of Religion*. Copenhagen: Museum Tusculanum Press, University of Copenhagen.

Reflections on Islamic Studies Series. 2014. *Bulletin for the Study of Religion* blog. http://bulletin.equinoxpub.com/?s=reflections+on+Islamic+studies (accessed August 1, 2017).

Safi, Omid. 2014. "Reflections on the State of Islamic Studies." *Jadaliyya*. http://www.jadaliyya.com/pages/index/16269/reflections-on-the-state-of-islamic-studies#.Uuvw6CkjVY4.facebook (accessed August 1, 2017).

Schalin, Jay 2014. "New Wave or Clever Ruse?" *Campus Watch: Monitoring Middle East Studies on Campus*. http://www.campus-watch.org/article/id/13907 (accessed August 1, 2017).

Stoneham, Carl. 2014. "Will it Ever Be 'Just about Bad Scholarship?': A Response to Aaron Hughes and Omid Safi." *Religion Bulletin*, http://bulletin.equinoxpub.com/2014/02/will-it-ever-be-just-about-bad-scholarship-a-response-to-aaron-hughes-and-omid-safi/

Tite, Philip. 2014. "Debating a Discipline, Contesting Identities, and the Future of Islamic Studies." *Bulletin for the Study of Religion* 43(4), November. https://doi.org/10.1558/bsor.v43i4.1

Wikipedia. "Aaron W. Hughes." https://en.wikipedia.org/wiki/Aaron_W._Hughes (accessed August 1, 2017).

Matt Sheedy is currently Visiting Professor in the North American Studies Program at the University of Bonn, Germany. His research interests include critical social theory, theories of secularism and religion, as well as representations of Christianity, Islam, atheism and Indigenous traditions in popular and political culture. He is currently completing a book on Jürgen Habermas's theory of religion in the public sphere. He is also working on a project that provides a discourse analysis of popular atheism in the Euro-West, with particular attention to how it has been reshaped in light of debates surrounding Islamophobia.

Part I
Theory and Identity Politics in the Study of Islam

1. The Modesty of Theory

Ruth Mas

> I only ask you to consider, Ladies and Gentlemen, whether the compulsion to do something here and now, and the tendency to fetter thought which it contains, does not bring thought to a standstill precisely where it ought to go further, in order to reach the place where something can really be changed.
> – Theodor W. Adorno (2002: 126)

The previous iteration of this essay was a pointed consideration of the links between theory and the politics of intellectual and critical exercise in an era where for many scholars of the Islamic tradition in the field of religious studies, the production of critical knowledge is embattled and precarious (Mas 2014a).[1] The problematic that I raised then came as a result of a dispute between Aaron Hughes[2] and Omid Safi (2014), which continues to allow for an elaboration of the

---

1 I would like to thank Carl Ernst, and the other colleagues at the Duke-UNC Consortium for Middle East Studies Annual Conference *Islam and Religious Identity: The Limits of Definition* (October 14, 2016) for the invitation to present the final version of the paper that is published here. I am especially grateful to Bruce Lawrence for his response to my presentation and his careful engagement with my text. The final version of this paper was completed in 2015 before the important change to the political landscape in the United States. As such, it should be read in conjunction with "The Time of Critique" (2018), which addresses this change and was written at the beginning of 2017.

2 A special issue of the journal *Method & Theory in the Study of Religion* launched this debate. See specifically articles written by Hughes (2012a and b) and McCutcheon (2012), and the responses including my own (2012), that were solicited. Since then, Hughes has expanded and developed his perspective in a monograph (2014b).

argument for theorizing in the face of politics. Their exchange and the responses that weighed in through various fora have been proof of how, as scholars of the Islamic tradition, we are pushed into very publicly defending our political positions and asserting the manner in which we have staked them within and outside the field.

At the time of writing, I had been struck by how cultural studies scholar Stuart Hall made a case for unrelenting critical reflection at the same time as he underscored the "necessary modesty of theory." It is from Hall that I borrow my title, but I also considered using the statement by Hannah Arendt, "All thinking demands a *stop-and-think*," which reflects her lifelong preoccupation with the risks stemming from the failure to think (1981: 78). For Arendt, behind that failure lies an important connection between thought and action. "What I propose," she elaborates in *The Human Condition*, "…is very simple. It is nothing more than to think what we are doing" (1998: 5). At first glance, the two options that I considered using for the title seem almost opposed especially given Hall's enduring insistence that to ignore the politics of intellectual work is to be let off the hook by theory (1992: 285). And yet, Hall's argument is also a nuanced reminder of "the essential nature of intellectual work and critical reflection, the irreducibility of the insights which theory can bring to political practice, insights which cannot be arrived at in any other way" (285). Our role as intellectuals, he insists, is to "really know, not just pretend to know, not just to have the facility of knowledge, but to know deeply and profoundly" (281).

If I have seemingly introduced a tension between Arendt and Hall, it is to highlight the importance of the relationship between thought and politics, and to ask what happens when politics is cheated of the process of thinking. My concern begins with the not-so-simple fact that there are few subjects of study like that of Islam, Muslims and the Islamic tradition that are thought about with such urgency. At worst, the condition of their location in modernity incites their arrest into the set calculations of politics or the abstractions of theory. In other words: the modesty of theory should not be taken for the modesty of thought. I will therefore persist in asking the same question I have asked before, and still from the other side so to speak – the side that believes you cannot cultivate political practice without also cultivating reflection. What happens when we are so overcome by a desire to make a difference and to have some effect on the world, that our political practice takes the place of intellectual work? This is still Hall's question but posed differently: Has the formulation of political projects, stances and questions that we hope will intervene in the world let us off the hook from thought?

Asking whether politics has let us off the hook is to recognize that there is undoubtedly something unrelenting and forceful that is at stake in the study of Islam because there has been no way of getting around its political aspects throughout the last decade and a half. To say that the field is as fraught as the extra-academic context with which it is so utterly intimate risks becoming the dreary pabulum of those who have hit intellectual walls – except for the part where speaking and writing can get us fired, and then the walls are political. The evidence of how political treachery is also structured into the academic world continues to expand and with it the thankless task of attempting to define the very broad concept of "politics." A glance at a common dictionary generally finds politics described as one of the fundamental grounds and objects of our writing, that is, the affairs of a state, its art and science of government. This meaning seems to have held steady for the past century and we find it in an essay delivered in 1919 during the German Revolution by Max Weber. The definition he assigns to politics is, he acknowledges, a limited one: "We wish to understand by politics only the leadership, or the influencing of the leadership, of a *political* association, hence today, of a *state*" (1958: 77). "Hence," he contends in a later passage, "'politics' for us means striving to share power or striving to influence the distribution of power, either among states or among groups of people within states" (78). If we recognize that beneath and within the state, and across states, there also exist all kinds of associations, it would seem then that the definition of politics is also tied to how we function as subjects in relation to the myriad aspects of interpersonal and institutional affairs. In this sense, politics also refers to the allegiances, principles, sympathies and opinions, and policies of governance pertaining to these affairs. This includes the activities, methods, maneuvers, strategies or the business concerned with the acquisition of power amongst and between individuals or parties. Politics, politicking, lobbying, pandering – however global their structural aspects or however local their relational aspects – demand a sustained consideration of how beholden we are to power, its distribution and the state. The stakes could not be any simpler nor could they be any less unyielding.

In the field of religious studies, these maneuvers, allegiances, opinions, these individuals, this striving, that's us. We academics couldn't be more implicated because our writing and speaking are bound to have political effects despite how objectively we want to teach our facts and whether we address politics in our writing or not. Our approaches and the differing qualities of our relations to politics itself more obviously skirt the agentive dimensions of our involvement with a closely surveilled, tirelessly publicized and ambitiously globalized world: advocacy and activism, the arts of our disputations and polemics, the implications of our academic writing and our journalistic writing,[3] demonstrating, striking, boycotting, signing, speaking out in the public sphere, electronically and otherwise, volunteering and mobilizing change in local community contexts, etc. I will necessarily disappoint readers by not completing what is fundamentally a never-ending list. Let me just say that, as Weber declared, it is difficult to exceed the grasp of politics even for those of us who don't make politics a vocation: "One may engage in politics, and hence seek to influence the distribution of power within and between political structures, as an 'occasional politician.' We are all 'occasional' politicians...." (1958: 83). Hence, if politics is also an avocation (83), its fabric is punctuated by our interventions into its occasions, whether or not we are purposefully public in our personal or academic practice. At the very least we are left with very serious doubt about the possibility of keeping separate "doing theory" (or, even more generally, doing academic work) from "doing politics."

The very fact of having put quotation marks around "doing theory" signals a by now generalized discomfort with how "theory" has been turned into the ongoing totalizing reification and instrumentalization of the activity and production of thought. In his discussion

---

[3] See Weber's discussion of the difference between journalists and academics (1958: 96–8).

of the "quotation market" established around theory, Derrida writes, "The demarcation by quotation marks or inverted commas means that these labels have the exchange value of currencies meant to circulate and make possible the circulation of goods…in some Wall Street of the academy" (1990: 74). The rise of theory's stock within the academy has been pushed by "concurrent forces of desire and power," and has produced both its "taxonomic objectivization" and "hierarching structure" (64, 65). A theoretical "monster" (67, 79) has emerged which totalizes, unifies and thereby dissolves different disciplines into "theory," so that it can be identified and replicated (82ff). This mutant breeding of theory is fed by the concentration and expenditure of emotional significance and energy – what Gasché calls a "theoretical cathexis" – by scholars in its singularity, uniqueness and exclusivity (2006: 148).

Although initially organized as a run up the ladder of capitalist drive, the democratization and dissemination of academic prestige invoked by "theory" eventually has to fall. Rabaté describes this decline in terms of the generating of "standard interpretations, repetitive or dull writing," and the streamlining and mass production of concepts that systematize theory into "simple conceptual tricks," "cool tools, handy handles or even better, 'power tools'" (2002: 98–100). "Boredom," Rabaté points out, "is indeed the reaction triggered by imitative discourses, and boredom was massively institutionalized in American universities when Theory gave birth to endless copy-cat readings killing any sense of the 'new' in texts" (100). The market forecast for theory is grim. Its performance is low. The academic corporatization of theory has meant that because theory has had only itself to run on, it has depleted itself and dissipated its own prestige. Bought high and then dumped, theory has been sold short by the Stockbrokers of Theory, and branded into a meaningless logo of academic accreditation.

It really isn't much of an irony to have a US-American president be the one who observes that, "The thing about branding is that you can be fact free" (Clinton 2015). This reflects the additional problem of how the over-investment in theory's standardizing objectivity risks obscuring its sectarianism and territoriality. For Gasché, theory is a regional commodity – a US-American one (2006: 149). Derrida couldn't agree more and contends that theory is "a purely North American *artifact*" (1990: 71) "which could only take form in the States" (81). In other words, any objectivity attributed to theory is only alleged and certain structures of both politics and power have already crept in at the moment of its fabrication. The impact that the regional commodification of theory has on the study of the Islamic tradition has to do with a cathexis that is ideologically loaded and situated within institutions that secure its geopolitical embrace. Against the promise of the pure and unadulterated elixir of theory stands the threat of both disciplinary dissolution and the encroachment of US-American priorities, nationalist state-politics and privilege. The two come together in the form of the jealous guardians of religious studies who police the internal processes of distilling theory.

The unfortunate result is that wariness about fact-free theory can also be ideologically loaded when it provincially takes over "objectivity" on behalf of a particular field – especially if that field pretends to be a discipline. What is especially alarming is the ease with which the totalizing and a-disciplined enterprise of "theory" can get displaced onto religious studies at the moment of its encounter with the study of Islam. One can easily picture a religious studies scholar gasping at the Jowls of Theory, "Oh, how universal you are!" And Theory salivating, "Yes, the better to trade you with." The Hunter that comes to the rescue is more often than not safely armed by a US institution and clears out a tabula rasa of the field, which, post-Mircea Eliade, pretends that "real" religious studies theory has inaugurated an authentic tradition of self-contained thinking.[4] But when he proudly scrambles to the top of the mountain, guns a' blazing, and realizes he's really only standing his ground on top of an insignificant boulder, his Iver Johnson goes limp at the sight of any foreigner. The actual problem of course, is that he has run out of disciplinary

---

4 In different versions, the hunter is a wood-chopper. (One can imagine a more modern version, one less honest about its aggression, in the figure of a jock, or a mountaineer of sorts.) On a different note, at the time of writing this article, I would never have predicted that the National Rifle Association in the United States would be rewriting fairy tales. One of these, "Little Red Riding Hood (Has a Gun)" by Amelia Hamilton, can now be accessed on the NRA website.

ammunition and has no theoretical guns to speak of. His delusions of renewed objectivity cannot be anything but fired blanks of smoke and hot air. (With great privilege – or power – comes great responsibility. Or something like that.)

The study of Islam is thus faced with the double jeopardy of echo and oblivion towards the state politics that condition and harness theory under the jaundiced eye of religious studies. No wonder that the mere suggestion of "doing theory" as divorced from the politicized and social circumstances of Muslim lives and experiences invites the kind of eye-rolling that it does. But the problem with resisting theory at any cost is that its potential for totalizing abstraction only gets intensified when we enforce the idea of "true religious studies theory" in a desperate attempt to render theory "authentic" to religious studies. The problem becomes even more acute when "true religious studies theory" singularly arises from the post-Christian or secularized Christian traditions of phenomenological thought. In that case, the study of Islam has to contend with the fact that it is situated within a field that is staving off alien allegiances and whose solution to the threat from outside is to identify Muslims with a gesture of pluralizing authenticity that tidily organizes "Muslim experience" within "etic" and "emic" distinctions. "One mosque, two mosques, three mosques, four. Count which Muslims walk through the door" becomes the reductive mantra of its contamination by Islam.

The fear of contagion can be measured by how insistently texts are translated into English, how quickly spelling is standardised,[5] how unrivalled Sufism and terrorism are as binary options of study, and how zealously scholars such as Asad and Foucault, rendered guilty of post-structuralist leanings, are brushed aside as thinkers that "we need to get beyond" – (Wait. Already?! We'd have to understand and systematically engage with their work first, no?). And yet, if anything, the study of Islam by way of these scholars has demonstrated that Islam as a tradition can be studied "anywhere," and that indeed it has to be studied "everywhere" temporally and spatially, and that doing

---

5 The editors have kindly indulged my insistence on this spelling of the word as a sign of my resistance to the way in which my text has been "Americanized."

so implies an engagement with and reconsideration of the categories that religious studies holds so dear. In other words, the relationship of Islam to theory works in that it holds the latter in expansive check by way of a thinking from within the field (and its disciplines) to outside of it, and then back again. It is through this constant movement, one that is attentive to and directed at the conditions of its locality, that religious studies theory sheds itself of its regional commodification. It isn't so much loyalty or faithfulness to the discipline which is owed here, but serious reflection on its terrain from a position of exteriority to politico-theoretical opportunism and colonizing imperial obligations.

Given the contentions around theory, it may seem propitious for scholars of Islam to join Rabaté in wondering whether "theory" should just be called "politics" (2002: 3). At least this would draw attention to how hegemony is disguised in the duds of objective applicability. Indeed, nobody would blame us if, like Judith Butler in the following statement, we'd like to go ahead and equate the two and get on with the business of doing our work: "If the political task is to show that theory is never merely *theoria*, in the sense of disengaged contemplation, and to insist that it is fully political (*phronesis* or even *praxis*), then why not simply call this operation *politics*, or some necessary permutation of it?" (quoted in Rabaté 2002: 2). Of course, underlying Butler's question is a long tradition dating back to at least the Greeks where, in the relationship of thought to a "life devoted to public-political matters," the former was an integral part of the *bios politikos*, or relegated to the lofty heights of contemplation (Arendt 1998: 12–13). Butler reflects the desire of many scholars to overcome the strict division of thought from practice that was solidified after Plato, especially within Christendom where contemplation was prioritized over practice (Arendt 1998: 16). Some scholars have even attempted to undo the parcelling out of theory from practice by in turn demarcating theory from thinking in the hopes that thinking can better approximate practice. Heidegger, for example, famously stated that "thinking acts insofar as it thinks" and also suggested that it is the highest form of praxis (Heidegger 1977: 193; Gasché 2006: 4). But this does nothing to satisfy our questioning of the way in which theory gets naturalized, nor by whom.

Still further, as Gasché points out, this mistakenly implies that "thinking is not of the order of the theoretical, for only theory stands in direct opposition to praxis" (2006: 8). In a most lucid elaboration of the necessary relationship between the two, Gasché explains that what gets lost is the importance of sustaining the deliberate moment of thinking within theory:

> A thinking that exceeds the theoretical does not leave it behind but comprises the confrontation of theory with the structural limits that its very enabling conditions impose on its totalizing and stabilizing enterprise. It also follows from this that thinking does not make theorizing obsolete – totalizing and mastery remain as necessary as ever, except that theory needs to face both the structural limits of its conditions of possibility and the metaphysical (but also ideological and political) character of many of its claims. Theory continues to have its place, but "reformed," as it were, within and with respect to thinking. (2006: 11)

In Gasché's statement we find not so much a defense of theory or a sidestepping of the problems with theory, as we do a qualification of its continued relevance. The point is that theory's value thrives in the persistence of thinking. To ignore this is to discount the issue of temporality that arises in that persistence, both in terms of the syncopation of theory and thinking but also in terms of how our resistance to theory may very well be symptomatic of a modern distortion of the past. Differently put, our present-day understanding of theory is "an extreme recasting" of the notion of "*theoria*" developed by the Greeks (Gasché 2006: 149). Maintaining a critical stance towards theory targets this untimeliness instead of degenerating into hostility (9–11). (After all, the anachronism is really ours and should not get rhetorically smuggled out into the purported territory of Islam.) "Declarations against theory," Gasché insists, "are hopelessly naïve, and even self-contradictory," and are made by those that "are terrified of becoming politically irrelevant by deferring to theory" (9–10). In this day and age, it would be a quite an achievement and a sad one at that for any scholar of Islam to manage to be politically expendable. One can only hope that the suspicion directed at theory is really a suspicion of how its totalizing enterprise risks being sustained or rendered hegemonic, and not simply an excuse for resisting thought. Besides, if there is anything that the study of Islam can offer theory, it is a confrontation with its structural limits and with the ideological and political and temporal character of its claims.

Another way of saying this is that the political relevance of either "theory" or "thinking" is not achieved by calling one or the other "politics" or even "praxis." There is a reason why Arendt implored us to "*stop*-and-think" and this has to do too with the necessary modesty of practice, not jumping the gun into action, and with thwarting the violence of non-thinking and of action without thought. This means ensuring a thinking about the political, which you cannot get away with *not* doing by simply saying "thinking is political." As the art of subtly bringing theory into crisis, thinking knows *when* to approximate itself to politics. It is practiced in resisting theory's embrace without rebuff. Taking critical distance from politics and political authority thus allows thinking to track them both down. Never entirely separate from action, thinking nonetheless has its own rhythm. It also has its own location, one from which, even so, it tries to abstract itself. It is more than knowledge in that it needs and thus, as Arendt tells us, begets judgment, namely a judgment of the imbrication of politics with power. Thinking begins by its own accord but in that begetting. This is how it propels us into the political and dangerously unpredictable sphere of speech, which it incites, and action.

Our sensibility to the necessary connection between politics and theory is not new. As Gasché writes, "The theoretical attitude is of Greek origin. Anything that would call itself 'theory' must confront what emerged in Greece as *theoria* in the fifth century B.C." (2006: 149). What's more, the way in which the signification we have made of theory that Gasché gestures towards has obscured what was theory's sensibility towards politics for the early Greeks. This has been highlighted by a number of scholars with respect to the way in which *theoria* indicated a delegate and representative of the state thus allowing for participation in its affairs (Rabaté 2002: 114; Gasché 2006: 201; Godzich 1994: 165). Gadamer has attended to the role of this delegate in his reading of the ancients by specifying that the etymology of "*theoria*" signals an onlooker (a *theoros*, that is, a spectator) who sees beneath the surface of things or facts (1988: 31). For Gadamer a fact "always referred back to a context of supposition and expectation, to a complicated context of inquiring understanding." When a little further on Gadamer says that "The secret of all government – the evil of its power and its counterpart, the wisdom of political assembly – is hidden here" (31), he is naming the politics of power that prejudice the context behind a fact and that needs to be thought through.

Thus, before we even start theorizing, the imaginings of power, its assurances and responsibilities, are already built into the ideas and concepts we engage. As a consequence, theorizing is representative of the operations of power at the same time as it allows us to unmask them. And we simply need to stop and think about how. Because, as academics we are theorists and this means that we must either attend to how our writing and our speaking may prescriptively and strategically intervene into political fields, or admit that we are just playing them both, politics and fields, as we vie for and profit from the power they exert. There is also, of course, the matter of how we ourselves are being played or whether we are even allowed to speak. And it is our recognition of the extents, strategies and mechanisms of all of these that will determine the imbrication of our theory and the quality of our credentials as academic subjects and actors. The state, its power and us: power is what cements us to the state and politics will tell us how, for whom, and by whom. And while theory may be political, there is nothing just "theoretical" about politics.[6]

What can we understand by "politics" as scholars of Islam in the field of religious studies? One thing we can understand is the kind of politics that has as its occasions our intercessions with the state and/or the public square for the actions, beliefs, sentiments, traditions, politics and practices of Muslims. This is only one example of course, and one that Steven P. Weitzman describes in a recent article as the "interventionist impulse" of scholars of religion. He writes,

---

6 Unfortunately, there is insufficient space here to track the shifts between different possible modalities of the intersections between theory and practice, such as theoretical practice, theoretical intervention, practice, intervention, political practice, political intervention and politics.

"What is in question here is not the utility of Religious Studies as a reference source, but its power to intervene in conflict, a power that it has claimed for itself both before and after 9/11" (2013: 987). Describing scholars in our field, Weitzman explains that "their ability to understand and explain religious mindsets and interpretation, their experience in moving between secular and religious mentalities – created possibilities for constructive intervention, for analysis, for advice, even for direct mediation" (962). It seems that we have cast ourselves as authorities with rather ambitious and urgent objectives, incited by a desire to "do more than theorize about how to overcome religious violence and conflict" (962).[7]

This configuration of violence warrants more attention but for now, let us be clear: Weitzman's account is a cautionary tale about those who have wanted to "help to prevent further terrorist attacks," to "illumine the mindset of suicide bombers," to "[review] different ways to 'cure' religious violence," or to make "policy recommendations for U.S. foreign relations" (2013: 960). As Weitzman knows, there have been prior events on US soil as well as extra-territorially that have inspired some scholars to believe that "academia could indeed help to peacefully resolve potentially violent crises" (970). Weitzman could not be brandishing a redder flag. Not only does he conclude that previous experience did not have "much impact on how things have developed" and "arguably exposes a mismatch between scholarly aspirations and reality" (972, 977), he both outlines how we have been subjected to the "ethos of heightened government surveillance and interference in academia" and reminds us of how intelligence about Muslim communities has been procured "in ways that threaten their civil liberties" (974).[8] Quite aside from the insufficiently

---

7 See Weitzman for a discussion of the receptiveness of government officials to scholarly efforts to "intervene against religious violence" (2013: 961–2).

8 Weitzman offers many reasons for the less-than-anticipated impact of scholars on government officials. He writes about the "insufficient or misguided training procedures that perpetuate outmoded or biased information and a relationship with Religious Studies that remains sporadic, unstructured and without clear guidelines or measures of success," the "institutionalized

balanced confidence of a scholar who pretends s/he can cure violence, prevent terrorist attacks or peer into the minds of dead suicide bombers, is there a clearer case for taking a step back from wanting to "do more than theorize" and beginning, perhaps, to interrogate the differences between intervention, collaboration and interpellation? Isn't this the point where we simply stop and ask with which concept of the state we are working, and, *before* we intervene, how exactly we understand the power that is available to us? The necessary modesty of the clarity of thinking here would seem to enable finely honed and measured strategy.[9]

If the opportunities for scholars of the Islamic tradition to act on their interventionist impulses with foreseeably satisfying results that they can control are really quite grim, it may be because of "the tragedy with which all action, but especially political action, is truly interwoven" (Weber 1958: 117). Or it may be because we realize that "a refusal to intervene can create an expertise vacuum that other kinds of experts are all too willing to fill and in ways that can be very harmful" (Weitzman 2013: 988). Perhaps Weitzman's account is not the only account, "perhaps" it is an "extreme" account, and yes, perhaps there are many other modes of conditional antagonism, mediation, arbitration, etc. that don't have to take on or collaborate with federal agencies, but he makes clear that what is hanging in the balance are the theoretical and political consequences of the state.

The ferocity of politics has been a long-standing feature in our field, which has always been in a state of interruption and disruption by extreme political forces that have ushered in new ideas and new spaces for theoretical work and that have guided our aspirations for political relevance. September 11, 2001 marks an event that has been very fracturing and nothing has branded our intellectual arena in

---

culture of ignorance about religion, the biases and stereotypes" and the "reorganization of the FBI" (2013: 975, 970, 973).

9 Of course, extreme modesty with regard to thinking can be terribly strategic with abhorrent consequences. When Hannah Arendt exclaimed, "Well, he was neither the first nor the last to be ruined by modesty," she was referring to one of the most horrific criminal masterminds of the Third Reich, who routinely refused his own judgment (1963: 284).

the recent past like these attacks.[10] This event was not only a crucial moment in the dissolution of a unified historical and political project but also the site where the advance of a liberal and secular politics has faltered. An event of this kind has also marked the field in significantly different ways than it has others. This difference merits attention so that the field can stake its own wager and its own critical project in the wake of this dissolution. Only then can we be clear about the critical projects that we want to produce (Hall 1992: 277–85).

The urgency that political events such as these fabricate and even force on us as scholars often makes our struggle to establish the space that connects critical reflection to politics seem insurmountable. But what if the problem is also that the manufacturing of this urgency has given politics its alibi – the alibi that allows politics to masquerade as theory and that can so quickly and acrimoniously fold back into a deafening (or deaf) contestation over who gets to speak and how, who gets to be represented as part of the field and even who gets to be ignored? This is a difficult question to ask when scholars are being run out of universities and fired for holding politically inconvenient views. But there is something more to be thought through here than a certain modality of power that can be made manifest as the dominating and subjugating force of state governance, and it has to do with the nature of theory itself and its relation to power and the vying forces behind its politics.

---

10 See Amir Hussain's discussion of the ensuing heightened expectations for scholars to intervene in public discourse, i.e., as "scholar citizens," and the reasons for the limits that he sets to his public appearances. Hussain argues that this marks an important shift for academics in the study of Islam (2008: 31) which, in light of the explicit targeting of Muslims in the United States, includes vast pedagogical transformations, extra-curricular work with student bodies, peace and justice groups, etc. His reminder of the conditions of empire and colonialism which sustain the histories and lives of Muslims in North America (229), is developed in terms of their globalization by Tazim Kassam in a carefully written essay on the risks for scholars of Islamic studies in the wake of September 11, 2001 (2003). See also Scott Elliott's inclusion of a section on the study of Islam after September 11, 2001 in his monograph on the discipline of religious studies (2014), and his interview with Matt Sheedy (2013).

When in a different lecture Weber warns us against being the "petty prophets" for "warring gods" in our lecture rooms, he reminds us that we are "placed upon the platform solely as teachers" and not as leaders. His fear is one that is shared by many scholars: that all we may "accomplish is to show that [we] are unaware of the decisive state of affairs" or that we may "create only fanatical sects but never a genuine community" (1958: 153, 149, 155). Even the famously activist Foucault declared, "I confess that I do not subscribe to the idea of the intellectual intervening or assuming the role of someone who gives lessons or advice regarding matters of political choice" (2014: 247). And more recently, in an insightful interview with anthropologist David Scott, Talal Asad has expressed skepticism with regard to academia's being "the special space of insight from which rational political action can be designed" (2006: 240). Notwithstanding their misgivings, for these intellectuals there is no facile shielding of the academic from "the political." A little further on Asad contends, "But the political world itself can be recalcitrant and treacherous – even if this does not free us from having to act when we must" (241). How this obligation is related to our scholarly endeavors for Asad is evident when he points out the "tension between the need for decisiveness in political commitment and the need for openness in anthropological inquiry" (301). Foucault recognizes in this tension between political action and theoretical investigation the encroachment of one on the other: "It seems to me that there was perhaps an easier way, or I would say a more immediately practical way, of posing the question of the relationship between theory and practice correctly, and that was to carry it out directly in one's own practice.... Second, I have always insisted that there take place within me and for me a kind of back and forth, an interference, an interconnection between practices and the theoretical or historical work I was doing.... I always insisted that this theoretical work not dictate rules with regard to contemporary practice, and that it pose questions" (2014: 248). Even Weber suggests that there is a need to interrogate politics when he advises teachers to teach their students how to recognize "inconvenient facts," by which he means "facts that are inconvenient for their party opinions" (1958: 147). What we may have here is not so much an issue of politics intruding on an academic safe place but one of whether theorizing obstructs our political practice.

Still, there is something that nags in the hesitation of these thinkers to make direct and simple associations or "make too tight a connection between intellectual work and political work" (Asad and Scott 2006: 255). We sense it when Asad cautions against reducing understanding to "moralistic judgment" (258). We sense it too when he expresses the desire to work "without eternally fixed foundations" (258). And it starts to emerge when we consider that it is the mobility of these foundations that constitute the movement of politics. Asad turns to this when he says, "The political implications of any theoretical work are not as tidy, as determinate as they might appear at first sight. 'Implication' is a logical term, but the political activity that someone might engage in (or reject) doesn't depend on relations of logic" (266–7). Foucault is also skeptical of a logic tied to fixed foundations and contends that the coherence between theory and practice is strategic and moves through one's subjective experience (2014: 266).[11] From there, Foucault also notes, "one can move on to other things in such a way that there is a real coherence, a schema, or a point of rationality that does not take as its foundation a general theory of man" (266).

Much more can be culled from the statements of these two intellectuals than there is room for here.[12] I shall just say that guiding their thought is a suspicion of the classical Marxist readings of ideology where there is a predictable structural causality that engulfs the subject and with it all the possibilities of action.[13] What this signifies

11 For Asad, this has meant "reconceptualizing the question of ideology in terms of the experience of the body-mind-heart" (2006: 267).

12 One example is how Asad sets the individual's engagement with language and emotion against the Marxist idea of a systematic distortion of reality by ideology (2006: 267). Noteworthy too is the significance of Foucault's engagement with the idea of alienation as a response to how dominantly it had been characterized by a conflation of "phenomenological-psychiatric-Marxist" perspectives (2014: 268).

13 Asad's distance from Marx is marked by, among other things, skepticism of revolutionary politics and the emancipatory potential of a rationalist politics (2006: 250, 255–6). Foucault's disassociation from Marx is pointed

specifically is their acknowledgment of the *relational* aspects of power as precluding an *already-made* continuity for the *full* impact of its variegated capacity.

Insofar as the possibilities for political action are held and formed by power, the question is how to read the many crisscrossing locations of politics back onto the construal of the state by somebody like Weber. We are immediately met here with a theoretical problem and obligation. How will our political commitments and practices target both the architecture of the continuities of power as well as each instance of its differences? Weber's argument that the state is intimately founded on violence and force (i.e., the violent means which are specific to it and the legitimate use over which it claims monopoly) (1958: 78) would seem to provide a clear and decided template for locations of political intervention. But what does this say about the politics that occurs in the moment of the relations between subjects? Especially when the institutionalization of politics is one of the signposts of power, and our relations are often its cover? Do we escape interpellation into those foundations of violence and force when they become the site of our interventions, and if so, how? It is all very well and good and, more often than not, easy to point fingers at the violence of *other* states, but things get immediately complicated when, as the "privileged hirelings of the state" – *our* state (or states) – it is assumed that we march under the banner of its benevolence. This is where the excess of the relational aspects of power, those that guide the behavior of others, rears its head.[14]

And so, the formulation of our political practices, stances and activism would have to account for how politics proliferates within the deeper and replicating structures of the operations of power while being cognizant of the twists, turns and detours these structures mobilize. We have to follow the politics and chase down its facts and its asymmetries before the grounds that authorize it escape us and take a

---

(1988: 11). He especially departs from Marx over the latter's emphasis on the foundationalism and superstructure of power (2014: 237–9).

14 The expression "privileged hirelings of the state" belongs to Weber (1958: 153). For a discussion of the intricacies of relational power see Foucault (1988: 2).

different form and shape. And then we have to tie the fact of politics to those movements and transformations. That is our theoretical duty. Accordingly, to require of a scholar to define her political project is in part to ask her to anticipate the uncharted grounds of power. What would happen to our political interventions if we took time to reflect on the locus, both continuous and unfixed, of the political fact? What tactics would it enable in the face of the capricious alacrity of power?

It worries me that I may be taken to mean that we have to get beyond – or worse, leave behind – the political activism, intervention and struggles for recognition that hound the debates within Islamic studies. This is not so. I want to be very clear that these interventions contest in very important ways the normative study of the Islamic tradition in the field of religious studies and produce some of the grist of the theorizing we do. They are the reminder that if nothing else, theory is not self-sufficient; it is already grounded in and in irresolvable tension with politics and needs to be politically fluent and relevant. I am simply asking that when we consider where to place our political commitments, we focus on why and how these debates come to be in the first place. Politics cannot be allowed to stand in for a serious, sustained and critical consideration of the *grounds* that authorize our practices. This is especially true if politics is produced at every moment of theory, because then, suddenly, our authoritative grounds are quite entangled. To be very precise, I think that engaging with these grounds is what will constitute the advance of the field. More often than not these grounds relate directly to our ideas of state power and governance, and what politics offers us is the opportunity to radically reconsider how they have been presented to us. Theory as deliberative practice is a necessary mode of intervention.

Because the constitution of theory is the moment of the constitution of politics we need to identify the conditions of its possibility so that we can spell out the grounds from which, and onto which, we intervene. In "Why Critique?" (2012), I called into question the specter of objectivity that pretends that our critical intellectual practices are impartial and scholarly when the foundations of humanistic enquiry, both theoretical and political, are established by the continual attachments of secularism to Christianity and the Enlightenment pretence that these are divided. What we have on the theoretical agenda is thus the need to examine in more detail the political significance of the modernist stance in the foundation of critique's relationship to tradition, and the contexts of colonialism and empire which continue to sustain it. These are the grounds that I am addressing here and the problem is that that they are now all over the map.

So, how do we get out of this difficulty, can we, and where would that leave us? Do we do it by finding within the Islamic tradition the source of the critique of the secular presuppositions of what is increasingly the normative understanding of intellectual practice? Maybe, but then we will also have to deal with the fact that in many ways this very tradition contributed to the project of European Enlightenment and has its own pre-modern (i.e., pre-secularizing) secular genealogies, however much it was later subjected to the government apparatus that the latter put into place. I am not convinced that simply delving into the past to find authentic notions of tradition, or modalities of being Muslim, is enough for these to be able to stand up to the post-Christian secular demands made by powerful modern states. And this has to do with the impossibility of authenticity, as much as it has to do with the force with which secular political and intellectual projects are promoted as impartial and, consequently, how aggressively Muslims, scholars, and Muslim scholars, are made to conform. It is right here that our commitments and the possibility of political intervention are located. But I am convinced that we must agree with Michel Foucault and refuse what he called the blackmail of the Enlightenment that obliges us to position ourselves as either for it or against it.[15] We are in it and, for good, for worse, for all of us, these are our grounds, whether they have been thrust upon us or not. We will each hold and enact different positionalities and interventions within them of course, some that are more resistant or reorienting than others.

---

15 Following Kant there is a long tradition established by intellectuals such as Nietzsche, Derrida, Foucault and Lyotard who use the critical reason deduced from the Enlightenment itself to reflect on those limits. See also James Schmidt's discussion (1996) of how quickly the Enlightenment underwent critical scrutiny, thus already making it the container for much of the criticism against it that exists today.

If we have to come to terms with an intellectual and political legacy that has been imposed on many of us by force, then the good news is that contained within this legacy is what Kant espoused as a "limit-attitude" that allows us to analyze and reflect on its limits, politically and theoretically. For Kant, the Enlightenment forces us to ask the question of who we are today, and, at this moment the questions that remain are: How are we going to reflect on those limits and for whom? What do these limits look like in the asymmetrical power relations of a globalized world? Will we be able to reform the Enlightenment and its limits, which harnessed the values of the modern state, with the Islamic tradition, that is, with something other than what the Enlightenment has *explicitly* produced and endorsed? It seems to me that, at the very least, the study of the Islamic tradition confronts and even contests the discriminating operation of Western theory. Can the Islamic tradition function as the limit case for the Enlightenment? In his discussion of limit-experiences, Foucault wrote that they were described as "borderline experiences that put into question the very things that were considered ordinarily acceptable" (2014: 238). A paraphrase of Foucault elucidates what it could mean to consider the tradition of Islam as a limit experience of the Enlightenment: Instead of interrogating the Enlightenment itself and how it could be founded, take the Islamic tradition as the point of rupture with regard to the system, and then take this point of view to ask, What is the Enlightenment then? (238).

What the theoretical turn of the field looks like will depend largely on what it acknowledges as having the privilege and authority to do that no other field does. It will thus have to contend first with the fact that September 11 has been able to exert such pressure on the field largely because of the *way* in which Islamic studies has attempted to meet the demand for rational, loving and liberal Muslim subjects to speak for the tradition in all-too-quotable sound bites. This has become the Muslim scholar's burden and indeed the burden for everybody working on the study of the Islamic tradition. All of us, Muslim and non-Muslim, are working within the very instantiation of the modernist enterprise of critical and theoretical projects; this is one of Talal Asad's great lessons for the field. We need to consider what this means for the study of Islam within the field of religious studies, a field that has so proudly defended the questions of religious experience and now the questions about the experience of people bound together by different traditions of belief and practice. Does it mean that scholars of the Islamic tradition can take for granted modernity's claim to critical objectivity or that Muslim scholars of Islamic studies should fashion themselves as the secular ethicists to members of their own communities in an effort to discipline their behavior? In the moment of our interventions, we cannot escape having to make explicit the ways in which our theoretical and political practices are indebted to state power.

Understanding the constitutive and political nature of the intervention of Muslim scholars can instill in us the need for serious theoretical work but only if we reflect on all of its complexity and think all its fronts together. Once you hit, politically and theoretically, the Enlightenment and how people continue to live and die for its values, the world's your limit. To stop at its politics is to miss the boat intellectually. Ultimately, it is also to pass up the chance for our political interventions to be strategically and effectively tactical. At a historical juncture in which political relevance has been foisted upon us, I am arguing for theoretical courage and for critical attention to be paid to the grounds that such a demand obscures. This is to say that we can never be off the hook theoretically. Aware of its own limits, theory's call to mobilize and to resist occurs precisely at the site where the political is asserted. This is the site where theory demands the most. *"What is the intellectual, if not one who works to prevent others from having such a clear conscience?"* (Foucault 2014: 250).

This essay is dedicated with esteem and gratitude to Frederick Denny.

Bibliography

Adorno, Theodore W. 2002. *Metaphysics: Concept and Problems*. Palo Alto, CA: Stanford University Press.

Arendt, Hannah. 1963. *Eichman in Jerusalem: A Report on the Banality of Evil*. New York: The Viking Press.

— 1981. *The Life of the Mind*. New York: Mariner Books; 1st Harvest/HBJ edition.

— 1998. *The Human Condition*. Chicago: The University of Chicago Press. https://doi.org/10.7208/chicago/9780226924571.001.0001

Asad, Talal and David Scott. 2006. "The Trouble of Thinking: An Interview with Talal Asad," in David Scott and Charles Hirschkind, eds., *Powers of the Secular Modern* (pp. 243–303). Palo Alto, CA: Stanford University Press.

Braun, Willi. 2005. "Rhetoric, Rhetoricality, and Discourse Performances," in Willi Braun, ed., *Rhetoric and Reality in Early Christianities*. Waterloo: Wilfrid Laurier University Press.

Clinton, Bill. 2015. Interview with Erin Burnett on *Erin Burnett OutFront*. September 29, 4:07pm. https://archive.org/details/CNNW_20150929_230000_Erin_Burnett_OutFront

Derrida, Jacques. 1990. "Some Statements and Truisms about Neologisms, Newisms, Postisms, Parasitisms, and Other Small Seismisms," in *The States of "Theory": History, Art and Critical Discourse*, edited with an introduction by David Carroll. New York: Columbia University Press.

Elliott, Scott. 2013. "Reinventing Religious Studies: An Interview with Scott S. Elliott, Part 2." Interview conducted by Matt Sheedy. *Bulletin for the Study of Religion* blog. http://www.equinoxpub.com/blog/2013/12/reinventing-religious-studies-an interview-with-scott-s-elliott-part-2/

—, ed. 2014. *Reinventing Religious Studies: Key Writings in the History of a Discipline*. New York: Routledge.

Foucault, Michel. 1988. "Power, Moral Values and the Intellectual: An Interview with Foucault." Interview conducted by Michael Bess. *History of the Present* 4: 1–2, 11, 13.

— 2014. "Interview with Christian Panier and Pierre Watté" and "Interview with Jean François and John De Wit," in *Wrong Doing, Truth Telling. The Function of Avowal in Justice* (pp. 247–52 and 253–69). Chicago: The University of Chicago Press.
https://doi.org/10.7208/chicago/9780226922089.001.0001

Gadamer, Hans Georg. 1988. *Praise of Theory*. New Haven, CT: Yale University Press.

Gasché, Rodolphe. 2006. *The Honour of Thinking: Critique, Theory, Philosophy*. Palo Alto, CA: Stanford University Press.

Godzich, Wlad. 1994. *The Culture of Literacy*. Cambridge, MA: Harvard University Press.

Hall, Stuart. 1992. "Cultural Studies and Its Theoretical Legacies," in Lawrence Grossberg et al., eds., *Cultural Studies* (pp. 277–94). New York: Routledge.

Hamilton, Amelia. 2016. "Little Red Riding Hood (Has a Gun)." The National Rifle Association blog. https://www.nrafamily.org/articles/2016/1/13/little-red riding-hood-has-a gun/

Heidegger, Martin. 1968. *What Is Called Thinking?* New York: Harper & Row.
— 1977. "Letter on Humanism," in *Basic Writings*, edited by D.F. Krell. New York: Harper and Row.
Horkheimer, Max. 1975. "Traditional and Critical Theory," in *Critical Theory: Selected Essays*, translated by Matthew J. O'Connell (pp. 188–243). New York: Continuum Press.
Hughes, Aaron. 2012a. "The Study of Islam Before and After September 11: A Provocation." *Method & Theory in the Study of Religion* 24: 314–36. https://doi.org/10.1163/15700682-12341234
— 2012b. "Provoked: Afterword." *Method & Theory in the Study of Religion* 24: 418–23. https://doi.org/10.1163/15700682-12341243
— 2014a. "When Scholarship Is Just Bad Scholarship: A Response to Omid Safi." *Bulletin for the Study of Religion* blog. http://www.equinoxpub.com/blog/2014/02/when-bad scholarship-is-just-bad-scholarship-a-response-to-omid-safi/
— 2014b. *Theorizing Islam. Disciplinary Deconstruction and Reconstruction*. New York: Routledge.
Hussain, Amir. 2008. "Thoughts on Being a Scholar of Islam and a Muslim in America Post 9/11," in Bryan Rennie and Philip L. Tite, eds., *Religion, Terror and Violence, Religious Studies Perspectives* (pp. 227–42). New York: Routledge.
Johansen, Baber. 1990. "Politics and Scholarship: The Development of Islamic Studies in the Federal Republic of Germany," in Tareq Y. Ismael, ed., *Middle East Studies: International Perspectives on the State of the Art* (pp. 71–130). New York: Praeger.
Kassam, Tazim. 2003. "On Being a Scholar of Islam: Risks and Responsibilities," in Omid Safi, ed., *Progressive Muslims: On Justice, Gender, and Pluralism* (pp. 128–44). Oxford: Oneworld Press.
Kristof, Nicholas. 2014. "Professors, We Need You!" *The New York Times*, February 15.
Mas, Ruth. 2012. "Why Critique?" *Method & Theory in the Study of Religion* 24: 389–407. https://doi.org/10.1163/15700682-12341246
— 2014a. "Follow the Politics…" *Bulletin for the Study of Religion* 43(4): 6–13. https://doi.org/10.1558/bsor.v43i4.6
— 2014b. "Has Politics Let Us Off the Hook?" *Bulletin for the Study of Religion* blog. http://www.equinoxpub.com/blog/2014/03/has-politics-let-us-off-the-hook reflections-on-islamic-studies/
— 2018. "The Time of Critique," in Lucian Stone and Jason Bahbak Mohaghegh, eds., *Manifestos for World Thought* (pp. 209–28). London: Rowman and Littlefield.

McCutcheon, Russell. 2012. "The State of Islamic Studies in the Study of Religion: An Introduction." *Method & Theory in the Study of Religion* 24: 309–13. https://doi.org/10.1163/15700682-12341239

Rabaté, Jean-Michel. 2002. *The Future of Theory*. Hoboken, NJ: Blackwell.

Safi, Omid. 2014. "Reflections on the State of Islamic Studies." *Jadaliyya*. http://www.jadaliyya.com/pages/index/16269/reflections-on-the-state-of-islamic-studies

Schmidt, James. 1996. *What Is Enlightenment? Eighteenth-Century Answers and Twentieth-Century Questions*. Berkeley, CA: University of California Press.

Taminiaux, Jacques. 1996. "Bios politikos and bios theoretikos in the Phenomenology of Hannah Arendt." *International Journal of Philosophical Studies* 4(2): 215–32. https://doi.org/10.1080/09672559608570832

Wampole, Christy. 2014. "In Praise of Disregard." *The New York Times*, February 16.

Weber, Max. 1958. "Politics as a Vocation" and "Science as an Avocation," in *Max Weber: Essays in Sociology*, edited and translated by H.H. Gerth, and Wright Mills (pp. 77–128 and 129–56). Oxford: Oxford University Press.

Weitzman, Steven P. 2013. "Religious Studies and the FBI: Adventures in Academic Interventionism." *Journal of the American Academy of Religion* 81(4): 959–95. https://doi.org/10.1093/jaarel/lft033

Ruth Mas is a scholar of Islam and Critical Theory currently based in Brooklyn, NYC. She has spent the last two years at the BGSMCS-Berlin Graduate School (for the Study of) Muslim Cultures and Societies at the Freie Universität as a Senior Visiting Research Fellow and has taught and held academic positions in Canada, the United States, England and Germany. She is one of the founding editorial board members of *ReOrient: The Journal of Critical Muslim Studies*. Mas's field and research sites include Morocco, Syria, France and Germany and her research commitments emphasize the intellectual and political dimensions of contemporary Islam. She is specifically interested in the secularization of the Islamic discursive tradition and is currently investigating the relationship between secularity and criticism. Her present writing addresses the nature of temporality in the exercise of critique and its relevance to current debates about Islam and Islamic thought.

2. "I Want My Discipline Back"

S. Sayyid

At one level the disagreement between the positions articulated by Omid Safi and Aaron Hughes about the nature of scholarship and the future of Islamic studies in the North American academy would appear to be only of esoteric interest, far removed from the concerns of a wider public. The battle-lines, however, are not only of Hughes and Safi's making: in one corner are those who believe that their venerable discipline has been invaded by "identity politics" or "political correctness" or "anti-Americanism" or whatever may be the current designation of the latest threat to the civilizing mission as we know it. In the opposite corner are those who see, in the claims to conduct business as usual on behalf of the discipline, the last vestiges of privileges and power. If one steps back from the often personalized and occasionally petty tones of these disputes on which academic reputations and careers are staked, it is possible to see the recurring pattern as a structural fault – signalling the unravelling of a paradigm which arose with the Age of Europe and which the shift to the post-Western seems to be leaving stranded.

In this chapter, I explore the spat between Omid Safi and Aaron Hughes by contextualizing its "larger, social, cultural and ideological structures" (Hughes 2012: 2). The conflict between Hughes and Safi is, of course, like most conflicts, over-determined, so my intention and interest is not to provide a commentary on its twists and turns. Rather, looking at it from far away across an ocean, the question that it raises for me is the purpose of Islamic studies in the heart of what Hardt and Negri (2000) describe as "Empire". Immediately, framing it in this way is bound to raise some hackles. For some, what is problematic is both the formulation of the Empire as well as the assumption that Islamic studies would be any different if it were being taught anywhere else in the world, other than the Empire. The question that I want to raise belongs to the genre of the geopolitics of knowledge.

Both Hughes and Safi acknowledge the impact of the geopolitical in the form of 9/11 and accept that it was a "game changer" (Safi 2014; also see Hughes 2014). They, however, focus on 9/11 not as the beginning of the process by which the "war on terror" became the grammar of the international order, but rather on 9/11 as a national disaster, and the effect it had on the academic provision of teaching on matters Islamicate. In other words, what seems to matter in their dispute is whether the discipline of religious studies specifically (but one could extend this to include other academic areas that study Islam and Muslims) is adequate to the task of understanding and explaining the role of the Islamicate in the in the aftermath of 9/11. For Safi, 9/11 has meant an expansion in the numbers of scholars tasked to teach and research Islam and Muslims. The academy has responded to the shock of 9/11 and to the American public's interest in trying to make sense of the trauma of those events, and the ongoing American occupations and interventions in Muslimistan.[1] Safi notes with some satisfaction that this expansion has also provided the space for an increasing number of Muslim scholars to become involved in the study of matters Islamicate, and he views this as a positive development which may help check what can be described as the Orientalizing gaze. Hughes's disagreement with Safi seems to be based on his objection to Safi's pride in Muslim scholars studying the Islamicate. He sees this intrusion of "identity politics" into the academy as a negative development that sullies the search for truth that is for him the core mission of the academy. For Hughes this influx of Muslim scholars is one aspect of the establishment of what he describes pejoratively as Islamic religious studies (2012: 3). Islamic religious studies is, according to Hughes, the heir to Edward Said's critique of Orientalism (1978), which (as is common in these circles) Hughes dismisses without really engaging with its central

---

1   By Muslimistan I basically refer to the countries in which Islam is socially, culturally and sometimes politically dominant. It basically corresponds with membership of the Organisation of Islamic Cooperation give or take one or two anomalies. See Sayyid (2010: 3–10).

arguments. This is a pity because, by focusing on the consequences of 9/11 for the academy, both Hughes and Safi neglect to contextualize the possibilities that the contemporary assertion of Muslim political subjectivity has for the production of knowledge.[2]

The dislocation caused by the disclosure of Islam in the world is not a disciplinary issue, but rather an epistemological one. That is, while there is a recognition that "Islam" represents a geopolitical and cultural challenge, there is less focus on the epistemological problems that it raises. It is the intersection between geopolitics and epistemology that was so powerfully evoked by Edward Said's *Orientalism*, which forms the backdrop to the Hughes-Safi dispute. In the first part of this chapter I will elaborate on the significance of the debate generated by *Orientalism*, since the ground for disagreement between Safi and Hughes was prepared by the inability of the discipline associated with the study of Islam and the Islamicate to exorcize the ghost of Said's critique.

Orientalism and Whiteness

For Said, Orientalism was the point where ideas of what is European (or Western) intersect with discourses on modernity and discourses on empire. Orientalism is not just another discipline or another division of knowledge production; it is the discursive formation that can be described as being tasked with holding the barbarians at bay, and thus enabling the articulation of whiteness as a form of rule. *Orientalism* (the critique) radically addressed the question of the geopolitics of knowledge production, and in the process delegitimized Orientalism (the discipline).[3] It thus unsettled the narrative of

---

2 For details of what I consider to be the main effects of the global assertion of Muslim political agency, see Sayyid (2014 and 2015).

3 It should be clear that I am expanding the notion of the Orient as a synonym for the residual Other of Europe. The Orient is no more a geographical idea than Europe is. The Orient in its various iterations and divisions came to connote different aspects of what Europe was not. The Orient, in the sense that I am using it, corresponds to Stuart Hall's formulation of the Rest. See Hall (1992).

academic achievements closely associated with the Enlightenment's belief that the production of knowledge required careful and accurate representation of reality and that such a representation could be undertaken in a language that was transparent, neutral, rational and universal: in other words, science.

In such a narrative the success of Western civilization and its conquest of the world was ultimately derived from its embrace of science. Science provided technology, both in terms of the hardware of iron and steel, steam engines and Gatling guns, and the software of double book accounting, cartography, disciplined military drill ..., that enabled Europe to become a continent and a template by which the rest of the world could be measured and understood. Science was the marker of European distinctiveness, and it also influenced other forms of knowledge production to the extent that the study of what we now consider to be the humanities was to be patterned on the achievements of science. The emergence of the "modern" university around the mid-19th century signaled the triumph of enlightenment epistemology, as institutions with precedents going back to the 11th and 16th centuries began to reorganize their teaching activities and, in the process, reorganized the production of knowledge that was attuned to the "European miracle." A positivist world-view centered on the claim that the epistemology and methodology that produced the great achievements of Western science and technology could be harnessed to producing knowledge about humans, with a similar prospect of success, was foundational to the modern Western university. Other forms of knowledge were directly suppressed, e.g., the actions of French colonial authorities in Algeria and British colonial authorities in Punjab in closing down madrasas. As a consequence, the institutional ensembles which sustained local production of knowledge in these colonized regions withered away.

Eurocentric narratives and cultural practices claimed that the triumph of Western forms of knowledge was simply the case of truth conquering falsehood. Europe did not merely discover the truth that was out there; the knowledge that was produced by the European colonial enterprise was empowered not because of its truth content, but because of its ability to shape the world so that it corresponded to its truth claims. The European colonial enterprise was not just the product of a Europe armed with science and imperial ambition setting out to master the world; rather, it was a project constitutive of Europe itself. In other words, the European colonial enterprise as a process of world-making also meant making Europe a part of the world made by Europe.[4] Europe, empire and episteme came together and it is that coming together which we continue to inhabit.

The economic, military, political and cultural dimensions of this process of world-making have been the subject of many investigations. The critique of the relations of exploitation and cruelty established by the European colonial enterprise in its various iterations and interactions has focused on the fostering of unequal and uneven relations of production and consumption. Explorations of the violence of the European colonial enterprise – the brutality of the plantation-enslavement complex, or the institutionalization of the intrusive tyranny of white rule, or the militarized campaigns of extermination – have been conducted, and while there is intense debate about the extent to which these acts of enslavement, torture and extermination were exceptional or were the normal workings of the exceptional states which constituted the European colonial empires, there is an agreement of sorts that massive acts of violence were committed. Even as all the major edifices of the European colonial world system have come under sustained and systematic attack (economy, politics, military, culture), the philosophical underpinnings of European world-making have, to a large extent, managed to be insulated from the process of decolonization. It is against the threat of deepening decolonization that the Hughes-Safi dispute is played out. It is therefore not surprising that, as one of the key custodians of the Western identity, Orientalism would become embroiled in this process.

---

4 The self-referential nature of the process "Europe makes Europe by making the world" recognizes the different registers in which Europe is evoked but also suggests why this process is constantly undisclosed: our very conceptual language for understanding the world is bound up in the construction of the world that it seeks to apprehend. This double bind, I argue, is one of the main obstacles that we face when trying to historicize the European colonial enterprise without decolonizing the episteme that is associated with it.

The significance of Orientalism as an academic discipline, as a cultural comportment or as a discursive formation derives from the way in which it inscribes the point where discrete elements of the European colonial enterprise converge. Orientalism is where European-ness as a form of science, European-ness as a form of racial rule and European-ness as a form of cultural exceptionalism come together. Said's choice of the Napoleonic invasion of Egypt as the ruptural moment that gave birth to Orientalism draws attention not only to the way in which knowledge of the Orient was predicated on the invasion of the Orient, but also to the way in which older ideas about the limits of what was considered to be Western, European and Christian were reinforced and given scientific foundations (1985: 87). The Napoleonic invasion is a metaphor for the entwining of modernity and Europeanness. The scholars who accompanied the soldiers of the Armée d'Orient did not need to wear uniforms and, no doubt, they were motivated by the best of considerations of scholarly intentions, they did not need to be critical or hostile to the Egyptians ... their personal feelings and attitudes are less important than the fact that their very mundane ability to study Egypt was predicated on being part of an occupying force. This is one of the main arguments Said advances in his critique of Orientalism: it was made possible by the exercise of European imperial power over the "Orient," and not the skill or learning of the Orientalists. It is because of the way in which Said's critique resonated globally and not just in the precincts of the academy that Orientalism, much to the chagrin of its adherents, has come to mean not so much an academic discipline but an extended apologia for the systematic cruelties and inequities associated with the European colonial enterprise.[5] Hughes's project seeks to restore the disciplinarity of Orientalism and rescue it from its seepage into a world that seems less and less anchored in the West.

The problem that most Orientalists have with *Orientalism* can be seen to have three major dimensions. First, the terms of Said's critique were associated with an epistemology that emerges from an

---

5   See Hughes (2012: 104) or Robert Irwin (2007). More rabid neo-conservative and Islamophobic accounts can be found on social media; for details see Lean (2012: 41–66).

articulation between the work of Foucault and Gramsci, in particular the marriage between the concepts of discourse and hegemony. This revolutionary coupling of Gramsci and Foucault that Said embraced, and the way it linked hegemony and discourse, helped to propel *Orientalism* beyond the confines of Oriental studies, but also hindered its reception in that field, since it hinted at an epistemological stance that was for most part considered to be alien and irrelevant by the discipline.[6] The mix of discourse and hegemony proved highly productive in contributing to the generation of postcolonial studies and post-structuralism. A number of fields began to see the value of this combination and produced interesting and compelling studies. Most in the field of Islamic studies and related fields, by training and to some extent by inclination, were dismissive of post-structuralist inflected studies. So when confronted with one of the pioneering texts of this intellectual transformation, there was a sense of bewilderment and incomprehension: how could such a "bad book" as *Orientalism* generate so much acclaim in so many circles of higher learning?[7] Wedded as Oriental studies was to positivism, in which epistemological questions were buried in the conventional wisdom of scholarship and the naturalization of Eurocentrism, it was difficult for the discipline to respond to an epistemological critique except by reiterating nostrums that simply could no longer be grounded.

The second problem was that the philosophical foundations of the humanities were laid in a conjuncture in which Europe connoted both an empire and an episteme. The episteme that underscored Western civilization can be described in various ways, with one such label being the metaphysics of presence. This metaphysics is the bedrock of the various infrastructures of the production of knowledge, which includes Orientalism. In the wake of the First World War, such metaphysics of presence began to be subject to sustained critique, most obviously associated with Heidegger and Wittgenstein. While this critique can be seen as uniquely philosophical, there are enough clues to persuade us that there was an awareness of the tangle of Western

---

6   Of course, there was some scholarship infused by Marxist categories but Marxism was not immune to Orientalism.

7   See in particular Robert Irwin's incredulity that such a piece of "charlatanism" has gained such a following (2007).

philosophy and Western civilization.[8] Wittgenstein's declaration at the beginning of his abortive work makes clear that his book is "different from the one that informs the vast stream of European and American civilization in which all of us stand."[9] As has been often pointed out, Wittgenstein was not prone to making comments on the public issues of the day, so his situating his remarks on philosophy not merely in philosophical terms but in civilizational terms should alert us to the possibility that the critique of metaphysics has a reach that goes beyond the merely philosophical (Sayyid 2015).

Finally, it was unlikely that any criticism of a discipline as discipline would not generate resistance from those who had invested a greater part of their life and social capital in the furtherance of that discipline. Thus the critique of Orientalism was seen by those who identified themselves as card-carrying Orientalists, and were unable or unwilling to let go of that attachment, as not only an assault on the intellectual legitimacy of their work, but a potential attack on their livelihoods and individual integrity.[10] Hence the pains to which many Orientalists went to demonstrate how much they and their academic ancestors loved the Oriental. That most scholars in the field were doing Orientalism from the best of motives and were not and had never been part of racist activities, and that many Orientalists were critical of European colonial rule and certainly could not be considered to be advocates and defenders of white rule. Perhaps this accounts for the highly personal tone of Orientalists responding to the criticism of Orientalism. As students of racism are aware, this kind of response is fairly common. The strategic selectivity of structures associated with white rule is translated into questions of culpability or otherwise of

---

8 This section is based very closely on my *Islamism as Philosophy* (forthcoming).

9 This claim is made in the foreword to Wittgenstein's *Philosophical Remarks*, which is the abortive early version of what became *Philosophical Investigations*. See Sayyid (2015).

10 Hughes (2012: 104) is not the only one who finds the pejorative use of the label Orientalist unfair. It is hard not to be moved by the scale of his incomprehension: "Am I ... an 'Orientalist' because I have criticized a number of authors in this volume on methodological grounds?"

individual white people, and in this process the institutional nature of racism is erased. Similarly, structural problems associated with the production of knowledge in the age of white rule become banalized into whether the motivations and intentions of individual Orientalists were benign or not.

Said's critique helped to disclose that the study of matters Islamicate was more about the articulation of the West than it was about understanding the Orient. The significance of Orientalism as a discourse exceeds its self-image as a quaint academic discipline. While this vision of Orientalism was flattering – on the one hand, Orientalists were charged with doing more than just writing dictionaries of Arabic or Aramaic, and on the other hand it implied the erosion of the hermetically sealed barrier between academia and the broader historical and social contexts. This is one of the reasons why so many critics of Said keep pointing out that he confused philologists with proconsuls, academics with adventurers, truth-seekers with profit-maximizers, for the vision the Orientalist scholars had of their field of study was as a closed space, an ivory tower, insulated from the imperial-colonial enterprise unfolding all around them. In its most profound form, by enlarging the conception of Orientalism as a narrative of Western identification in contrast to the non-Western, Said's critique challenged Orientalists to think outside the box of even a sociology of knowledge. It pointed to the imbrication of the process by which the production of knowledge was organized with the process of nation-empire formation.

The defenders of Orientalism have spent the last forty years since the publication of *Orientalism* staging a series of rearguard actions against the advances of the critique. However, despite the institutional and financial resources available to the dons of Orientalism, they have found it difficult to hold back the loss of authority. They have on occasion (and some more than others) tried to find cultural explanations for this state of affairs. They have seen the relative success of *Orientalism* as part of the process by which Western plutocracies have lost their hold on rationality besieged by cultural relativists, uppity Muslims and postmodernists, and seem to believe that is the main reason why their rejection of Said's critique has not been sufficiently persuasive.[11] In general, they have launched three main counter-attacks against *Orientalism*. First, they have tried to show with autodidactic zeal that Said's scholarship is full of elementary mistakes; second, they claim that Said has erased the heterogeneity of Orientalists, some of whom were good and some of whom were bad; and third, they argue that the fundamental relationship between power and knowledge that Said makes so much of is deeply flawed and does not hold. In a series of rebuttals they have sought to argue that Said was an amateur in the field of Oriental studies, and simply did not know enough about the topic to present a sustained critique of it.[12]

The problem with criticisms that focus on the various empirical errors of Said's work is that none of these purported errors is sufficient to dismantle Said's argument as such. The main thrust of the argument that Said makes derives from advancing an epistemology that the defenders of Orientalism tend to dismiss as "faux postcolonialism studies." The argument that Said's conception of the link between power/knowledge or European imperialism and Orientalism was flawed has rested a great deal on the counter-example of German Orientalism. Since some of the greatest and most productive Orientalist scholarship was carried out by Germans, and Germany did not have colonies in West Asia, it follows that the causal connections that Said makes between imperialism and Orientalism cannot be sustained.[13]

---

11 Compare this to Andres Breivik's 1,000-page screed justifying his killing of over 77 people as part of his crusade against Muslims, Marxists and multi-culturalists, and reproducing almost exactly a chain of equivalence that circulates among neo-con-Islamophobes.

12 If one of the charges held against Said is that he was is an interloper in the discipline, then certainly Marshal Hodgson's work cannot be so faulted. In the first volume of Hodgson's *The Venture of Islam* there is, in fact, a critique of Orientalism, which does not necessarily go through the route of Gramsci and Foucault, but nevertheless shares many of Said's misgivings.

13 This also has consequences for Foucault's linking of power/knowledge. The absence of a large German empire in Muslimistan would allow a liberal account of power to prevail in which knowledge and power were distinct phenomena. One of the consequences of such a move is to make it possible for academics and other knowledge-makers to speak truth to power.

This counter-example has become a staple of the commentary defending Oriental studies.[14]

The trouble with such a criticism is that most of those who make it (despite their oft-repeated claims of academic rigor) often lack anything other than a rather rudimentary understanding of the operations of European imperialism. They fail to understand that European colonial empires were divided nationally but united racially.[15] In other words, European colonial empires were racial states: instruments of white rule. Thus the privileges of whiteness were not contained within the nation-states but transcended it, in the same way as nation-states such as France and Britain could represent themselves as distinct from their respective empires. German Orientalists could leverage their whiteness in the context of a European colonial enterprise in which white rule was institutionalized on a global scale. It is not only nationalist iterations but white rule that signals the causal link between imperialism and Orientalism.[16]

Speaking truth to power becomes one of the roles that many academics take upon themselves, including Omid Safi and Aaron Hughes, who in their very different ways want to see the production of truth to be the key role of academics. Safi would want to take this truth out of the classroom, whereas Hughes, with a certain faith in neo-liberal osmosis, would want to see such truth to be contained in the classroom, but trickle down into general culture.

14 For example, David Schimmelpenninck van der Oye's study of Russian Orientalism endorses this criticism levied against Said (2010: 8).

15 One only has to watch a film like *55 Days in Peking* (1963) to see how national divisions could be reconciled by white unity. This film, starring Charlton Heston and David Niven, depicts the events of a siege of the diplomatic enclave in the Chinese empire during the "Boxer Rebellion," in which Americans, British, Germans and Japanese, i.e., the civilized nations, cooperate to fend off Asiatic hordes. The inclusion of Japan makes the point that whiteness is a political rather than a phenotypical category.

16 To be clear, the institutionalization of white rule does not mean that there were no intra-Western rivalries. By the beginning of the 20th century future wars between varying permutations of white great powers were imagined both in dread and fascination. The color line began to be eroded as the exigencies of existential struggle began to impact on the European colonial order, otherwise it would be hard to explain the deployment of "colored" troops in European theaters of war.

Similarly, while Orientalists who assume that the academy is somehow hermetically sealed from the broader culture are unable to cash this claim; in their inability to see diversity in the university as anything but a sign of academic decadence they reflect wider social anxieties and concerns.

Orientalism faces a double challenge, for not only does the critique of the metaphysics of presence destabilize its epistemological claims, but the slow unravelling of the European colonial enterprise undermines its structural centrality too. The crisis of Orientalism is a symptom of the way in which white rule (and all the privileges that it entailed for the bearers of whiteness) is under sustained, if varyingly intense, attack. The nostalgia for a world in which whiteness as a mode of regulation and governance was established has found its most vocal expression in the Tea Party movement. The Tea Party started off as a peculiarly American movement in 2009, with its reference to the American revolution and its belief that the US Constitution was being subverted by a variety of social forces which had taken hold in the 1960s and turned America away from the path laid down by its Founding Fathers. While it is the case that the Tea Party movement has a number of obsessions which do not circulate beyond the United States (e.g., the right to bear arms) there is, however, an argument to be made that the Tea Party has a resonance that transcends US particularisms and describes an intellectual-cultural and political project characterized by the demand for a restoration. During the election campaign of Barack Hussein Obama, a white woman nearly in tears, protesting at the prospect of a Black Muslim President (sic), made a poignant plea: I want my country back. The desire to reclaim their lost country has become a battle cry for the Tea Party. The project of restoration is implicit in the idea that the world has lost its bearings. This sense of lost bearings I would describe as a manifestation of the global crisis of whiteness.[17]

---

17 In its British, French and Austrian iterations it can be seen at work behind the vote for Britain to leave the European Union, behind the support for far-right political parties and behind the institutionalization of Islamophobia across large swaths of Europe.

This explains why some dons of Orientalism can seem to be channeling the doyens of the Tea Party, regardless of their party political affiliations and tendencies, for at the heart of the Tea Party is Eurocentrism, and Eurocentrism does not divide neatly along lines of Left and Right. Rather it could be argued that in relation to the Islamicate, Left and Right become almost meaningless, as socialists, nationalists, liberals and libertarians can all find ways of endorsing Islamophobia. In other words, it is more and more difficult to read one set of political positions around issues such as the role of government in economy and state, and another on policies towards Muslim demands for autonomy.

This significance of Said's *Orientalism* is not really about disciplinary or methodological issues but, rather, about the epistemological changes that come about when the episteme focused on Europe begins to unravel. In other words, Orientalism is about narrating the centrality of the Western enterprise by policing the boundary between the West and the Rest, and therefore it cannot but help be affected by the shift towards a world which is postcolonial. That is, a world in which the institutions and protocols which established and maintained the European colonial process of world-making are disintegrating.[18] The postcolonial is neither a chronological category nor is it exhausted by literary and cultural productions. The postcolonial refers to the process by which European colonial world-making is placed sous rature.[19] That is, we have not been able to replace the world order built by the European colonial enterprise, but we can no longer assume its continued naturalization. This postcolonial condition has many ramifications: cultural, geopolitical and philosophical. In the next section of this chapter I want to draw out the consequences of the postcolonial thus defined to address the question: How should Islam, the Islamicate and Muslims be studied?

---

18 This is why scholars and researchers of East Asia, Eastern Europe, Africa and Latin America have found *Orientalism* such a fruitful text, able to generate insights in a wide variety of temporal and spatial settings.

19 I am using postcolonial in the sense similar to that used by Stuart Hall (1996), but my emphasis is on the postcolonial as a category of political analysis.

The study of Islam and related topics, whether organized in religious studies, or areas studies, or philology, has become politicized in a manner that many of its early scholars would probably not recognize. The politicization of the study of Islam is an extension of the disintegration of Orientalism's hegemony over the constitution and representation of the non-West. This politicization can be seen in the activities of neo-McCarthyite outfits like Campus Watch or Jihad Watch, the machinations of bigoted billionaires and also the disputes among academics about the purpose of such studies. The paradigm that governed the production of knowledge about Islam is less and less able to do so. This unraveling means that most of the verities of Oriental studies are being challenged and interrogated. There are two major developments which have contributed to the politicization of study of the Islamicate: firstly, the Israeli-Palestinian conflict and its leakage into American campuses, and secondly, the increasingly frequent criticism of US foreign policy in Muslimistan.

Since at least perhaps the 1970s, there has been a gradual but clear shift in the world regarding the Israeli-Palestine conflict. There are a number of reasons for this, which we do not need to detail but which include the increasing identification of the Zionist project as an extension of European settler colonialism. By describing Zionism in these terms it has been possible to see in the conflict between Israel and the Palestinian people a metaphor for the conflict inaugurated by the European colonial enterprise. Given how far-reaching this form of white rule was, many in the Global South have increasingly come to understand Zionism in a radically different manner than those in European nations who tended to see the representation of Zionism through the suffering inflicted by racism in the form of Nazism. The shrinking space of the hegemonic narrative of Zionism has meant that its supporters have become far more active in its defense. An intellectual-moral struggle has become joined as an issue that has increasingly become a metaphor for wider struggles, where the floating signifier of Palestine circulates beyond the borders of Israel or Palestine. This is similar to the process by which the anti-apartheid struggle began to be waged outside South Africa, and became a floating signifier by which a critical discursive field was unified, and onto which many social demands could coalesce. With the relative strength of the civil society movement and its achievement in undermining the overt state-sponsored racial segregation in South Africa, the ability of the apartheid state to intellectually defend white rule was heavily circumscribed. Campaigns by various civil society organizations to disinvest in the country created the conditions by which the South African version of racism came to be considered to be outside the pale of acceptable forms of white rule. The anti-colonial struggles that led to dismantling of white rule in European colonies also contributed to making the conditions for the continuation of white rule within Western plutocracies far more complicated. The most intense period of challenge to global white rule came when anti-racist struggles, which challenged white rule in Western metropoles, were combined with anti-colonial struggles, which challenged white rule in the Southern periphery.

The Israel-Palestine conflict shares some of these features with the anti-apartheid struggle and, as a consequence, the study of the Islamicate becomes increasingly contested around the attempts to make the Zionist narrative hegemonic and the resistance to that attempt. The Israeli-Palestinian conflict is over-determined, which is one of the reasons why its study and analysis cannot be resolved empirically or algorithmically. For example, on September 14, 2016, UC Berkeley suspended a one-credit student-led course, "Palestine: A Settler Colonial Analysis," apparently after protests by Zionist organizations that the course was anti-Semitic. Leaving aside the details of this specific case, what it illustrates is the way in which scholarship in contested terrains cannot be insulated from non-academic factors. Therefore, academic rules and algorithms cannot stand above the fray. For example, in the above case, the argument made was that a course that seemed to be calling for a decolonized Palestine was axiomatically anti-Semitic. In the absence of algorithms or rules, we have a process that is inherently political, that is dominated by rule-making rather rule-following. In this regard, the Orientalist establishment wants to assert a scholarship that follows rules, but its efforts are stymied by the increasing numbers of people who recognize that rules are not neutral or transparent and that, ultimately, these rules are the results of the naturalization of a previous array of power relationships. Thus, Orientalism's tendencies to demand disciplinary rigor and the following of rules, if not orders, is met with incredulity by those who are aware that such demands are not themselves innocent or transparent.

The second major development leading to the politicization of the study of the Islamicate is linked to the way in which US foreign policy has become more directly involved in Muslimistan, which has led to an increase in the demand for forms of knowledge that will serve the purposes of US interventions. This demand has given scholarship of the Islamicate an increasingly general relevance. These developments have reinvigorated the classical relationship central to Orientalism – that between empire and episteme. As we have seen, one of most telling indictments that Said made was about the complicity between imperialism and Orientalism. The dismantling of direct European empires appeared to break this relationship down and promise the liberation of Orientalism from suspicion. The emergence of the "war on terror" as the grammar of the international order and the imbrication of the United States in the Islamosphere has led to a demand for specialists who can guide the conduct of US interventions and operations. One of the best examples of this is provided by the Human Terrain System (HTS) launched in Afghanistan in 2007. This was a major initiative by the US military which weaponized social science, and tried to turn it directly into an instrument of US-led occupation and attempted pacification.[20] At least three academic members of the HTS have been killed in action. What is interesting about the HTS is that precisely the subjects that were considered the staple of Oriental studies – linguistics, religious studies and anthropology – have become central to the exercise of American military power in Muslimistan. Invasion, occupation and systematic torture – all these deployments of American might – have been aided and abetted by academics. Inevitably this has weakened the attempts by the Orientalists to suggest that scholarship should be disinterested and unbiased. The idea of good scholarship that is motivated by a desire to produce the truth and bad scholarship that is motivated by the desire to defend a

---

20 See Price (2011) for an account of the deployment of experts from the fields of anthropology and other social sciences in the service of US interventions and occupations in many parts of Muslimistan.

particular identity disintegrates when scholarship becomes part and parcel of military campaigns. (It is one of the central conceits of white rule, that only others have politics based on identity – analogous to the manner in which whiteness is commonly asserted not to be an ethnicity.) By its having to respond in various ways to the demands of the US interventions in the Islamosphere, Orientalism's dream of presenting itself as a de-politicized and self-contained disciplinary field has been subverted.

Islamic Studies and Empire

So far in this chapter I have argued that the Hughes-Safi dispute can be understood as another skirmish between those who want to hold on to Orientalism and what it represents, and those who are uneasy about what it is and what it represents. I have argued that in many ways these tensions are part of a broader process that can be described as the de-centering of the West (Young 1990; Sayyid 2015 [1997]). One of the main responses to this provincialization has been the emergence of an Eurocentric coalition whose members range from "the deplorable"[21] to the new atheists, to those who see in the Pentagon the revolutionary vanguard, to demagogues of the alt-right, muscular liberals and decent folk ... what unites this disparate cast of characters is a script based on the theme of the restoration of the West as the center of the world and the template for the universal.

21 The category of "deplorables" is one that Hillary Clinton deployed in a speech on September 16, 2016: "You know, to just be grossly generalistic, you could put half of Trump's supporters into what I call the basket of deplorables. Right? The racist, sexist, homophobic, xenophobic, Islamophobic – you name it. And unfortunately there are people like that. And he has lifted them up. He has given voice to their websites that used to only have 11,000 people – now 11 million" (http://www.latimes.com/nation/politics/trailguide/la-na-trailguide-updates-transcript-clinton-s-full-remarks-as-1473549076-htmlstory.html). For a particularly acute analysis of muscular liberalism and the relationship that I am drawing out in this chapter see Klug (2015: 67–70) who dissects the Munich speech of former British Prime Minster David Cameron and the opposition that it presents

I have argued that in this context the geopolitics of knowledge production cannot be bracketed and we have to ask the question of how the Islamicate can be studied from inside the Empire. I am not sure Hughes would recognize this as a legitimate question or concern. Safi may recognize the challenge but his response seems to be something like that the influx of Muslim scholars will help undermine the specific structures that imprison the study of Islam and Muslims. The problem with the latter line of argument is twofold. First, it turns the epistemological problem at the heart of the critique of Orientalism into a methodological problem that can be resolved by the production of "insider" accounts. This anthropological solution, however, does not resolve the epistemological problem. There are many reasons why we should welcome the fact that more and more Muslim scholars are entering the academy and teaching and researching about all matters Islamicate. It is not the case, however, that a change in University demographics will, in itself, transform the production of knowledge of Islam.

While it is the case that it would be considered to be perverse to have a department of Women studies, or African-American studies, without a single woman, or African-American academic, such an absence is often the norm for departments of Islamic studies.[22] What has made the wider participation of women and African-Americans in the academy a transformatory experience (however, contested) is the way in which both feminist and African-American scholarship's entry into the academy was to a large extent based on the success of political struggles. It is not just that the Civil Rights movement opened up the academy for black scholars but rather the fact that it constituted a black political subject in the first place. The articulation of a black political subject enabled the experience of blackness to have a significance that was general rather than individual, and that

---

between "state multiculturalism" and muscular liberalism – an opposition to be found among the diverse members of a broad coalition that seeks to defend Eurocentrism by defending its own version of the Enlightenment.

22 Of course such an observation is restricted; there are many parts of the UK where it perfectly possible to have African studies without African academics, as well as Islamic studies without Muslims.

experience was part of an assemblage of commitments and horizons that inform to lesser or greater degree African-American scholarship. The infusion of black scholars in the academy especially (perhaps mainly) in the United States has been because of the articulation of a black political subjectivity with scholarship. To dismiss such a process as an expression of "identity politics" misses the point about how knowledge is produced.

In other words, the extent to which Muslim participation in the field of the Islamicate would be transformative and could address the epistemological lacuna produced by the critique of Orientalism and the de-centering of the West depends on the degree to which Muslim refers to a political rather than an ethnographic (or even religious) category. That is, to what extent and how many Muslim scholars coming into the American academy bring with them not only their experiences but the means to read these experiences not purely biographically but historically. The most productive outcome of the Safi-Hughes dispute would not be the victory of one side or another (whatever such a victory may mean) but rather the ability to see the study of matters Islamicate in a new light, and in doing so, change the way in which we learn and teach.

So how should we study Islam, Muslims and the Islamicate in the postcolonial West? What is perhaps not particularly helpful is to put together a manifesto of sorts with commandments such as: "Islamic studies must appeal to other theoretical disciplines," or that it should not be open to "soft disciplines like post-colonialism," or that you should be allowed to criticize Islam without being called a neo-con (Hughes 2012: 125). This form of special pleading may serve some therapeutic function to those who need discipline and order, but the quest for a post-Orientalist approach to all matters Islamicate, to be a productive one, has to understand post-Orientalism as an epistemological rather than a chronological category. The lack of discipline that some see in the field is, as I have argued in this chapter and in other forums, best understood not in moral terms that scholars have become corrupted by the siren calls of multiculturalism, political correctness or "soft disciplines," but rather that the paradigm (and behind it the episteme) of the given order is no longer hegemonic.

To understand the post-Orientalist means being able to come to terms with the critique of Orientalism. Without being prescriptive, I would suggest that there are two types of critique: a sociological approach and a philosophical approach. The first I describe as "weak orientalism" and the second as "strong orientalism" (Sayyid 2015 [1997]: 32–4). In weak orientalism the problem is the persistence of bias caused by undue influence on scholarship by the sponsorship of corporations, governments, etc. In strong orientalism the problem is not that Orientalists distort the Orient due to self-interest or undue influence, but rather that Orientalism constitutes the Orient. In which case, the problem cannot be of ill-informed writers trading in stereotypes, because the purpose of Orientalism is to represent the West by articulation of a series of binary oppositions which give it cohesion (for example, the West symbolizes democracy, because the Orient is despotic, the West is modern because the Orient is traditional, the West is individualistic because the Orient is collectivist, etc.). Categories such as democracy, modernity, individualism and their cognates only have an identity because they can be contrasted with their opposites. If we understand the post-Orientalist as post-"strong Orientalism" then it seems to me that the only approach one can take is a decolonial one.[23] In relation to the study of matters Islamicate, a decolonial approach is what I describe as "Critical Muslim Studies."

All the social sciences are silently comparative, in that our identification of problems and issues revolves around an accepted and often unstated assumption of the criterion of the normal, the natural, the ordinary, the ways things are when they are the way they are supposed to be. For example, to what extent the is category of religion, in both its expert and popular formulations, derived as it is from an Enlightenment understanding of Western Christianity at particular historical conjunctures, a useful way of understanding the complexes and associations that bear the designation of Hinduism, Judaism, Buddhism, Islam? As Tomoko Masuzawa points out, the development of the category of world religions reflected transformations in European geopolitical positioning and the "reconstitution" of

---

23 For more details on decoloniality see Mignolo (2011); for a decolonial approach in relation to the Islamicate see Sayyid (2015 [1997]).

its identity vis-a-vis a world order centered on the signifier of Islam (2005: 180). Thus, while on the one hand the taxonomy of world religions was an attempt to demarcate and discipline a range of social organizations and human experiences, the Archimedean point of that edifice was Christianity re-articulated to be the embodiment of Europeanness.

As long as the contrast with the normal by which the social sciences respond to a problem is occupied by Eurocentric accounts, the analyses that follow will tend to be infelicitous especially when the capacity for the West to use its power to hammer round pegs into square holes becomes diminished. The organized production of knowledge as response requires a recognition of a problem; in this sense knowledge is primarily an activity of discovering and resolving puzzles. What tips something into being a puzzle is crucial. One could make the argument that in the long 19th century the development of social sciences was also an attempt to constitute and normalize a distinct Western identity, and to ensure that normal as settled, in contrast to which a problem that arose was based on a Western reading of its own destiny. Hence, the social sciences cannot but be affected by transformations of the position of the Western enterprise. The shift from so-called "hard disciplines" to "soft disciplines" may reflect something other than academic decadence; it may reflect an uncertain, hesitant attempt to recognize the unraveling between the universal and the Western. When the world stutters in reproducing Westernese, the silence of the silent comparator has to be broken. At its best this is what critical scholarship has done, be it feminism, be it critical race theory, be it whiteness studies … to speak about the silence.

The project of Critical Muslim Studies is not a set of prescriptions let alone commandments, or perhaps even a manifesto, but rather an opening gambit. A gambit built around two moves: a recognition of the way in which world history has been dominated by a historiography centered on the figure of the West (Goody 2007: 13) and a recognition of that philosophical edifice on which the social sciences were erected in the 19th century and which has been subject to a series of profound critiques that require a response other than pretending to stay calm and just carry on. So it is in this sense that Critical Muslim

Studies is post-Orientalist, post-positivist and decolonial (Sayyid 2014: 11–14). As the opening statement of the journal *ReOrient* puts it: "Critical Muslim Studies is characterized by a series of epistemological orientations rather than substantive properties, permanent categories or persistent methodologies" (Klug 2015: 6). The orientations that guide Critical Muslim Studies recognize that the challenge of Eurocentrism is inscribed in the very analytical tools that we use to understand the world around us.

The Safi-Hughes exchange carries with it echoes of an ongoing struggle between those alarmed by the prospect of a white population losing its majority and those who are impatient to imagine a rainbow nation. This is why the slogan "I want my country back" has resonated in some recent debates in Western plutocracies. At the same time, a number of universities founded by the European colonial enterprise in many parts of the world have been confronted by students asking: "Why is my curriculum white?" These two slogans existing at the same time, but rarely drawn together, illustrate the fissures that the de-centering of the West seems to be triggering. The desire to have their discipline back that seems to animate so many doyens of Orientalism is not simply an attempt to assert ownership over an academic field, it is also a simultaneous attempt to regulate the production of knowledge along specific lines: to discipline a disciplinary field. If asked why the curriculum is white, one answer would be because the curriculum is based on the truth. Another answer would be that the disciplines that we teach were the products of a world that is no longer what it was, and that we need to come to terms with it. The study of matters Islamicate or the Orient or whatever iterations of whatever is defined as non-West cannot simply be an affair of good or bad scholarship, because the criterion of what constitutes such a distinction is itself a product of a particular history, a history that we need to know but not necessarily a history that we are bound by. In such circumstances, a lack of discipline is perhaps nothing more than a recognition of the necessity of decolonizing the Eurocentric episteme.

References

Goody, J. 2007. *The Theft of History*. Cambridge: Cambridge University Press. https://doi.org/10.1017/CBO9781139197151

Hall, S. 1992. "The West and the Rest: Discourse and Power," in S. Hall and B. Gieben, eds., *Formations of Modernity* (pp. 275–331). Cambridge: Polity Press.

— 1996. "When Was 'the Post-colonial'? Thinking at the Limit," in I. Chambers and L. Curti, eds., *The Post-colonial Question. Common Skies, Divided Horizons* (pp. 242–60). London: Routledge.

Hardt, Michael and Antonio Negri. 2000. *Empire*. Cambridge, MA: Harvard University Press.

Hodgson, Marshal. 1974. *The Venture of Islam, Vol. 1: The Classical Age of Islam*. Chicago: Univeristy of Chicago Press.

Hughes, Aaron W. 2012. *Theorizing Islam: Disciplinary Deconstruction and Reconstruction*. Durham, UK: Acumen.

— 2014. "When Bad Scholarship Is Just Bad Scholarship: A Response to Omid Safi." *Bulletin for the Study of Religion*, http://bulletin.equinoxpub.com/2014/02/when-bad-scholarship-is-just-bad-scholarship-a-response-to-omid-safi/

Irwin, Robert. 2007. *For Lust of Knowing: The Orientalists and Their Enemies*. Middlesex: Penguin Books.

Klug, Brian. 2015. "Fawlty Logic: The Cracks in Cameron's 2011 Speech." *ReOrient* 1(1): 61–77. https://doi.org/10.13169/reorient.1.1.0061

Lean, Nathan. (2012). *The Islamophobia Industry*. London: Pluto Press.

Masuzawa, Tomoko. 2005. *The Invention of World Religions*. Chicago: University of Chicago Press. https://doi.org/10.7208/chicago/9780226922621.001.0001

Mignolo, Walter. 2011. "Epistemic Disobedience and the Decolonial Option." *Transmodernity: Journal of Peripheral Cultural Production of the Luso-Hispanic World* 1(2). http://escholarship.org/uc/item/62j3w283

Price, David H. 2011. *Weaponizing Anthropology: Social Science in Service of the Militarized State*. Petrolia and Oakland, CA: CounterPunch and AK Press.

Safi, O. 2014. "Reflections on the State of Islamic Studies." *Jadaliyya*, http://www.jadaliyya.com/pages/index/16269/reflections-on-the-state-of-islamic-studies (accessed March 17, 2015).

Said, Edward W. 1978. *Orientalism*. London and Henley: Routledge & Kegan Paul.

— 1985. "Orientalism Reconsidered." *Cultural Critique* 1 (Autumn): 89–107.
Sayyid, S. 2010. *Thinking Through Islamophobia: Global Perspectives.* New York: Columbia University Press.
— 2014. *Recalling the Caliphate: Decolonization and World Order.* London: Hurst.
— 2015. "Towards a Critique of Eurocentrism: Remarks on Wittgenstein, Philosophy and Racism," in M. Araujo and Silvia R. Maeso, eds., *Eurocentrism, Racism and Knowledge: Debates on History and Power in Europe and the Americas* (pp. 80–92). New York: Palgrave.
https://doi.org/10.1057/9781137292896.0009
— 2015 [1997]. *A Fundamental Fear.* 3rd edn. London: Zed Press.
— forthcoming. *Islamism as Philosophy.* London: Bloomsbury Academic.
Schimmelpenninck van der Oye, David. 2010. *Russian Orientalism.* New Haven, CT: Yale University Press.
Young, M. 1990. *White Mythologies.* London: Routledge.

S. Sayyid is Professor of Social Theory and Decolonial Thought and Head of the School of Sociology and Social Policy at the University of Leeds. He is the author of *A Fundamental Fear* (1997, which was banned by the Malaysian government; a 3rd edition was published in 2015) and *Recalling the Caliphate* (2014).

Part II
Critique and Identity in Qur'anic Studies

3. Religion, History, Ethics

Rethinking the Crisis of Western Qur'anic Studies

Alexandre Caeiro and Emmanuelle Stefanidis

What reading practices and literary sensibilities are appropriate for understanding scripture?[1] How are different modes of historical inquiry linked to various socio-political projects? What is the proper function of critique in a (post)secular world? These timely questions constitute the stakes underlying contemporary debates in the field of Qur'anic studies (QS). In this essay we trace the emergence of a mode of practical history concerned with the relation between historical inquiry and ethical commitment. This historiographic mode, prompted by the reconfiguration of Qur'anic studies in the aftermath of 9/11, contrasts with the resilient ideal of disinterested scholarship that has dominated the field for most of its modern history. The onset of practical history coincides with broader institutional transformations that have unsettled the field's regime of truth, expressed in a set of oppositions between secular reason and religious commitment, science and politics, the West and Islam. Rather than the widely-invoked methodological challenge posed by revisionist approaches to the history of the Qur'an, it is perhaps the blurring of these constitutive binaries that best explains why the diagnosis of "crisis" and "disarray" has proliferated in spite of the field's obvious vitality.

The history of the Western study of the Qur'an narrated by its modern practitioners is closely modeled on secularism's own

---

1 This article is a revised version of a paper presented at the eighth SOAS Conference on The Qur'an: Text, Society & Culture, London, 2013. We thank the organizers and the participants for their comments.

self-representation. It typically posits the Enlightenment as a key rupture, shifting the study of the Qur'an from the realm of medieval polemics into the secular world of academic objectivity, and it construes Christianity as an ambivalent force. The rise of historical criticism is sometimes depicted in terms of a struggle of secular reason against religious myth. At other times, the method appears as the distinctive achievement of Christian thinkers, whose openness to reason and metaphor stands in contrast to Muslim readings of their scripture.

Like secularism's own historiography, this narrative is increasingly under strain. On the one hand, the idea of pre-Enlightenment polemics has been complicated by studies that show the complex range of reading practices and attitudes that medieval Christians brought to bear on the Qur'an (Burman 2007; Elmarsafy 2009). On the other, the notion of post-Enlightenment objectivity has been rendered problematic by the recognition of the prejudice and speculation that has driven much of field's recent scholarship (Saleh 2003; Schöller 2004). When non-Western views are taken into account, the Enlightenment rupture becomes simply a matter of perspective. The postcolonial Muslim subject interpellates scholarly practices (and secular politics), revealing biases hidden behind universal definitions and prompting scholars (and political philosophers) to search for alternative narratives. As linear claims of exclusive ownership over critical inquiry give way to more nuanced discussions about the relation between Western and Islamic traditions of scholarship, debates in QS bespeak a broader interrogation of the secular academic – that "placid order" (Masuzawa 2012: 186) of knowledge that has been for too long taken for granted by professional scholars. This interrogation must be placed in the context of knowledge production in a multivocal world: what kind of knowledge of the other can be produced and how it should be articulated (Clifford 1988), and even what constitutes the "other" in the first place. These questions, raised most famously by Edward Said (1978) in relation to the study of Islam, have maintained their significance: Is there a Western will to power underlying the accumulation of Oriental knowledge? If so, how is this will actively sustained or tacitly acquiesced? Can it be resisted, tamed, reversed? Are there ethical limits to the pursuit of knowledge?

21st-century Disarray

Western Qur'anic studies constitutes a privileged case-study for probing the secular nature of academia. Moribund for decades, the field is currently undergoing rapid expansion and renewal. The vitality of the field is demonstrated by an impressive number of recent monographs, dictionaries, translations, companion volumes and encyclopedic works in all the major European languages.[2] This is partly the outcome of the general expansion of Islamic studies across Western universities: scholars of the Qur'an seem to be the greatest beneficiaries of the increased public and academic interest in Islam in the aftermath of 9/11.[3] The surge of interest in the Qur'an occurs however at a peculiar moment in the discipline – a moment that is now frequently described as one of crisis, confusion and disarray. The diagnosis is shared by scholars positioned at the center as well as in the margins of the field; recently, it has become part of a wider public debate in Europe and North America.[4] The reasons for this state of affairs are multifaceted. While some are common to Islamic studies, and perhaps to academia in general, others appear more specific to the field of QS. We discuss three factors below: the protracted debate about Orientalism; the revisionist challenge; and the emergence of an ethical question.

As a subdiscipline of Islamic studies, the field of QS has reached the 21st century reeling from the debates provoked by Edward Said's critique of Orientalism and what goes derogatively in the field by the name of "postmodern skepticism." Although Said's work urged

---

2 This vitality has led one scholar to ask whether we are currently witnessing a "golden age" in the study of the Qur'an (Reynolds 2011).

3 As Ernst and Martin argue, "very frequently a job in Islamic studies is defined exclusively as the study of classical Arabic texts such as the Qur'an and the foundational texts of Islamic law" – a practice inherited from "the heyday of Orientalism" (2010: 13–14).

4 Glen Bowersock, "In the Shadow of the Sword by Tom Holland – review," *The Guardian*, May 4, 2012; Tom Holland, "Tom Holland responds to Glen Bowerstock's review of In the Shadow of the Sword," *The Guardian*, May 7, 2012.

scholars to rethink the relation between knowledge and power, its main impact upon QS has been methodological rather than political.[5] The conceptual moves underlying *Orientalism* challenged scholars to keep up with insights developed in the humanities and social sciences. Practitioners of QS have often struggled to combine the hefty demands of the field with knowledge of recent advances in other disciplines (Schöller 2004: 196). Because of this, QS is frequently depicted as a field based on outdated methodologies, while the reverse question of how the study of the Qur'an might help to advance debates in the wider disciplines seems almost unthinkable.

The diagnosis of methodological obsolescence in QS, to some extent shared with the field of Islamic studies, is accentuated here by the lingering influence of a set of questions related to the origins of the Islamic scripture. A significant body of QS scholarship has been geared towards uncovering the meaning and context of the Islamic scripture. Drawing on biblical historical criticism and associated Enlightenment understandings of science and reality, scholars have undertaken a "genetic" search for the authentic Qur'an, the "urtext" from which the current scripture derives. The relevance of the question lay partly in an older motive of Western scholarship: the understanding of Islam as a (corrupted) offshoot of Judaism and Christianity. The pull of the approach drew also on historicist assumptions about the role of the past in the making of collective identities, accentuated by an Orientalist conceit about the pervading impact of religion in the so-called "Islamic society." As Wilfred Cantwell Smith and other scholars of religion have pointed out, the search for origins is fraught with essentialisms: the idea that a religion is best understood

---

5   Attempts by scholars of the Qur'an to respond to Edward Said are quite rare. In "Orientalism in Oriental Studies? Qur'anic Studies as a Case in Point," Neuwirth (2007) draws upon Said's methodological critique of Orientalism (the alterity of the Orient, requiring exceptional methodologies) to suggest innovative ways out of the field's methodological predicament without explicitly mentioning Said's name. The political dimension of Said's critique – the relation between knowledge and power in Orientalism – is left largely unaddressed. The same is true of Chase Robinson's baffling description of Patricia Crone as a post-Orientalist scholar (Robinson 2014).

in its inaugural moment, and through the study of its sacred text, and that it is more productive to focus on causes rather than historic consequences.[6] In recent decades some voices have started to question the excesses of the positivism inherent in the search for origins, to emphasize Islam's originality rather than its debt to other monotheistic traditions, and to call for studies not of the Qur'an's textual truths but of its contextual meanings. As a field however, QS seems to have only started to make its assumptions about historical causality and the historicity of meaning explicit and debatable.

QS scholarship in the 21st century has also inherited the polarizing debates prompted by John Wansbrough's revisionist works (1977, 1978) and accentuated by Christoph Luxenberg's more recent polemic (2000). Revisionism radically questioned the reliability of Muslim sources, throwing the field's basic assumptions (from the person of Muhammad to the setting and language of the Revelation) into question. Although it might be reductionist to divide QS in terms of a traditionalist-revisionist line, the impact that revisionism has had on the field is demonstrated by the number of responses it continues to elicit, and by its usual identification as the primary (if not unique) reason for the "dire" and "sorry" state of the field (Saleh 2003: 143; Sinai and Neuwirth 2010: 1).

The failure to reach a consensus on the basic questions does not seem to have undermined the principled confidence of practitioners in the ability to approximate historical truth (Madigan 1995; Böwering 2008). In practice, however, historical criticism has not yielded the rewards it promises. As the authoritative *Encyclopedia of the Qur'an*'s review of the "Post-Enlightenment Academic Study of the Qur'an" (Schöller 2004) suggests, the results of modern scholarship have been so frequently disappointing that the very assumption of cumulative knowledge in the field needs perhaps to be questioned. The nature of the Qur'an as an "open text" (Stefanidis 2008) and the scarcity of reliable historical evidence have repeatedly frustrated attempts to rescue the scripture from the generic past and make it

---

6   See Smith (1980), Madigan (1995), Ernst and Martin (2010), Sinai and Neuwirth (2010: 4).

available for historical inquiry.[7] This has forced scholars to adopt ambivalent positions regarding speculation: at times they seem to hail the place of "educated guesses," the role of "sheer speculation," the virtues of "independence of thought" and "methodological experimentation" (Donner 2011: 28, 30, 32; Rippin 2004: ix); more frequently, they decry the "musings," "conjectural claims," "useless speculation," "circumstantial evidence" and excessive reliance on "hypothetical" scenarios (Abdel Haleem 2008; Saleh 2003; Schöller 2004).[8] The speculative nature of much of the scholarship has often blurred the boundary between history and fiction, making it difficult to arbitrate between conflicting theses and contributing to the sense of confusion. The literary turn of QS – initiated by Wansbrough himself and taken up by various scholars – may be seen as a response to this predicament, shedding the burdens of proof associated with historical inquiry for a more creative approach to Qur'anic intertextuality.

The quest for the authentic Qur'an that drives much of the field has placed QS practitioners in an awkward position toward standard Muslim belief. Some scholars have tried to justify their work (and pre-empt Muslim criticism) by drawing upon discourses that emphasize the tensions between (Christian) belief and (biblical) historical criticism.[9] Western attitudes toward the Qur'an have also been reminiscent, however, of the anthropology of error, fetishism and myth. Elaborated in colonial contexts, these constructs share the idea that non-Europeans mistakenly sacralize objects that Europeans recognize as profane. The long-standing association of QS with missionary

---

7   We are indebted to Michael Oakeshott and Hayden White for the distinction between generic and historical pasts.

8   The late Fazlur Rahman (1984: 75) had a trenchant take on this kind of studies: "such attempts, in the judgment of the Qur'ān itself, are no more than *Ahwā'*, uncontrolled desires and wishful thinking with a singular indifference to canons of sound scholarship and objectivity."

9   See for example Harvey (1966) quoted in Donner (2011). The relation between biblical criticism and Christian theology is more complicated than authors such as Donner would have it. It would be mistaken to place biblical criticism within a secular grand-narrative of textual liberation from theological constraints, since many theologians championed the methods of textual criticism.

postures, colonial projects and cultural animosity continues to haunt the field.[10] Until recently it was possible to more or less openly subscribe to the 19th-century Scottish philosopher Thomas Carlyle's description of the Qur'an as "A wearisome confused jumble, crude, incondite; endless iterations, long-windedness, entanglement; most crude, incondite; – insupportable stupidity, in short!" More "sympathetic" approaches to the Qur'an can also be found but the possibility that Western scholarship on the Qur'an might be appreciated by Muslims seems nevertheless so distant that when it does happen, scholars find it worth mentioning (Rippin 2004: x).

If the 20th-century professionalization of the discipline has allowed historians to marginalize ethical concerns, the ethical turn ushered in by postcolonial studies (and the increasing Muslim presence in the academy) has forced scholars to confront the epistemic violence of their claims and face the existence of Muslim communities whose textual practices exceed the interests of "objective" scholarly research. Mirroring the emergence of an insider/outsider problem in the study of religion (McCutcheon 1999) and debates about the politics of representation in anthropology (Clifford and Marcus 1986), a reflection about the proper management of Muslim sensitivity has irrupted in the field. Montgomery Watt's concern "not to offend Muslims gratuitously" (1970: vi) constitutes perhaps one of the earliest expressions of a new ethical awareness that has led to recurrent debate.[11] As we show below, this ethical dilemma will be thrown into sharp relief

---

10 The racial prejudice and dubious politics of scholars in the field is sometimes recognized, but always discarded as inessential to the scholarship they produce.

11 While the ethical debate is common to all the disciplines once subsumed under Orientalism, QS is frequently singled out by Muslim critics as particularly problematic. A long article by Toby Lester in *The Atlantic* magazine provides a useful overview of scholarly positions at the dawn of the new century (Lester, "What Is the Koran?" *The Atlantic*, January 1999). For scholarly texts before and after 9/11 on the question of Muslim sensitivity see inter alia Abdul-Rauf (1985), Adams (1985), Bennett (2010, 2013), Donner (2011), Ernst and Martin (2010), Esack (2005), Neuwirth (2007), Rahman (1984), Reynolds (2011).

in the aftermath of 9/11, reshaping both the field's methodological debates and its structures of justification.

21st-century Rearrangements

In introductions to companion volumes, as in reviews of individual monographs, it has become commonplace in the 21st century to link the vitality of QS to the present political predicament. These linkages range from sober references to the timeliness of scholarly works (Rippin 2006a: x) to emphases on their vital necessity (Arkoun 2005: 249). While it seems exaggerated to claim that 9/11 changed "everything" (McAullife 2005: 616), the attacks produced a crucial reorientation of QS in two main directions.

In the context of an important social demand for an Islamic Reformation, a premium has been placed on scholarship that can help along the reform process while simultaneously building bridges with Muslims. Reform and bridge-building were not totally unknown in QS (nor do they exhaust its current dynamics), but they have acquired great urgency in the 21st century. The idea of reform has sometimes been linked to controversial projects such as INARAH (Institute for Research on Early Islamic History and the Koran) and dismissed as irrelevant to mainstream scholarship. As we demonstrate below, the demand for reform has nevertheless impacted the field well beyond its margins. Rather than casting QS scholars as agents of a (variously-appraised) Western civilizing mission, as many have claimed, our aim is to highlight more modestly how scholarship in QS has been mediated by the opportunities and constraints presented in public and policy debates. One does not have to impute hidden ideological motives to individuals in order to grasp how the imperatives of reform and bridge-building have reshaped the manner in which scholars in QS seek funding, devise research projects, decide the composition of research teams, extend conference invitations and publicly assert the relevance of their scholarship.

It is widely acknowledged today that the security concerns which have funded much of post-9/11 Western research on Islam have also reshaped QS's relation to the state and the wider public. As one scholar pointedly put it, "in the popular mind the Qur'an is a ticking bomb that needs somehow to be defused" (Madigan 2008: xii). The privileged status of the Qur'an as the literal word of God in mainstream Islam is read as a sign of Islam's unique dangerosity – an obstacle to Muslim integration in the West, to democratization in the Muslim world and to Western interests worldwide.[12] Public debates have thus contributed to authorize the kind of critical reading of Islam's sacred text deployed in Western academia, reversing the decline of historical-philological work prefigured in the post-Saidian debates on Orientalism.[13] The link between the academic study of the Qur'an in the West and a global Islamic Reformation has become a cliché often cautioned by academics and liberal Muslim intellectuals. At stake lies no less than the question of "how to reconcile Islam with the modern world"; and the Muslim reaction to Western QS is scrutinized as "a sensitive test" of its "readiness" to accommodate critical thinking.[14]

In this configuration, QS scholars have been compelled to participate in debates about the nature of Islam, the integration of Muslims in the West or the rise of Islamophobia (Qureish and Sells 2003; Rippin 2007; Wild 2009; Ismael and Rippin 2010). Urged by the wider public to "explain" the putative absence of critical Muslim scholarship on the Qur'an, scholars have also taken a renewed interest in the writings of modern Muslim intellectuals. If they sometimes

---

12 See for example *The Economist*, "Muslims and the Koran: In the beginning were the words," December 31, 2011. Specialists in Qur'anic studies have sometimes provided justification for this view (e.g., Prémare 2004: 106–7). Mahmood (2006) provides a critical analysis of the mode of thinking that underlies this mode of reasoning: "the recalcitrant Muslim is faulted for his inability to recognize that the truth of Quranic scripture is grounded not in its theological claims but in culture and history."

13 Maxime Rodinson was justified in writing in 1980 that advances in social sciences might not render philology obsolete, but would significantly diminish its relevance (Rodinson 2003 [1980]: 99; see also Pollock 2009). The new configuration forces us to nuance the assessment. As Angelika Neuwirth (2013: 189–90) sharply put it, the 9/11 attacks "rescue[d] philology from Said's polemic."

14 Andrew Higgins, "The Lost Archive," *Wall Street Journal*, January 12, 2008.

lament the "uphill battle" that methods of historical-critical analysis face outside Euro-America, scholars celebrate the rare Muslim voices that are willing to brave the dangers that confront them (Wild 2006) or adapt their interpretations to suit the Western contexts (McAuliffe 2005). In the foreword to one such study, Andrew Rippin captured the field's reconfiguration perfectly when he praised the role that QS plays in "pushing the [Muslim] community to face the issues and undertake open debate" and pronounces the obsolescence of "the customary alibi of scholarship that pretends that [academic work] is just 'there', to be accepted or rejected by the Muslim community with no value judgment or even concern attached to the impact of the study" (Rippin 2006c: x; see also Rippin 2013a: 59).

Western universities are now routinely expected to provide opportunities for engagement with Muslim scholars. Series of lectures by "Muslim intellectuals" are organized in the context of projects that otherwise consider Muslim tradition irrelevant; scholars seek to quote Muslim authors even when they seem removed from the argument at hand; and leading academics present their work to select audiences in the Muslim world. The absence of Muslim voices from collective volumes becomes an issue frowned upon by reviewers (Renard 2011: 684). The need to build bridges arises partly from the realization that Muslims are now a part of the West, and increasingly active in the academic study of Islam (McAuliffe 2005). It echoes and reinforces the dialogue initiatives promoted by high-profile political instances and testifies to a gradual change of power relations between Islam and the West.[15] The imperative of reform, on the other hand, stems from the widespread perception that the "mythical history" that Muslims tell about their scripture has "dramatic consequences" (Chabbi 2008: 24; see also Reynolds 2010: 173–203). The teleology guiding many of these initiatives can be seen in lecture titles such as "On the Way to a Critical Reappraisal of the Koran," and in the disappointment

---

15 The most relevant development here is perhaps the establishment of chairs of Islamic studies generously funded by Arab donors. The anxiety that this funding may lead to "self-censorship" despite the recognized lack of "strings attached" is highlighted in Davidson (2012: 98–104).

frequently expressed by scholars upon their return from meetings in the Muslim world.

Unsettled Binaries

Projects such as Corpus Coranicum[16] and the International Qur'anic Studies Association (IQSA)[17] reveal the contradictions induced by the

---

16   Perhaps the most important of several large-scale research projects initiated in the Western academy after 9/11, the Corpus Coranicum is an eighteen-year study funded by the Brandenburg Academy of Science which seeks to provide a long-awaited "critical edition" of the Muslim scripture (http://koran.bbaw.de/). In a newspaper article published in 2007, a leading commentator (Frank Schirrmarcher) hailed Corpus Coranicum as a project that "might overthrow rulers and topple kingdoms," comparing the impact of a critical edition of the Qur'an to the Paleolithic discovery of fire, and speculating on the outrage it would spark amongst Muslims. The claim prompted a swift rebuttal from the research team, eager to re-cast the project in terms compatible with Muslim exegetical traditions. As the researchers explained in their response letter, the idea that Corpus Coranicum may undermine fundamentalist readings and threaten authoritarian regimes is mistaken and unhelpful, since it reinforces the perception of Orientalist scholars as politically-motivated agents. This in turn endangers the scientific integrity of the project, making cooperation with Islamic scholars more difficult. Although the project addresses primarily a European audience, the researchers are keen to establish "a productive culture of debate" with Muslim scholars; while they recognize the "obvious dissonance" between the Qur'anic text and the values of "Western modernity," they wish to relativize the significance of the sacred injunctions in the problems facing the contemporary Muslim world. The attempt to de-politicize Corpus Coranicum expressed in this exchange is interesting because the leader of the project, Angelika Neuwirth, has explicitly embraced a political stance elsewhere in her scholarly work (2007, 2009, 2010). The gap expressed here between academic and media discourses highlights the difficulties that scholars face when translating the politics of method in terms intelligible to the wider community of readers, funders and policy-makers.

17   Established in May 2012 by two North American scholars, the International Qur'anic Studies Association seeks explicitly to promote

injunction to cast scholarship on the Qur'an as consequential beyond the academy. They highlight the tension that obtains between the double imperative of reform and bridge-building on the one hand, and the field of QS as it has historically developed in the Western academy. The primary significance of the post-9/11 transformations lies precisely in their unsettling of the constitutive binaries of QS: the distinctions between (secular) Reason and religious commitment, Science and politics, the West and Islam, are destabilized, and need to be reinstated – or renegotiated.

Modern QS has historically been predicated on ideals of disinterested scholarship and historical objectivity, understood here as "a sprawling collection of assumptions, attitudes, aspirations and antipathies."[18] Despite the widespread assault against these notions, QS practitioners have largely continued to rely on a principled distinction between scholarship and politics, refusing to reflect on the effects their work might produce. This line of argumentation has had two

---

"mutual understanding through scholarship." Seizing the opportunity presented by the controversial circulation of a demeaning video on the life of the Prophet of Islam, Gabriel Reynolds and Emran El-Badawi stated their vision and ambition for IQSA in the pages of *The Christian Science Monitor*. The increased public interest in the Qur'an, religiously-motivated violence in the Muslim world, and the polarization of scholarly positions in QS provide the justification for an association which seeks to provide a forum for sharing insights, publicizing discoveries and encouraging exchanges between scholars in the West and those in the Muslim world. The stated objective is to "build bridges between adherents of the Abrahamic faiths." This seems to involve a process of mainstreaming Islam. "Thinking evolves over time," the reader is candidly reminded, and just as an 18th-century prohibition on printing the Qur'an was subsequently abandoned, perhaps other Muslim beliefs can also be liberalized, the authors imply. If Muslims "may have reservations about this project," they should be reassured: IQSA "is intended to show that academic inquiry is inherently an act of deep respect for the subject"; as long as "its members do the work they love," understanding and peace will follow.

18 See Novick (1988: 1). Although objectivity and neutrality do not have to be conflated, they have historically been part of a common conceptual structure of historical inquiry.

major consequences. On the one hand, it allowed practitioners to cast Muslim opposition to their scholarship in terms of a category mistake: Muslims who may feel that their tradition is misrepresented or threatened in QS "fail to understand the radical discontinuity that separates belief from history," as one scholar put it (Donner 2011: 36).[19] On the other hand, this line of argumentation prevented QS scholars from adequately responding to the perceived instrumentalization of QS for Islamophobic polemics. The use of mainstream as well as revisionist QS works in overtly anti-Muslim discourse (as in the works of Ibn Warraq) has created an "uneasy feeling" (Donner 2011: 37), making a distinction between "scholarship" and "polemic" (Rippin 2006b: 235, 245) necessary if elusive. The ambivalence expressed here is perhaps inherent in the project of secular critique, hovering uneasily between what Foucault (1997: 42) once called "the high Kantian enterprise and the little polemical professional activities." QS's unreflective reliance on Enlightenment ideals has made it even more difficult to provide clear criteria for drawing a clear dividing line. The moral neutrality of the disinterested scholar has become in many cases synonymous with political naïvité.

If the notion of "disinterested scholarship" could be problematic prior to 9/11, its usefulness has been radically undermined in the aftermath. Unconvincing to many outsiders, "disinterested scholarship" is increasingly unable to secure the position of QS scholars within academia and beyond it. It is powerless against the Islamophobic uses of their scholarship – and is now de-authorized by the imperatives of reform and bridge-building.

The problem, we would like to suggest, has its roots in the partiality of the account provided by QS practitioners. History and philology, the field's main disciplinary homes, are part of a critical project that has often been understood as a transformative and redemptive undertaking, destined to "save" readers from "naïve" and "immature" forms of readings (Warner 2004: 15). The ability to acquire and

---

19 Donner's argument might be contrasted to that of Petra Bahr: that history is the ground on which truth claims are made for monotheistic traditions founded on historical moments of revelation (Bahr 2005: 1). Bahr is concerned with Judaism and Christianity, but Islam would fit in too.

transcend a proper historical consciousness has been tied to Reason and to Modernity in ineluctable ways. The representation of Western Qur'anic scholarship as simply apolitical thus contrasts sharply with a long-standing understanding of critique as "a moral and political project that links the production of meaning to the possibility for human agency, democratic community, and transformative social action" (Warner 2004: 14–15). It contradicts the link between philology and the public sphere that lies at the heart of the academic modern. Muslim understandings of the Qur'an as the literal Word of God can only be seen in this context as misguided – an improper reading practice that fails to recognize the proper work of history and language.

The relation between the historical inquiry conducted in the Western university and Muslim accounts of their history has thus become a key stake in QS. Twentieth-century scholars seemed largely content with separating their historical work from Muslim narratives. This separation often contained an implicit hierarchy but it didn't need to make explicit the underlying assumption that there is a single correct relationship to the past, and that the professional historian alone is able to determine which relationship is correct. The link between the academic study of the Qur'an and the project of the Islamic Reformation posited in the aftermath of 9/11 renders the assumption explicit, forcing scholars to start confronting the relations and inequalities between the different kinds of historical commitments.[20]

---

20 The work of Jacqueline Chabbi, a leading French specialist in the history of early Islam, is paradigmatic here. In *Le Seigneur des tribus*, her first book on the subject published in 1997, Chabbi surmised that "historians have nothing to say to theologians" (1997: 22), a claim repeated in the French media (Xavier Ternisien, "Le Coran en question," *Le Monde*, September 7, 2001). In her second monograph, *Le Coran décrypté* (2008), Chabbi radicalizes her critique of the Muslim "denial of history," framing her work as an attempt to "dépasser un syndrome collectif" – to go beyond this collective characteristic. The project would be "less important", Chabbi adds, if the mythical account of Islamic history espoused by Muslims did not lead to the "dramatic developments recently witnessed on the world stage" (Chabbi 2008: 22–5; see also Zabbal 2011).

It is in this context that *practical history* becomes a privileged mode of historiography. We adapt the notion from Michael Oakeshott to suggest a mode of historical inquiry that is critically concerned with the present and the future. Our claim is not simply that contemporary QS scholars display today a willingness to perform social functions beyond the confines of the academy. Such willingness was present in the writings of scholars such as Montgomery Watt, who argued in the 1970s that "Islami[ci]sts ... have to help their fellows understand more fully the cultures of the orient, to learn their weaknesses and their strengths and the ways in which they differ from our own culture, and above all to appreciate the universal human values they enshrine" – a task that becomes particularly urgent in the context of Muslim migration to Europe (Watt 1976: 41). Watt's humanism, however, lacked the practical ambition of the new mode of historiography. Practical history points to the more or less conscious attempt to intervene in the field of Muslim subjectivity by retelling "scientifically" the story of Islamic origins and the history of the Qur'an. It is part of the reconfiguration of the academic study of the Qur'an as an instrument of governance.

In order to capture the novelty of the current situation, we have focused on developments that suggest ruptures, rather than tracing the permanence of entrenched modes of thinking. But the far-reaching effect of the transformations seems unmistakable. These changes may also help to explain the pregnancy of talk of crisis in QS in spite of the field's obvious vitality. Rather than a simple reflection of key methodological issues (the lack of historical sources, the elusiveness of the Qur'anic text, the inability to come to terms with the revisionist challenge), the widespread sense of crisis is perhaps best understood in relation to the disintegration of the field's constitutive binaries described here.[21] As Reinhart Koselleck famously pointed out, a crisis points to that critical moment that "tip[s] the scales," requiring decisions to be made between stark alternatives (Koselleck

---

21 The striking contrast between current discourses and those of the 1990s – as seen for example in the sober tone adopted by the editors of *Approaches to the Qur'an* (Hawting and Shareef 1993) – supports our hypothesis.

2006: 358). The study of the Qur'an in the West has perhaps reached one such moment; until principled choices are made, depictions of QS as a field in crisis are only likely to proliferate.

A Single Tradition?

The desirability of helping the reform process has encouraged scholars to embrace an *interested* and *performative* view of QS – either as an objective aim or (more frequently) as a collateral benefit.[22] The imperative of building bridges, on the other hand, has contributed to blur another binary of QS as it was institutionalized in the Western academy: the clear separation between Muslim and non-Muslim subjects.

Scholars may continue occasionally to refer to the "West" as the antonym of "Muslim" (Donner 2011: 25), to write nostalgically about a time when Orientalists did not have to worry about the politically-correct (Gilliot 2012: 116), and to celebrate the dominance of non-Muslims in QS (Berg and Rollens 2008: 278). The border between Western and Muslim has nevertheless become increasingly porous – and the comforts of a shared habitus perhaps irremediably lost. If Muslim contributions to Western QS date back to the days of Fazlur Rahman (1919–88), their voices have become much more

22 The differences between "scientific" projects and "polemical" works collapse here. Dedicated to "pure scholarship" ("reineswissen"), the researchers of the controversial INARAH project claim that, "any impact on the enlightenment of Islamic cultures would be merely a fortunate side-effect" (http://www.inarah.de/cms/). Celebrating "the critical scientific method" as the "most magnificent intellectual contribution of [Western] modernity," the respectable Amir-Moezzi hopes that his *Dictionnaire du Coran* may fulfill the "civic task" of secularizing the Muslim world (Amir-Moezzi 2007: xiii–xiv; see also Chabbi 2008: 22–5 and Prémare 2004: 28 for similar arguments). These animated statements from Europe have more sober counterparts in North America: Andrew Rippin (2012: 6) "would like to think of...translations [into Muslim languages] of [Euro-American] scholarly work on the Qur'an as evidence of an evolving research partnership that recognizes both the value of the work but also, ultimately, its relevance to the larger community of Islam."

prominent in the last two decades. Scholars from Muslim backgrounds articulate a wide range of perspectives, including a radical critique of the "violence" inherent in Western QS, a denunciation of the field's "farces," an appreciation of its critical method and an open invitation to subvert Muslim orthodoxies. The fragmentation of Muslim positions highlights the conceptual flaw of bridge-building exercises: the assumption of a stable Muslim subjectivity implied in the latter has become impossible to establish empirically.

The relation between the Western and Muslim traditions of scholarship has turned into an object of reflection and concern. An approach that seeks to collapse or relativize the differences between the "two streams" of scholarship (Smith 1991) has become increasingly attractive to a range of scholars, including figures such as Jane McAuliffe, Angelika Neuwirth and Andrew Rippin. Does the porosity between Muslim and Western scholarship herald the emergence of a single tradition? If the move to collapse differences resembles the more familiar attempt to dissolve the "West" as a category, perhaps we should ask – as Talal Asad (2003: 15) urges us – what and whose politics are served by it.

The work of Andrew Rippin anticipates and addresses many of the developments highlighted in this article and is therefore of particular interest here. From the mid-2000s onwards, Rippin has chosen to emphasize the similarities between Western and Muslim approaches, closer to each other than "a Muslim living in Europe" or "an academic working in a North American university" would like to admit, and to relativize the idea of disinterested scholarship (2006b: 235). In recasting the history of Western QS as consistent with the Muslim tradition (2006b), Rippin is not only pointing to a (carefully selected) set of common assumptions; he is also rewriting the history of the field in light of 21st-century demands. This response, however, is not entirely coherent. If Euro-American scholarship is always in some sense "interested" (Rippin 2012: 8 fn. 21), then the idea that the interests of academics based in the West do not differ from those of scholars in the Muslim world would need to be proven rather than implied. The attempt to relativize the truth claims of both traditions (2006b: 247) and the failure to engage the differential powers invested in the production of discourses on the Qur'an betray the comforts of a North

American scholar reflecting from afar on some of the consequences of globalization.[23]

Conclusion

We have argued so far that the aftermath of 9/11 has reshaped the field of Western QS by placing a new emphasis on a mode of practical history oriented towards building bridges with Muslims and reforming Islam. We have suggested that this reconfiguration has contributed to unsettling the field's constitutive binaries, explaining why the diagnosis of crisis permeates informed discussions in spite of the field's evident dynamism. In order to understand the possibilities of success of reform and bridge-building (and the extent to which the boundary between Muslim and Western traditions of Qur'anic scholarship has become blurred), it seems necessary to consider the impact of Western QS in the Muslim world. If our analysis so far has been correct, one should expect that Muslim reception becomes the object of a particular concern in the West, perhaps even a measure for evaluating the achievements of current scholarship. There is some evidence supporting the idea that, under the current configuration of the field, Muslim reception of Western QS has become a "problem" that needs to be explicitly addressed.[24] While Western scholars did not have

---

23 Rippin also appears to view favorably the incorporation of the Qur'an into the canon of world literature (2006b: 243). This move reverses a centuries-old denigration of the literary qualities of the Qur'anic text (Wild 1994), but seems insufficiently reflective of the function of world literature as a concept. As Aamir Mufti (2010) and Michael Allan (2016) have shown, world literature is a concept indebted to the disciplines of colonial schooling that presupposes a particular set of literary sensibilities. World literature does not entail the cultivation of character and manners; instead it relies on an understanding of reading as a private and silent act, essential to liberal self-government. The adoption of these reading practices to the Qur'an has been at the heart of American attempts to refashion the Muslim world in the aftermath of 9/11 (Mahmood 2006).

24 Stefan Wild's oral account of his participation in a 2006 conference on "Orientalist studies on the Qur'an" held under the auspices of the King

to burden themselves with the issue in the past, the imperatives of reform and bridge-building have created new expectations and novel constraints.[25]

Fahd Complex for the Printing of the Holy Qur'an, Medina provides a paradigmatic expression of this issue (Wild 2010). The German scholar reflected on the lack of interest in Western scholarship from the "majority of religious scholars" in the Muslim world in these terms: "This for me is the real challenge ... I don't really know how to go about to change this because ... we are sort of dependent on this ... what sense does it make when somebody like me or Angelika Neuwirth has a wonderful idea and most Muslims say, we are not really interested, maybe true maybe not true, but this is not anything interesting ... that is very very regrettable, and I don't have a cure for this."

25 A recent special issue of the *Journal of Qur'anic Studies* underscores the current importance given to Muslim reception. Drawing on a typology developed by a Dutch historian of religion, the guest editor divided reception into three types: "parasitic interaction," "apologetics," and "reform." Apologetics seemingly constitutes the dominant Muslim response – one that fails to distinguish between "true scholarship" and "polemics" and is ultimately expressive of an irrational "protest against Western domination" (Rippin 2012: 3–4). Both claims are odd: Rippin (2006b) himself has shown how unclear the difference between "true scholarship" and "polemic" is. In relation to the second claim, borrowed from Jacques Waardenburg, it is not clear whether Rippin is denying the fact of Western domination, or whether he considers protest against it morally wrong. If the answer is neither, as Rippin has suggested elsewhere (Ismael and Rippin 2010), then the idea that Muslims protest against Western domination would seem unrelated to the validity of their claims. The reader is led to believe that the only acceptable Muslim position is the uncritical acceptance of Western scholarship – a strange claim given the contested nature of much scholarship in the West. This line of argumentation is indicative of a refusal to think about the corporate dimensions of knowledge production and to consider the situatedness of Western conceptions of scholarship. For some recent engagements with Western QS not mentioned by Rippin, see Raḍwan (1992), Azami (2003), Hajj (2003), Sayyid (2007), Hirmās (2013) and the proceedings of the November 2006 international conference "Al-Qur'ān al-karīm fi-l-dirāsāt al-istishrāqiyya" organized by the King Fahd Complex for the Printing of the Holy Qur'an in Medina (http://www.ahlalhdeeth.com/vb/showthread.php?t=85757). A comprehensive bibliography of Arabic language works on Western scholarship on the Qur'an is provided in Namla (2010).

An account of contemporary Qur'anic scholarship in the Muslim world requires a much larger effort than what can be attempted here. Below we simply highlight some recent developments in the Arab world – a region where the field of QS is in a noticeable state of renewal and expansion too.[26] From Morocco and Egypt to Syria and Saudi Arabia, specialized research institutes have been established, and new editorial strategies (as well as new actors) have expanded the range of approaches to the Muslim scripture available to the educated masses. Although some of the publications have proved short-lasting, they testify to a renewed vitality in the field. New research institutes include the Tafsir Center for Qur'anic Studies (*Markaz Tafsīr li-l-Dirāsāt al-Qur'āniyya*) founded in 2008 in Riyadh (www.tafsir.net), the Center for Qur'anic Studies at the Imām al-Shāṭibī Institute (*Ma'had al-Imām al-Shāṭibī li-l-Qur'ān wa 'Ulūmihi*) established in Jeddah in 2005 (www.shatiby.edu.sa), and the Center of Qur'anic Studies of the Muhammadian Union of Muslim Scholars (*Rābiṭa Muḥammadiyya li-l-'Ulamā*) opened in Rabat in 2006 (www.alquran.ma). At least four specialized journals

---

26 Secondary literature on contemporary QS in the Muslim world is sparse. The contributions by Koç, Karimi-Nia, Albayrak and Al-Akoub to the special issue of JQS edited by Rippin (2012) provide important material. Developments in the Arab world seem comparatively speaking less researched, perhaps because of the perception that academic production is less dynamic there. A recent study of *tafsir* in four Muslim countries argues for example that "Arab commentaries ... are considerably more conservative with respect to issues like the status of women, the attitudes towards non-Muslims, or slavery. Their image of God is distinctly more fear-inducing and less loving than that of the Indonesian and Turkish commentaries" (Pink 2010: 74). Arab scholars are also seen as less interested in early reformist exegesis, in Jewish and Christian sources, and in philosophy. Overlooking national differences within the Arab world seems justified in light of the shared language and the increasing accessibility of scholarship across the region in our electronic age. The academic study of the Qur'an represents of course only a small part of the activities associated with the scripture in Muslim contexts. As McAuliffe (2003) has pointed out, the Qur'an's "persistent power" draws on mutually-reinforcing carnal, conceptual and communal dimensions.

– *Majallat Ma'had Al-Imām al-Shāṭibi li-l-Dirāsāt al-Qur'āniyya* (Saudi Arabia, 2006–), *Al-Buḥūth wa-l-Dirāsāt al-Qur'āniyya* (King Fahd Complex for the Printing of the Holy Qur'an, Saudi Arabia, 2006–), *Majallat al-Dirāsāt al-Qur'āniyya* (Muhammad Ibn Sa'ud Islamic University, Riyadh, 2007–) and *Al-Majalla al-Dawliyya li-l-Dirāsāt al-Qur'āniyya* (Egypt, Qatar and United Kingdom, 2009–) have been initiated in the last decade. As these examples suggest, the expression *al-dirāsāt al-qur'āniyya* (Qur'anic studies) borrowed from European languages is steadily replacing the traditional *'ulūm al-qur'ān* (Qur'anic sciences) in Arabic usage. The new buzzwords in the study of the Qur'an are *dirāsāt naqdiyya* (critical studies) and *qirā'āt mu'āsira* (contemporary readings).[27]

Attempts at reform and bridge-building clearly underlie several current initiatives in Muslim contexts. As has been noted, translations of Western QS works into "Muslim" languages have accelerated in the 21st century (Rippin 2012). Conference invitations are now frequently extended to Western scholars, who are also occasionally invited to publish in local journals, serve as board members of specialized publications, write in festschrifts of prominent Muslim intellectuals, and are offered prizes for their scholarly achievements. While the Eurocentrism that drives current initiatives in Western QS has not gone unnoticed in the Arab world (Hirmās 2013: 226–9), Western scholars have become interlocutors in attempts to evaluate the scholarly merits of Orientalism in Medina (Wild 2006); delineate the scope of modern hermeneutical approaches appropriate to the study of the Qur'an in Rabat (Neuwirth 2013); rethink the sacred text in Ankara (Rippin 2013b); tackle the problem of political manipulation of religious scripture in Kairouan; and confront Islamophobic depictions of the Qur'an in Teheran. Even when Western scholars are not present in scholarly meetings, their absence becomes an issue of concern. As a Saudi scholar recently put it at an international conference held in Medina in February 2013, Muslims should seize the

---

27 See inter alia Budra' (2013) and the collective volumes entitled *Qirā'āt Mu'āsira fi-l-Naṣṣ al-Qur'ānī* (2008) and *Al-Ta'wīl wa-l-Harmīnūṭīqā – Dirāsāt fi Āliyyāt al-Qirā'a wa-l-Tafsīr* (2011) published by the Shi'i Markaz al-Ḥaḍāra li-Tanmiyya al-Fikr al-Islāmī.

opportunity presented by Western bridge-building efforts, even if the underlying motives and intentions are doubtful, and move from critique at home towards positive engagement abroad.[28]

Bridge-building efforts are facilitated by the demographic changes in Western academia, the electronic accessibility of Western scholarship and the growing participation of Muslim scholars in meetings such as the biannual SOAS conferences on the Qur'an. Other reasons include European state efforts to establish new Faculties of Islamic Studies (often in collaboration with institutions in Muslim countries), the intensification of exchange programs and the growing financial clout of universities in parts of the Muslim world. Collaboration with Western scholars and institutions confers "academic prestige" upon local initiatives. It also allows institutions in the Muslim world to demonstrate their "moderation" at a time when Islamic education has come under intense global scrutiny. In the aftermath of 9/11 the Turkish Minister of Foreign Affairs (not of Education) found it necessary to issue a decree calling upon Qur'anic scholars to "establish an atmosphere in which it would be possible to engage in scientific dialogue [with] orientalist authors" (Koç 2012: 43–4). Bridge-building efforts in the field of QS can thus be seen as one part of larger state attempts to foster a "dialogue of civilizations" – one that is underlined by the shared interest of authoritarian Arab political regimes and Western democracies in depicting violence as the result of misguided hermeneutics.

It is common for scholars in the Arab world to depict these efforts at bridge-building as marginal and politically-driven. Much of the intellectual energy spent in the engagement with Western scholarship is still devoted to unmasking the biases and distortions of Orientalists. Western QS scholarship generally lacks persuasiveness: it is possible for Muslim scholars to publicly dismiss it on grounds of Western scholars' poor understanding of the language, culture and history of the Arabs. Yet, bridge-building efforts enable new collaborative projects, provide new career prospects and connect variously to the

---

28 Comments by ʿĀdil b. ʿAlī al-Shadī, a professor of Qur'anic sciences at King Saʿud University, at the first panel of the 2013 International Conference for the Development of Qur'anic Studies.

ongoing reconfiguration of Qur'anic studies in the Muslim world. They may however produce effects rather different than in the West. In order to succeed, making space for Orientalist scholarship will require a valorization of notions of disembodied, objective and depoliticized scholarship in the Muslim world. Instead of an engagement with practical histories, this will entail a reconfiguration of the complex epistemological structure and sensory organization that traditionally shaped the study of the Qur'an in the Muslim world.

References

Abdel Haleem, M.A.S. 2008. "How to Read the Qur'an: *Sūrat al-Ḥadīd* (Q. 57)." *Journal of Qur'anic Studies* 10(2): 124–30.
https://doi.org/10.3366/E1465359109000485

Abdul-Rauf, Muhammad. 1985. "Outsiders' Interpretations of Islam: A Muslim's Point of View," in Richard Martin, ed., *Approaches to Islam in Religious Studies* (pp. 179–88). Oxford: Oneworld Publications.

Adams, Charles. 1985. "Foreword," in Richard Martin, ed., *Approaches to Islam in Religious Studies* (pp. vii–ix). Oxford: Oneworld Publications.

Allan, Michael. 2016. *In the Shadow of World Literature: Sites of Reading in Colonial Egypt*. Princeton, NJ: Princeton University Press.
https://doi.org/10.1515/9781400881093

Amir-Moezzi, Mohammad Ali. 2007. "Préface," in M.A. Amir-Moezzi, ed., *Dictionnaire du Coran* (pp. xi–xiv). Paris: Robert Laffont.

Arkoun, M. 2005. *Humanisme et islam: Combats et propositions*. Paris: Librairie philosophique J. Vrin.

Asad, Talal. 2003. *Formations of the Secular: Christianity, Islam, Modernity*. Stanford, CA: Stanford University Press.

Azami, M.M. al-. 2003. *The History of the Qur'ānic Text from Revelation to Compilation: A Comparative Study*. Leicester: UK Islamic Academy.

Bahr, Petra. 2005. "Religious Claims of Truth versus Critical Method: Some General Remarks on a Complex Relationship in Western Tradition," in Helwig Schmidt-Glintzer, Achim Mittag and Jörn Rüsen, eds., *Historical Truth, Historical Criticism, and Ideology: Chinese Historiography and Historical Culture from a New Comparative Perspective* (pp. 1–12). Leiden: Brill.

Bennett, Clinton. 2010. *Studying Islam: The Critical Issues*. London: Continuum.

—, ed. 2013. *The Bloomsbury Companion to Islamic Studies*. London: Continuum.
Berg, Herbert and Sarah Rollens. 2008. "The Historical Muhammad and the Historical Jesus: A Comparison of Scholarly Reinventions and Reinterpretations." *Studies in Religion / Sciences Religieuses* 37(2): 271–92. https://doi.org/10.1177/000842980803700205
Böwering, Gerhard. 2008. "Recent Research on the Construction of the Qur'an," in Gabriel Reynolds, ed., *The Qur'an in Its Historical Context* (pp. 70–87). London and New York: Routledge.
Budra', Abd al-Rahmān. 2013. *Al-khiṭāb al-qur'ānī wa manāhij al-ta'wīl: naḥūw dirāsa naqdiyya li-l-ta'wīlāt l-mu'āṣira*. Rabat: Markaz al-Dirāsāt al-Qur'āniyya/Al-Rābiṭa al-Muhammadiyya li-l-'Ulamā'.
Burman, Thomas E. 2007. *Reading the Qur'an in Latin Christendom, 1140–1560*. Philadelphia: University of Pennsylvania Press.
Chabbi, Jacqueline. 1997. *Le Seigneur des tribus: L'islam de Mahomet*. Paris: Editions Noésis.
— 2008. *Le Coran décrypté. Figures bibliques en Arabie*. Paris: Fayard.
Clifford, James. 1988. *The Predicament of Culture: Twentieth-Century Ethnography, Literature, and Art*. Cambridge, MA: Harvard University Press.
Clifford, James and George Marcus, eds. 1986. *Writing Culture: The Poetics and Politics of Ethnography*. Berkeley/Los Angeles/London: University of California Press.
Davidson, Christopher. 2012. *After the Sheikhs: The Coming Collapse of the Gulf Monarchies*. London: Hurst.
Donner, Fred. 2011. "The Historian, the Believer, and the Qur'an," in Gabriel Reynolds, ed., *New Perspectives on the Qur'an: The Qur'an in Its Historical Context 2* (pp. 25–37). London and New York: Routledge.
Elmarsafy, Ziad. 2009. *The Enlightenment Qur'an: The Politics of Translation and the Construction of Islam*. Oxford: Oneworld Publications.
Ernst, Carl and Richard C. Martin. 2010. "Introduction: Toward a Post-Orientalist Approach to Islamic Religious Studies," in Carl Ernst and Richard C. Martin, eds., *Rethinking Islamic Studies: From Orientalism to Cosmopolitanism* (pp. 1–19). Columbia, SC: University of South Carolina Press.
Esack, Farid. 2005. *The Qur'an: A User's Guide*. Oxford: Oneworld Publications.
Foucault, Michel. 1997. *The Politics of Truth*. Los Angeles, CA: Semiotext(e).
Gilliot, Claude. 2012. "Miscellania Coranica I." *Arabica* 59: 109–33. https://doi.org/10.1163/157005812X618925

Hajj, 'Abd al-Rahmān al-. 2003. "Ẓāhira al-Qirā'a al-Mu'āṣira li-l-Qur'ān wa Idiyūlūjiyā al-Ḥadātha." *Al-Tasāmuh* 1. http://www.altasamoh.net/Article.asp?Id=14

Harvey, V. 1966. *The Historian and the Believer: The Morality of Historical Knowledge and Christian Belief.* New York: Macmillan.

Hawting, G.R. and Abdul-Kader Shareef, eds. 1993. *Approaches to the Qur'an.* London: Routledge.

Hirmās, 'Abd al-Razzāq. 2013. "Fahm al-Qur'ān fī Ḍaw' Manāhij al-'Ulūm al-Insāniyya al-Gharbiyya: munṭalaqātuhā wa ḥaqiqatuhā wa afāquhā." *Buḥūth al-Mu'tamar al-Dawlī li-Taṭwīr al-Dirāsāt al-Qur'āniyya* 1: 179–250.

Ismael, Tareq Y. and Andrew Rippin, eds. 2010. *Islam in the Eyes of the West: Images and Realities in an Age of Terror.* London and New York: Routledge.

Koç, Mehmet Akif. 2012. "The Influence of Western Qur'anic Scholarship in Turkey." *Journal of Qur'anic Studies* 14(1): 9–44. https://doi.org/10.3366/jqs.2012.0036

Koselleck, Reinhart. 2006. "Crisis." *Journal of the History of Ideas* 67(2): 357–400 (trans. Michaela W. Richter). https://doi.org/10.1353/jhi.2006.0013

Luxenberg, Christoph. 2000. *Die syro-aramaische Lesart des Koran. Ein Beitrag zur Entschlusselung der Koransprasche.* Berlin: Das Arabische Buch.

Madigan, Daniel. 1995. "Reflections on Some Current Directions in Qur'anic Studies." *The Muslim World* 85: 345–62. https://doi.org/10.1111/j.1478-1913.1995.tb03627.x

— 2008. "Foreword," in Gabriel Reynolds, ed., *The Qur'an in Its Historical Context* (pp. xi–xii). New York and London: Routledge.

Mahmood, Saba. 2006. "Secularism, Hermeneutics, Empire: The Politics of Islamic Reformation." *Public Culture* 18(2): 323–47. https://doi.org/10.1215/08992363-2006-006

Masuzawa, Tomoko. 2012. "Secular by Default? Religion and the University before the Post-Secular Age," in Philip Gorski et al., eds., *The Post-Secular in Question: Religion in Contemporary Society* (pp. 185–214). New York: NYU Press. https://doi.org/10.18574/nyu/9780814738726.003.0008

McAuliffe, J.D. 2003. "The Persistent Power of the Qur'an." *Proceedings of the American Philosophical Society* 147(4): 339–46.

— 2005. "Reading the Qur'ān with Fidelity and Freedom." *Journal of the American Academy of Religion* 73(3): 615–35. https://doi.org/10.1093/jaarel/lfi072

McCutcheon, Russell, ed. 1999. *The Insider/Outsider Problem in the Study of Religion*. London: Cassell.
Mufti, Aamir. 2010. "Orientalism and the Institution of World Literatures." *Critical Inquiry* 36: 458–93. https://doi.org/10.1086/653408
Namla, 'Al Ībn Ibrāhīm al-. 2010. *Al-Mustashriqūnwa-l-qur'ān al-karīmfī-l-marāji' al-'arabiyya*. Beirut: Dār Bīsān.
Neuwirth, Angelika. 2007. "Orientalism in Oriental Studies? Qur'anic Studies as a Case in Point." *Journal of Qur'anic Studies* 9(2): 115–27. https://doi.org/10.3366/E1465359108000119
— 2009. "The Late Antique Qur'an: Jewish-Christian Liturgy, Hellenic Rhetoric, and Arabic Language." Lecture at the Institute for Advanced Study, Princeton University, June 3.
http://www.youtube.com/watch?v=qHCeYSvazY4
— 2010. *Der Koran als Text der Spätantike. Ein europäischer Zugang*. Berlin: Verlag der Weltreligionen.
— 2013. "Al-Ta'wīl fi-l-Dirāsāt al-Qur'āniyya al-Gharbiyya – Lamḥa Tārīkhiyya." Paper presented at the conference *Al-Ta'wīl: su'āl al-marja'iyya wa muqtadiyyat al-siyāq*, Rabat, June 26.
Novick, Peter. 1988. *That Noble Dream: The "Objectivity Question" and the American Historical Profession*. Cambridge: Cambridge University Press. https://doi.org/10.1017/CBO9780511816345
Pink, Johanna. 2010. "Tradition, Authority and Innovation in Contemporary Sunnī *tafsīr*: Towards a Typology of Qur'an Commentaries from the Arab World, Indonesia and Turkey." *Journal of Qur'anic Studies* 12: 56–82. https://doi.org/10.3366/jqs.2010.0105
Pollock, Sheldon. 2009. "Future Philology? The Fate of a Soft Science in a Hard World." *Critical Enquiry*, 35: 931–61.
Prémare, Alfred-Louis de. 2004. *Aux origines du Coran. Questions d'hier, approaches d'aujourd'hui*. Paris: Téraèdre.
Qureish, Emran and Michael A. Sells, eds. 2003. *The New Crusades: Constructing the Muslim Enemy*. New York: Columbia University Press. https://doi.org/10.7312/qure12666
Raḍwan, 'Amr b. Ibrahim. 1992. *Arā' al-Mustashriqīn hawla al-Qur'ān al-Karīm wa tafsīrihi: dirāsa wa-naqd*. 2 vols. Riyadh: Dar al-Taybah.
Rahman, Fazlur. 1984. "Some Recent Books on the Qur'an by Western Authors." *Journal of Religion* 64(1): 73–95.
https://doi.org/10.1086/487077
Renard, John. 2011. "Review Essay – New Qur'anic Studies: Reading Islam's Sacred Text." *Religion and the Arts* 15: 680–6.
https://doi.org/10.1163/156852911X596282

Reynolds, Gabriel S. 2010. *The Qur'an and Its Biblical Subtext*. New York and London: Routledge.
— 2011. "Introduction: The Golden Age of Qur'anic Studies?" in Gabriel S. Reynolds, ed., *New Perspectives on the Qur'an: The Qur'an in Its Historical Context 2* (pp. 1–21). New York and London: Routledge.
Rippin, Andrew. 2004. "Foreword," in John Wansbrough, *Quranic Studies: Sources and Methods of Scriptural Interpretation* (pp. ix–xix). Amherst, NY: Prometheus Books.
—, ed. 2006a. *The Blackwell Companion to the Qur'ān*. Malden: Blackwell Publishing.
— 2006b. "Western Scholarship on the Qur'an," in J.D. McAuliffe, ed., *The Cambridge Companion to the Qur'an* (pp. 187–204). Cambridge: Cambridge University Press.
— 2006c. "Foreword," in Abdullah Saeed, *Interpreting the Qur'an: Towards a Contemporary Approach*. London and New York: Routledge.
—, ed. 2007 (ed.) *Defining Islam: A Reader*. London and Oakville: Equinox.
— 2012. "The Reception of Euro-American Scholarship on the Qur'an and *tafsir*: An Overview (Editorial Preface)." *Journal of Qur'anic Studies* 14(1): 1–8. https://doi.org/10.3366/jqs.2012.0035
—. 2013a. "Qur'anic Studies," in Bennett (2013: 59–74).
— 2013b. "First International Symposium on Rethinking the Qur'an." http://iqsaweb.wordpress.com/2013/05/13/ankara-symposium/
Robinson, Chase. 2014. "Patricia Crone and the End of Orientalism," in Behnam Sadeghi et al., eds., *Islamic Cultures, Islamic Contexts: Essays in Honor of Professor Patricia Crone*. Leiden: Brill. https://doi.org/10.1163/9789004281714_023
Rodinson, Maxime. 2003 [1980]. *La fascination de l'islam suivi de Le seigneur bouguignon et l'esclave sarrasin*. Paris: Editions La Découverte.
Said, Edward. 1978. *Orientalism*. New York: Vintage.
Saleh, Walid. 2003. "In Search of a Comprehensible Qur'an: A Survey of Some Recent Scholarly Works." *Bulletin of the Royal Institute for Inter-Faith Studies* 5(2): 143–62.
Sayyid, Radwan al-. 2007. "Jawānib min al-dirāsāt al-qur'āniyya al-ḥadītha wa-l-muʿāṣira fi-l-gharb." *Al-Tasāmuḥ* 17. http://www.altasamoh.net/Article.asp?Id=385
Schöller, Marco. 2004. "Post-Enlightenment Academic Study of the Qur'an," in J.D. McAuliffe, ed., *Encyclopaedia of the Qur'an* (Vol. 4, pp. 187–208). Leiden, Boston, Köln: Brill.
Sinai, Nicolai and Angelika Neuwirth. 2010. "Introduction," in Angelika Neuwirth, Nicolai Sinai and Michael Marx, eds., *The Qur'an in Context:*

Historical and Literary Investigations into the Qur'anic Milieu (pp. 1–24). Leiden: Brill. https://doi.org/10.1007/978-90-481-9710-1_1

Smith, Wilfred Cantwell. 1980. "The True Meaning of Scripture: An Empirical Historian's Nonreductionist Interpretation of the Qur'an." *International Journal of Middle East Studies* 11(4): 487–505. https://doi.org/10.1017/S0020743800054830

— 1991. "A Note on the Qur'an from a Comparativist Perspective," in Wael Hallaq and Donald Little, eds., *Islamic Studies Presented to C.J. Adams* (pp. 183–92). Leiden: Brill.

Stefanidis, Emmanuelle. 2008. "The Qur'an Made Linear: A Study of the *Geschichte des Qorâns*' Chronological Reordering." *Journal of Qur'anic Studies* 10(2): 1–22. https://doi.org/10.3366/E1465359109000394

Wansbrough, John. 1977. *Quranic Studies: Sources and Methods of Scriptural Interpretation.* Oxford: Oxford University Press / Amherst, NY: Prometheus Books.

— 1978. *The Sectarian Milieu: Content and Composition of Islamic Salvation History.* Oxford: Oxford University Press.

Warner, Michael. 2004. "Uncritical Reading," in Jane Gallop, ed., *Polemic: Critical or Uncritical?* (pp. 13–38). New York and London: Routledge.

Watt, W. Montgomery. 1970. *Richard Bell's Introduction to the Qur'an.* Edinburgh: Edinburgh University Press.

— 1976. "On Interpreting the Qur'an." *Oriens* 25: 41–7. https://doi.org/10.2307/1580655

Wild, Stefan. 1994. "Die schauerliche Öde des heiligen Buches. WestlicheWertungen des koranischen Stils," in A. Giese and J.Ch. Bürgel, eds., *Gott ist schön und er liebt die Schönheit* (pp. 429–47). Berlin: FS A. Schimmel.

— 2006. "Political Interpretation of the Qur'an," in J.D. McAuliffe, ed., *The Cambridge Companion to the Qur'an* (pp. 273–89). Cambridge: Cambridge University Press.
https://doi.org/10.1017/CCOL0521831601.014

— 2009. "Muslime in Deutschland. Dialog, Konflikt und Koexistenz," in Cusanuswerk, *Jahresbericht* (Annual Report), Bonn (pp. 56–67).

— 2010. "The History of the Qur'an: Why Is There No State of the Art?" H.A.R. Gibb Arabic and Islamic Studies Lecture (October 26), http://cmes.hmdc.harvard.edu/node/2271

Zabbal, Francois. 2011. "L'islamologie des universitaires musulmans en France. Entre exégèse coranique et méthode critique," in François Pouillon and Jean-Claude Vatin, eds., *Après l'orientalisme. L'Orient créé par l'Orient* (pp. 179–92). Paris: IISMM-Karthala.

Alexandre Caeiro is Assistant Professor at the College of Islamic Studies, Hamad Bin Khalifa University, Doha. His research interests include religion in the Gulf, the modern transformations of Islamic normativity, and the politics of knowledge production. Caeiro's work has been published in journals such as *Die Welt des Islams*, the *International Journal of Middle Eastern Studies* and *Archives de sciences sociales des religions*.

Emmanuelle Stefanidis is a PhD candidate at the University of Paris IV – Sorbonne. Her dissertation examines the structure and function of diachronic readings of the Qur'an in Muslim exegesis and in Western historical-critical scholarship. She has published in the *Journal of Qur'anic Studies* and contributed to *The Qur'an Seminar Commentary: A Collaborative Study of 50 Qur'anic Passages* (De Gruyter, 2016).

4. Identity Politics and the Study of Islamic Origins

The Inscriptions of the Dome of the Rock as a Test Case[1]

Carlos A. Segovia

Misconstructing the Past: Identity Politics and the Traditional Narrative of Islam's Origins

In spite of their contrasting intellectual backgrounds, different understandings of the scholarly endeavor and dissimilar views on many of the problems inherent in the present-day situation of a discipline that, whether we like it or not, still needs to find a proper place within the field of religious studies, Aaron Hughes and Omid Safi seem nonetheless to agree upon one urgent task that scholars of Islam today must undertake – namely, the incorporation of the theoretical and methodological frameworks that are being successfully explored in other neighboring disciplines. As Hughes writes:

> [T]he academic study of Islam and the academic study of religion [need] to cross-pollinate …. [I]n many ways, this has happened. However, when this cross-pollination has occurred, Islamic studies has largely overlooked, or ignored, those discourses within the larger field of religious studies that are highly critical of the status quo. Instead, the academic study of Islam

---

[1] I would like to thank Guillaume Dye and Ian Morris for their comments and insights on an earlier draft of this chapter, as well as Emilio González Ferrín for unintentionally inspiring to me to add a slight philosophical flavor to its argument.

has migrated toward the more regnant ecumenical and phenomenological discourses within religious studies that are primarily interested in adjudicating truth, authenticity, experience, and meaning. ... Despite calls to the contrary, ... there have been virtually no attempts to connect Islamic data to the critical methods and discourses supplied by certain subsections within the larger field of religious studies. Instead we are presented, time and again, with special pleading and attempts to convey the uniqueness of Islamic data. It is important to reorient the field from such special pleading to a critical study in tune with other discourses in the larger discipline in which Islamic Religious Studies finds itself. Reorienting an entire subdiscipline, especially one about which the majority of those associated with it see nothing problematic, is, however, a daunting task. (2012: 2, 118)

And Safi writes in turn:

> Religious Studies programs create the possibilities for scholars of Islam to be an integrated part of the humanities, and a vital part of almost every university in America. For us to do so, however, it will be vital particularly for the Muslim scholars of Islamic studies to avoid the kind of minefields of proselytism that would be seen as violations of religious studies approaches. We can and should situate our own persons, but to do so would mean that we would have to become fully conversant with the theoretical insights of anthropology, post-colonialism, feminism, African-American studies, and other disciplines. Many scholars of Islamic studies are very open to that, but there are far too many who have adopted a polemical attitude which sees these fields as foreign, secular, and Western impositions upon "authentic" Islamic values. The more we situate Islam as being oppositional to these fields, the more we run the risk of self-marginalizing – and ultimately becoming irrelevant. (2014)

In contrast to Safi's "friendly critique," Hughes's has been accused of being "an over-generalization that indicts hundreds, if not thousands of people in dozens of countries at hundreds of academic institutions doing work in multiple languages as somehow engaging in an almost conspiratorial silence on issues such as the historical origins of the Qur'an or the career of the Prophet Muhammad" (Curtis 2014: 22). I do not agree. For that "conspirational silence" exists – it is simply unconscious, and hence non-conspirational, as I believe Hughes himself would acknowledge. It is, moreover, the offshoot of an obsolete "orientalist" paradigm that first emerged in the conservative theological circles of 19th-century Germany (Shoemaker 2012: 124–6), and is now seasoned with an explicit and well-agreed-upon dose of postcolonialist political correctness plus a tacit dose of colonialist paternalism; as though Muslim beliefs should be defended against any positivist intrusion and kept as an exotic piece in our collection of pre-modern irrational ideas. Thus in a documentary recently produced by the Franco-German TV network ARTE, *Jésus et l'islam* (2015), more than 20 competent scholars of Islam's origins were interviewed apropos the dawn of Islam, Muhammad and the Qur'an. One of the questions some of them were asked was: "Who authored the Qur'an?" Tellingly enough, most of them declined to respond, pretexting that this was too delicate and potentially too controversial a question.

Besides, if Hughes's critique has been accused of being an over-generalization, Safi's claim to adjust Islamic studies to the scholarly standards of the humanities while simultaneously accepting the essentials of the Islamic tradition (Safi 2008: 114–16; 2009) may be described as paradoxical at best; and as amounting to the very self-imposed marginalization that he criticizes.

An illustration of this self-imposed marginalization is the way in which scholars of Islam, be they Muslims or not, tend to misrepresent the making of Islam in late antiquity. Religious identity-making builds upon a number of power/knowledge discursive strategies whose purpose is to emphasize distinctiveness as the outcome of an exceptional founding event and to heighten a community's sense of uniqueness and stability. Selective remembering of the past, mythical and hyperbolic reworking of elusive historical data, ethnic and genealogical self-legitimation, artificial distinctions of sameness and otherness, adaptation of previous textual materials in a polemical fashion and a more or less systematic historicization of dogma all conspire to inscribe religious renewal as divinely sanctioned rather than politically achieved due to more mundane reasons – and thus contribute

Identity Politics and the Study of Islamic Origins   101

to (re)present self-identity as an unproblematic notion. Postmodern scholars of formative Judaism and Christianity are well familiar with these insights. Conversely, scholars of Islam very seldom seem to notice their crucial implications, as though the texts they study could be seen as either being ultimately self-referential (the Qur'an) or little more than embellished reports about what need not be de- and re-constructed otherwise (e.g., Muhammad's *Sīra*).

Let me offer two examples of this. One is the way in which the Qur'an is usually approached. As Gabriel Said Reynolds underlines, "[t]he student of the Qur'ān should be always alert to the conversation that the Qur'ān conducts with earlier texts, and in particular to its intimate conversation with Biblical literature" (2010: 36). Despite a few significant exceptions, however, scholars of the Qur'an tend to interpret this "intimate conversation" as being little more than evocative of the biblical stories, and hence refuse to engage in an intertextual exploration of the Qur'anic corpus (Segovia 2015b: 9–14). In short, they often overlook that just as new religions take shape only after some kind of dialectal variation is allowed within a given religious milieu (for these are always complex and dynamic in their very nature), new normative texts usually spread out of a common multi-dimensional stock of previous writings inside a multifaceted, and again dynamic, scribal milieu, thus reinforcing the view that the Qur'an exceptionally stands, and must ultimately remain, as a self-referential document (see further Reynolds 2014).

Another example is to be found in the way in which the "data" of the Islamic tradition are uncritically assumed by most scholars of early Islam. Only few among these would admit, for instance, that Ibn Isḥāq's "biography" of Muhammad is a fictional work. To be sure, many modern scholars would concur that it does contain, and elaborate on, a number of legends that fall under the hagiographic, rather than biographical, genre. Yet not many seem to know that Ibn Isḥāq's original work merely aimed at emending the Judeo-Christian history of salvation (*Heilsgeschichte*) from a theological point of view (Newby 1989; Berg 2012; Segovia 2015b: 108–9; cf. Schoeler 2011). It was only with Ibn Hišām that Ibn Isḥāq's fictional material was reframed as, and confused with, a historical account of both Muhammad's life and the beginnings of Islam.

I do not mean to say that no progress at all has been made in the subfield of early Islamic studies over the past decades. There is no denying that an increasing number of scholars of early Islam are reluctant to accept the Islamic tradition in the positive uncritical manner it has heretofore been assumed (Segovia 2015b: 1–20). Established in 2012 as a group related to the Society of Biblical Literature (SBL), the International Qur'anic Studies Association (IQSA) welcomes both traditional and innovative approaches to the study of the Qur'an. In turn, in 2014 Guillaume Dye, Manfred Kropp, Emilio González Ferrín, Tommaso Tesei and I launched the Early Islamic Studies Seminar (EISS), a learned society dedicated to the renewed study of Islamic origins that works in conjunction with the Enoch Seminar: International Scholarship on Second Temple Judaism, Christian, Rabbinic, and Islamic Origins. More than 60 scholars – including Qur'anic and biblical students, historians of late-antique Arabia, Byzantium and Persia, specialists in Jewish, Christian and Manichaean studies, epigraphists and archaeologists – have already agreed to join our project. Things are visibly changing, therefore. However, we are still a minority, and more often than not we are labeled "revisionists," a term that would hardly make sense in the neighboring field of early Christian studies despite the fact that, as James Crossley underlines, the latter is still far from being "free from the dominance of theology" (2014: 33).

In short, one has the overall impression that the complex process that led to the gradual emergence and establishment of the Islamic religion, its time frame and its context must be examined afresh. Accordingly, my purpose in this essay is to problematize the traditional account of Islam's origins, according to which Islam was fully formed in Muhammad's lifetime and subsequently spread by the *rāšidūn* caliphs and the Umayyads between 632 and 750, by exploring the following interrelated questions: (a) Is it possible to speak of Islam as a well-defined religion before the last decade of the 7th century? And (b) to what extent do the Kufic inscriptions of the Dome of the Rock, which date to 692, bear witness to an Islamic identity that is generally assumed to have been well-established before that time? Ultimately, this unwarranted assumption defines the often unexamined core of the identity politics that, following the Islamic tradition, scholars of Islam in their majority tend to project onto a period that is too nebulous to be described in black-or-white categories, and that they consequently misread as a closed process over-determined by its results. Therefore, questioning it should prove helpful to show that, like other religious identities, Islam initially was the product of a complex symbolic negotiation.

Rethinking the Past's Elusive Present: Identity Politics and the Ambivalent Confessional Rhetoric of the Dome of the Rock Inscriptions

As Robert Hoyland insightfully notes, we cannot approach the study of the early "Islamic" conquests by uncritically relying on the views put forward by later Muslim historiographers (Hoyland 2015: 5–6; see also Borrut 2014: 41–2). There is, to start with, no material evidence that Islam was the main reason behind the Arab takeover of West Asia and parts of North Africa. Nor is there evidence that the latter followed a linear development. In fact, it is difficult to speak of a unified Arab state, and of Islam as a new religion for that matter, until the late 7th century.

Indeed, between the 620s and the early 690s all we unambiguously know is that different Arab groups, with apparently similar albeit not necessarily identical religious ideas more or less dependent upon strict monotheistic and/or Christian beliefs, strove to achieve political hegemony in the Arabian peninsula and its adjacent regions. That one of such groups, presumably led by a prophet named Muhammad, partly succeeded in that effort between the 620s and the 630s. That from the 630s to the early 690s different Arab leaders, though probably not all of them, claimed to be heirs to Muhammad's polity in the Ḥiǧāz, Syria and Iraq. And that by the early 690s a new, unified Arab state with its capital in Syria was fully established at last. For it is only with 'Abd al-Malik b. Marwān (r. 692–705) and his successor al-Walīd I (r. 705–715) that the foundations of an Arab state were laid and that Islam emerged as a new religion, the official religion of this Arab state (cf. Sharon 1988; Nevo and Koren 2003: 271–95; Johns

2003; Robinson 2005: 59–128; Donner 2010: 194–224; Segovia 2019; see for discussion Hoyland 2006).

'Abd al-Malik is generally depicted as a reformer. He reformed law, theology and ritual, as well as the administration and the army. He also transformed the coinage by removing all previous Christian imagery from it and by adding on every minted coin a formulaic reference to Muhammad. Likewise, he had numerous milestones incorporating such reference placed all over his kingdom. Furthermore, he rebuilt the Ka'ba and established Mecca, together with Jerusalem, as a compelling religious symbol for all his subjects. He delivered sermons and letters to make his authority all the more effective among them. Most likely, he had the Qur'an (i.e., a non-uniform set of writings of miscellaneous nature dating between the early 7th century and his own days, which, similar to the Hebrew and Christian scriptures, had been composed by several authors) collected for the first time and expanded (Prémare 2010; cf. Robinson 2005: 100–4). And last but not least, he built the Dome of the Rock in the midst of the Temple Mount in Jerusalem as the official emblem of his rulership – an emblem that questions the mainstream Christian belief that Jesus is the son of God and that additionally displays a Muhammadan creed whose only known precedent is a Zubayrid confessional formula of the mid-680s (Johns 2003: 426–7; Hoyland 2006: 396–7).

Yet even if one assumes that 'Abd al-Malik set forth (to win over the Zubayrids?, i.e., one of the competing parties of the 680s) a specific Muhammadan policy to which his inscriptions on the Dome of the Rock bear witness, and that such policy reflects a carefully-studied anti-Christian political maneuver (Van der Velden 2011), the fact is that their content remains largely ambiguous. Who is, one may legitimately ask, the referent of the titles "Servant," "Prophet," and "Messenger" in the inscriptions? Muhammad, as it is commonly thought, or Jesus, as it has recently been suggested? In my view, this crucial question cannot be straightforwardly answered due to what I propose to call the *elusiveness* of the referent of such titles and the *ambivalence* of the rhetorical framing of the inscriptions themselves. However, this intriguing ambiguity may well provide a *symptomatic* clue as to their setting, as we shall see.

There are two Arabic Kufic inscriptions on the Dome of the Rock in Jerusalem: one on the outer face of its octagonal arcade (hereinafter Inscription A) and one on its inner face (hereinafter Inscription B). I will consider them separately.

Inscription A

Inscription A reads as follows:

> In the name of God, the Compassionate, the Merciful. There is no god but God alone. He has no associate. Say, "He is God, the One! – God, Indivisible!" He does not beget nor was he begotten, and no one is equal in rank to him. Muhammad/ Praised be the messenger of God. May God bless him. In the name of God, the Compassionate, the Merciful. There is no god but God alone. He has no associate. To him [belongs all] sovereignty and to him [belongs all] praise. He gives life and makes [people] die. He is almighty. Muhammad/Praised be the messenger of God. God and his angels bless the prophet. O you who believe, implore [God's] blessing and grace/peace upon him! God bless him, and may [God's] grace/peace and mercy be upon him. Say, "Praise belongs to God, who has no child nor partner in his rule. He is not so weak as to need a protector. Proclaim his limitless greatness!" Muhammad/Praised be the messenger of God. May God bless him, as well as his angels and messengers, and may God's grace/peace and mercy be upon him. In the name of God, the Compassionate, the Merciful. There is no god but God alone. He has no associate. To him [belongs all] sovereignty and to him [belongs all] praise. He gives life and makes [people] die. He is almighty. Muhammad/Praised be the messenger of God. May God bless him. And accept his intercession for his community. In the name of God, the Compassionate, the Merciful. There is no god but God alone. He has no associate. Muhammad/Praised be the messenger of God. May God bless him. This dome was built by God's servant :: al-Ma'mūn ::[2] in the year 72. May God accept it from him and be pleased with him. Amen, Lord of Creation. The will is God's.

2 The dome wasn't built by al-Ma'mun, who many decades later, after restoring the building, introduced his own name therein, instead of 'Abd al-Malik's name.

For the sake of clarity I will divide its content into eleven sections (A1–11), each containing an uneven number of meaningful sentences or groups of sentences differentiated by a vertical bar (|) and eventually reflecting more or less "accurate" "Qur'anic" quotations. I give the Qur'anic references in curly brackets ({}), preceded by a * when the wording slightly differs from the so-called Uthmanic or canonical wording. A few key terms and expressions to which I shall return below are given in square brackets ([]). Thus we have:

- (A1) In the name of God, the Compassionate, the Merciful. | There is no god but God alone. He has no associate. | {112} Say, "He is God, the One! – God, Indivisible!" He does not beget nor was he begotten, and no one is equal in rank to him.
- (A2) Muhammad/Praised be the messenger of God [*mḥmdrswl 'l'h*]. | {*33:56} May God bless him.
- (A3) In the name of God, the Compassionate, the Merciful. | There is no god but God alone. He has no associate.
- (A4) Muhammad/Praised be the messenger of God [*mḥmdrswl 'l'h*]. | {33:56} God and his angels bless the prophet [*'lnby*]. O you who believe, implore [God's] blessing and grace/peace upon him! | God bless him, and may [God's] grace/peace and mercy be upon him.
- (A5) {17:111} Say, "Praise belongs to God, who has no child nor partner in his rule. He is not so weak as to need a protector. Proclaim his limitless greatness!"
- (A6) Muhammad/Praised be the messenger of God [*mḥmdrswl 'l'h*]. | {*33:56} May God bless him, as well as his angels and messengers, and may God's grace/peace and mercy be upon him.
- (A7) In the name of God, the Compassionate, the Merciful. | There is no god but God alone. He has no associate. | {*64:1 + 57:2} To him [belongs all] sovereignty and to him [belongs all] praise. He gives life and makes [people] die. He is almighty.
- (A8) Muhammad/Praised be the messenger of God [*mḥmdrswl 'l'h*]. | {*33:56} May God bless him. | And accept his intercession for his community.

- (A9) In the name of God, the Compassionate, the Merciful. | There is no god but God alone. He has no associate. {*64:1 + 57:2}
- (A10) Muhammad/Praised be the messenger of God [mḥm-drswl 'l'h]. | {*33:56} May God bless him.
- (A11) This dome was built by God's servant :: al-Ma'mūn :: in the year 72 [= 692]. May God accept it from him and be pleased with him. Amen, Lord of Creation. The will is God's.

Put differently, this first inscription consists of four more-or-less homogeneous thematic sections (AI–IV):

AI	A1, A3, A7, A9
AII	A2, A4, A6, A8, A10
AIII	A5
AIV	A11

The "Qur'anic" quotations(?) (whatever we make out of them, on which see below) strongly confirm this thematic distribution, as sections AI, AII and AIII incorporate different "Qur'anic" verses:

Q {*64:1} + {57:2}	A1, A3, A7, A9	AI
Q {*33:56}	A2, A6, A8, A10	AII
Q {33:56}	A4	AII
Q {17:111}	A5	AIII

There certainly are some unique elements, namely A5 in full, the reference to a "prophet" in A4 and the concluding sentence in A8. Now, if we leave aside A11, which merely provides information on the building of the Dome itself (notice, however, that ʿAbd al-Malik's original name is replaced therein by that of al-Ma'mūn, the seventh Abbasid caliph [r. 813–833]), this results in an almost symmetrical scheme with A5 at its core:

| A1(a) → | A2(b) → | A3(a) → | A4(b) → | **A5** |
| A6(b) ← | A7(a) ← | A8(b) ← | A9(a) ← | + A10(b) |

Or in a more dynamic fashion:

1	2	3
A1 →		
	→ A2	
A3 →		
	A4 →	
		A5
	A6 →	
A7 →		
	→ A8	
A9 →		
	+ A10	

It is clearly possible to read AI and AII as a double *šahāda* (the Islamic creed that God is one and Muhammad is his prophet). But should we? As Luxenberg suggests, *mḥmd* in A2, A4, A6, A8 and A10 need not be a name ("Muhammad") but a gerundial passive participle meaning "praised be" (*muḥammad*); cf. the analogous Predicate > Subject structure of Psalm 118:26 and Matt 21:9 in the Arabic Bible: *mubārakunal-atī bi-smi r-rabb* (Luxenberg 2010: 130). Of course, this would make problematic, and ultimately turn unclear, the referent of the title "messenger" (*rswl*) in A2, A4, A6, A8 and A10, as well as that of "prophet" (*nby*) in A4. But, as we shall see, *rswl* is three times explicitly applied to Jesus on Inscription B (cf. B2, B3, B5) – in addition to "servant" (*'bd*), which interestingly enough is appended in B2 to the formula displayed in A2, A4, A6, A8 and A10 ("Muhammad/Praised be the servant of God and his messenger"), thus rendering even more problematic its referent! This obviously makes Luxenberg's argument not so overarched as it could a priori seem (see also von Sivers 2014).

In short, the rhetoric is ambiguous at best; and the "Qur'anic" quotations(?) are of no help at this juncture – if they can be defined as such, that is: for there simply is no complete extant Qur'an from this early period. Only a few dispersed "Qur'anic" fragments have survived to this day, that match to about 40% or 50% the text of the so-called "Uthmanic Vulgate"; to put it plainly then, we have no evidence of the type of document(s?) those fragments originally belonged to, but one thing is sure: projecting onto them the concept of a pre-Marwanid canonical Qur'an (whose *ductus* the inscriptions themselves do not fully match) makes little sense (see Dye 2015). Besides, if, as I have suggested, A5 is the core of the message contained in this first inscription (which Inscription B in turn expands, see below), the whole text can then be said to be about Jesus – or, a polemical text whose purpose is to question Jesus's divine sonship (which, of course, is not the same as to say that it aims at questioning Christianity per se [Segovia 2019], although it can, and possibly must, be interpreted in that way given its historical-political setting, which I have already alluded to). This does not necessarily imply, however, that the referent of the titles "servant," "prophet" and "messenger" in A2, A4, A6, A8 and A10 should be Muhammad: it could well be Jesus without affecting that polemical intent.

Inscription B

In turn, Inscription B reads thus:

> In the name of God, the Compassionate, the Merciful. There is no god but God alone. He has no associate. To him [belongs all] sovereignty and to him [belongs all] praise. He gives life and makes [people] die. He is almighty. Muhammad/Praised be the servant of God and his messenger. God and his angels bless the prophet. O you who believe, implore [God's] blessing and grace/peace upon him! God bless him, and may [God's] grace/peace and mercy be upon him. O people of the Scripture, do not ∴ exaggerate // err ∴[3] in your religion/judgment and do not tell anything but the truth about God. Verily the Messiah, Jesus son of Mary, is the messenger of God and his Word, which he infused into Mary along with his Spirit. So, believe in God and in his messengers and do not say "Three!"; cease [doing that], it is better for you. Verily God is a unique God – may he be praised! How then could he have a child!? To him belongs all there is in the heavens and upon the earth. For God is sufficient

3 Two optional readings.

as a helper [to mankind]. The Messiah would not disdain to be God's servant, nor [would] the angels standing near [to God]. Whoever disdains to serve him and himself behaves haughtily, such people he will [one day] call together in his presence [lit.: to himself]. O God, bless your messenger and servant Jesus son of Mary! Grace/Peace [be] upon him on the day when he was born, on the day when he will die, and on the day when he will be resurrected. Such is Jesus, son of Mary, the word of truth about whom you fight with one another. It does not become God to [adopt] a child – may he be praised! When he decides something, he only needs to say "Be!" – and it comes into being. God is my lord and your lord, so serve him – this is a straight path. God has warned [us] that there is no god besides him. And the angels as well as the learned people confirm [according the truth]: There is no god besides Him, the Powerful, the Wise! The right religion/judgment is agreement/conformity [with this truth]. Those to whom the Scripture was given fell [into disagreement] after receiving knowledge, [thus] disputing amongst themselves. Whoever denies the signs of God, [let her/him know that] God is swift in reckoning!

This inscription may be divided into seven sections (B1–7), each containing, once more, an uneven number of meaningful sentences or groups of sentences differentiated by a vertical bar (|) and eventually reflecting, again, more or less "accurate" "Qur'anic" quotations. As in the former case, I give the Qur'anic references in curly brackets ({}), preceded by a * when the wording slightly differs from the canonical wording. A few key terms and expressions are also given in square brackets ([]). Thus we have:

- (B1) In the name of God, the Compassionate, the Merciful. | There is no god but God alone. He has no associate. | {*64:1 + 57:2} To him [belongs all] sovereignty and to him [belongs all] praise. He gives life and makes [people] die. He is almighty.
- (B2) Muhammad/Praised be the servant of God and his messenger [mḥmd 'bd 'l'hwrswlh]. | {33:56} God and his angels bless the prophet ['lnby]. O you who believe, implore [God's] blessing and grace/peace upon him! | God bless him, and may [God's] grace/peace and mercy be upon him.

- (B3) {4:171} O people of the Scripture, do not ∴ exaggerate // err ∴ in your religion/judgment [*l' tglw' // t'lw' fydynkm*] and do not tell anything but the truth [*'lḥq*] about God. Verily the Messiah, Jesus son of Mary, is the messenger of God and his Word, which he infused into Mary along with his Spirit [*'l-msyḥ 'ysy 'bnmrymrswl 'l'hwklmth 'lqyh' 'lymrymwrwḥnmnh*]. So, believe in God and in his messengers [*rslh*] and do not say "Three!" [*l' tqwlw 'tlth*]; cease [doing that], it is better for you. Verily God is a unique God – may he be praised! How then could he have a child!? To him belongs all there is in the heavens and upon the earth. For God is sufficient as a helper [to mankind].
- (B4) {4:172} The Messiah [*'l-msyḥ*] would not disdain to be God's servant [*'bd 'l'h*], nor [would] the angels standing near [to God]. Whoever disdains to serve him and himself behaves haughtily, such people he will [one day] call together in his presence [lit.: to himself].
- (B5) O God, bless your messenger and servant Jesus son of Mary [*'llhmṣly 'lyrswlkw'bdk 'ysy b. mrym*]! | {19:33–6} Grace/Peace [be] upon him on the day when he was born, on the day when he will die, and on the day when he will be resurrected. Such is Jesus, son of Mary [*'ysy 'bnmrym*], the word of truth [*qwl 'lḥq*] about whom you fight with one another. It does not become God to [adopt] a child – may he be praised! When he decides something, he only needs to say "Be!" – and it comes into being. | {*43:64 & 5:117} God is my lord and your lord, so serve him – this is a straight path.
- (B6) God has warned [us] that there is no god besides him. | And the angels as well as the learned people confirm [according the truth]: There is no god besides Him, the Powerful, the Wise!
- (B7) {3.19} The right religion/judgment [*dyn*] is agreement/conformity [*'slm*] [with this truth]. Those to whom the Scripture was given fell [into disagreement] after receiving knowledge, [thus] disputing amongst themselves. | Whoever denies the signs of God, [let her/him know that] God is swift in reckoning!

112 Identity, Politics and the Study of Islam

The thematic division of this second inscription is somewhat simpler, as it consists of two instead of four major sections:

BI	B1, B2
BII	B3, B4, B5, B6, B7

BII, i.e., the longer one, is up to B5 an expansion of A5, as I have already pointed out, while BI reproduces the double "*šahāda*" in AI and AII (on which see above). Yet one may additionally divide BII into two complementary subsections:

BIIA	B3, B4, B5
BIIB	B6, B7

BIIA being the expansion of the "Christological" text in A5, and BIIB drawing a few supplementary coda ("God has [therefore] warned that there is no god besides him," "The right religion/judgment is agreement/conformity [with this truth]") on the message displayed on it. Thus we now have:

B1(a)	+ B2(b) →	**B3**	**B4**	**B5**	+ B6	+ B7

or in a more dynamic fashion:

1	2	3	4
B1 ↪			
	B2 ↪		
		B3	
		B4	
		B5	
			↪ B6
			B7

As to the "Qur'anic" quotations(?) present on this second inscription, this time one finds:

Identity Politics and the Study of Islamic Origins 113

Q {*64:1 + 57:2}	B1	B1
Q {33.56}	B2	B1
Q {4:171}	B3	BIIA
Q {4:172}	B4	BIIA
Q {19:33–6}	B5	BIIA
Q {*43:64}	B5	BIIA
Q {5:117}	B5	BIIA
Q {3:19}	B7	BIIB

Therefore, the largest part of this second inscription, and hence its thematic core, is once more (like A5) a polemical text (B3–5) whose purpose is, again, to question Jesus's divine status (notice especially the thematic parallels between A5 and B5).

Yet there are a number of additional elements worthy of comment in BII:

First, Jesus's titles in B3 (Q 4:171 actually being the longest Qur'anic passage in terms of what might be labeled as denominational Christology): Jesus is successively presented therein as "the Messiah, Jesus son of Mary" (*'l-msyḥ 'ysy 'bnmrym*; cf. B4 [*'l-msyḥ*] and B5 [*'ysy 'bnmrym*, twice]); as "God's messenger" (*rswl 'l'h*); as "his word" (*klmth*; cf. Q 3:45 [*klmhmnh*]); and as "a spirit from him" (*rwḥnmnh*). Jesus's name (*'ysy* = *ʿĪsā*, on which see Dye and Kropp 2011) and his description as "the Messiah son of Mary" (which as far as I can discern perfectly matches Mary's common Eastern-Christian description as *Christotókos* rather than *Theotókos*) have clear parallels in Dyophysite/Nestorian, and hence Eastern-Syriac, Christianity (Segovia 2015a, 2018); thus they could have likewise been acceptable for at least some Christians of late antiquity. The term *klmth*, on its part, suggests an implicit, if imprecise (cf. *qwl 'lḥq* in B5), Logos Christology. Finally, the expression *rwḥnmnh* can be interpreted in a very straightforward, even provocative manner if it is read in light of the tacit depiction of Jesus as the second or true Adam (after Hebrews 1:6?) that results from comparing Q 21:91 (*fa-nafaḥnāfīhā min rrūḥinā*) and 66:12 (*fa-nafaḥnāfīhi*[sic!] *min rrūḥinā*), on the one hand, and Q 15:29 and 38:72 (*fa-'iḏā ... nafaḥtufīhi min rrūḥī*), on the other hand – the wording in these passages being symptomatically reminiscent of Genesis 1:26–7 and 2:7.

Second, Jesus coming into being in B5 (cf. Q 3:59) draws on an argument introduced elsewhere in the Qur'an to explain Mary's pregnancy (Q 3:47). Its inclusion in B5, as also in Q 3:59 and 19:35, could be witness perhaps to the re-adaptation of an originally non-polemical argument within a different, now polemical, context.

Third, it is Jesus himself who bears the titles of "messenger" in B3 and B5, and "servant" in B4 and B5, which, as I have earlier underlined (see above my concluding comments on the elusive referent of such titles in A2, A4, A6, A8 and A10), complicates their plain attribution to "Muhammad" – and the same applies to the title "prophet" in A4 and B2.

Lastly, even if trinitarianism is explicitly rejected in B3 (*l' tqwlw 'tlth*), this does not imply that *dyn* ought to be read as "religion" rather than "judgment" therein and in B7. Besides, Luxenberg (2010: 137) persuasively argues that *l' tglw' fydynkm* in B3 can also be read *l't 'lw' fydynkm*, as the consonantal skeleton naturally lacks the diacritical dot over the second letter of the second word, which thus can be rendered as either ' or *g*; and *l't 'lw' fydynkm*, therefore, as a crypto-Syriac expression meaning "do not err in your judgment." Likewise, the final reference to a judgment (again, *dyn*) in conformity to the truth that Jesus is not to be seen as God's son (let alone as God) does not make of the word *'slm* (*islām*) a noun that denotes (the foundation of) a new "religion."

In conclusion, both inscriptions, while implicitly witness to the official promotion of a new confessional creed centered around the figure of Muhammad as God's servant, prophet and messenger – and hence to the official inscription of a new religious identity based upon a somewhat innovative confessional symbol – show that the time in which those very same titles were rather applied to Jesus was not distant enough to avoid some very significant conceptual ambivalences. In other words, they evince a moment of transition in the process of identity-making instead of representing the official sanction of an already existing one or a clear-cut new start within that process (see further von Sivers [2014], who rightly points to this ambivalence and persuasively explores its religious-historical background).

I have previously alluded to the elusiveness inherent in the referent of the charismatic titles displayed on the Dome of the Rock inscriptions. I should like to conclude this essay by stressing that their ambivalent rhetoric points to an inescapable and arguably broader type of *elusiveness*: that which corresponds to every present when it is seen from *within* as an open dynamic process instead of being misrepresented in light of its contingent results.

References

Berg, H. 2012. "The Needle in the Haystack: Islamic Origins and the Nature of the Early Sources," in C.A. Segovia and B. Lourié, eds., *The Coming of the Comforter: When, Where, and to Whom? Studies on the Rise of Islam and Various Other Topics in Memory of John Wansbrough* (pp. 271–302). OJC 3. Piscataway, NJ: Gorgias Press.

Borrut, A. 2014. "Vanishing Syria: Periodization and Power in Early Islam." *Der Islam* 91(1): 37–68. https://doi.org/10.1515/islam-2014-0004

Crossley, J. 2014. "Is the Grass Greener? A View from Biblical Studies." *Bulletin for the Study of Religion* 43(4): 29–33. https://doi.org/10.1558/bsor.v43i4.29

Curtis IV, E.E. 2014. "Ode to Islamic Studies: Its Allure, Its Danger, Its Power." *Bulletin for the Study of Religion* 43(4): 21–5. https://doi.org/10.1558/bsor.v43i4.21

Donner, F.M. 2010. *Muhammad and the Believers: At the Origins of Islam*. Cambridge, MA: Harvard University Press.

Dye, G. 2015. "Pourquoi et comment se fait un texte canonique: quelques réflexions sur l'histoire du Coran," in Ch. Brouwer, G. Dye and A. van Rompaey, eds., *Hérésies: une construction d'identités religieuses* (pp. 55–104). PHR. Brussels: Éditions de l'Université de Bruxelles.

Dye, G. and M. Kropp. 2011. "Le nom de Jésus ('Īsā) dans le Coran, et quelques autres noms bibliques: remarques sur l'onomastique coranique," in G. Dye and F. Nobilio, eds., *Figures bibliques en islam* (pp. 171–98). Religion et Alterité. Fernelmont, BE: Éditions Modulaires Européennes.

Hoyland, R. 2006. "New Documentary Texts and the Early Islamic State." *Bulletin of the School of Oriental and African Studies* 69(3): 395–416. https://doi.org/10.1017/S0041977X06000188

— 2015. *In God's Path: The Arab Conquests and the Creation of an Islamic Empire*. Oxford and New York: Oxford University Press.

Hughes, A. 2012. *Theorizing Islam: Disciplinary Deconstruction and Reconstruction*. Sheffield, UK, and Bristol, CT: Equinox. Reissued in Durham, UK: Acumen, 2014.

Johns, J. 2003. "Archaeology and the History of Early Islam: The First Seventy Years." *Journal of the Economic and Social History of the Orient* 46(4): 411–36. https://doi.org/10.1163/156852003772914848

Luxenberg, Ch. 2010. "A New Interpretation of the Arabic Inscriptions in Jerusalem's Dome of the Rock," in K.-H. Ohlig and G.-R. Puin, eds., *The Hidden Origins of Islam: New Research into Its Early History* (pp. 125–51). Amherst, NY: Prometheus Books.

Nevo, Y.D. and J. Koren. 2003. *Crossroads to Islam: The Origins of the Arab Religion and the Arab State*. Amherst, NY: Prometheus Books.

Newby, G.D. 1989. *The Making of the Last Prophet: Reconstruction of the Earliest Biography of Muhammad*. Columbia: University of South Carolina.

Prémare, A.-L. de. 2010. "'Abd al-Malik b. Marwān and the Process of the Qur'ān's Composition," in K.-H. Ohlig and G.R. Puin, eds., *The Hidden Origins of Islam: New Research into Its Early History* (pp. 189–221). Amherst, NY: Prometheus Books.

Reynolds, G.S. 2010. *The Qur'ān in Its Biblical Subtext*. RSQ. London and New York: Routledge.

— 2014. "Islamic Studies in North America, or Reflections on the Academic Study of the Qur'an." *Islamochristiana* 40: 55–73.

Robinson, Ch.F. 2005. *'Abd al-Malik*. MMW. Oxford: OneWorld.

Safi, O. 2008. "Between the Seventh and the Twenty-first: Musing on Texts and Contexts in the Early Twenty-first Century." *American Journal of Islamic Social Sciences* 25(3): 111–18.

— 2009. *Memories of Muhammad: Why the Prophet Matters*. New York: HarperOne.

— 2014. "Reflections on the State of Islamic Studies." *Jadaliyya*.
http://www.jadaliyya.com/pages/index/16269/reflections-on-the-state-of-islamic-studies#.Uuvw6CkjVY4.facebook

Schoeler, G. 2011.*The Biography of Muḥammad: Nature and Authenticity*. English translation by U. Vagelpohl. Edited by J.E. Montgomery. RSCI. London and New York: Routledge.

Segovia, C.A. 2015a. "Abraha's Christological Formula *Rḥmnn w-Ms¹ḥ-hw* and Its Relevance for the Study of Islam's Origins." *Oriens Christianus* 98: 52–63.

— 2015b. *The Quranic Noah and the Making of the Islamic Prophet: A Study of Intertextuality and Religious Identity Making in Late Antiquity*. JCIT 4. Berlin and New York: De Gruyter. https://doi.org/10.1515/9783110405897

—2018. "The Jews and the Christians of Pre-Islamic Yemen (Ḥimyar) and the Elusive Matrix of the Qur'ān's Christology," in F. del Río Sánchez, ed., *Jewish Christianity and Islamic Origins* (pp. 91–104). JAOC 13. Turnhout: Brepols.

—2019. "A Messianic Controversy behind the Making of Muḥammad as the Last Prophet?" Forthcoming in G. Dye, ed., *Early Islam: Rethinking the Religious Milieu of Late Antiquity.* LAMINE. Chicago: Chicago Oriental Institute.

Sharon, M. 1988. "The Birth of Islam in the Holy Land," in M. Sharon, ed., *The Holy Land in History and Thought* (pp. 225–35). Leiden and Boston: Brill.

Shoemaker, S.J. 2012. *The Death of a Prophet: The End of Muhammad's Life and the Beginnings of Islam.* DRLAR. Philadelphia: University of Pennsylvania Press. https://doi.org/10.9783/9780812205138

Van der Velden, F. 2011. "Die Felsendominschrift als Ende einer christologischen Konvergenz text ökumene im Koran." *Oriens Christianus* 95: 213–46.

von Sivers, P. 2014. "Christology and Prophetology in the Early Umayyad Arab Empire," in M. Groß and K.-H. Ohlig, eds., *Die Entstehungeiner Weltreligion III. Die heilige Stadt Mekka – eine literarische Fiktion* (pp. 255–85). ISFIK 7. Berlin: Hans Schiler.

Carlos A. Segovia is lecturer in religious studies at Saint Louis University, Madrid Campus. He works in the philosophy of religion (from a postmodern perspective), the history of religions (with special focus on the renewed study of Islam's origins) and the anthropology of religion (at the crossroads of Amazonian mythology, political theory and postcolonial studies). Among his latest publications are *The Quranic Jesus: A New Interpretation* (De Gruyter, forthcoming) and "Social Theory, Conceptual Imagination, and The Study of Pre-State Societies: From Lévi-Strauss to Pierre Clastres" (*Palimpsestos: Revista de Arqueología y Antropología Anarquista*, forthcoming).

Part III

Comparative Views from Outside Islamic Studies

5. Jews, Jewish Studies and the Study of Islam

Sarah Imhoff

The field of Jewish studies is full of Jews. This is obvious. It is also surprising, for two reasons. First, the diversity of Jewish studies scholars compares unfavorably with other religion-related fields. Islamic studies currently has a sufficient mix of Muslim and non-Muslim scholars to create a heated debate about epistemology, apology and the study of Islam. Jewish studies still has relatively few non-Jewish scholars of Judaism, although the number is slowly growing. Second, the paucity of non-Jewish scholars is surprising because, as recent debates about the Jewishness of Jewish studies show, most scholars of Judaism today would agree that there should be more non-Jews in Jewish studies.[1] It is desirable for non-Jews to study Judaism as full members of the scholarly community not only because of the value of the diversity of persons, but also because the health of the discipline depends of the diversity of methods and perspectives. So why doesn't the make-up of the field reflect this desire?

It is, in part, a matter of history. But it's also a matter of how we tell that history. While Islamic studies in America traces much of its history through Orientalism – non-Muslims studying Muslims and Islamic civilizations – the dominant narrative of Jewish studies begins with Jews studying Judaism. Although Jewish studies is my

---

1   Aaron Hughes, "Is Jewish Studies Too Jewish?" *Chronicle of Higher Education*, http://chronicle.com/article/Jewish-Studies-Is-Too-Jewish/145395/ (March 24, 2014, accessed June 29, 2015); Zak Braiterman, "Response to Aaron Hughes," *Jewish Philosophy Space*, http://jewishphilosophyplace.wordpress.com/2014/05/08/too-jewish-studies-response-to-aaron-hughes/ (May 8, 2014, accessed June 29, 2015).

primary field, I have found that reflecting on Islamic studies has made me think more clearly about Jewish studies. I hope the reverse also proves true – that reflecting on Jewish studies will offer fruitful parallels with, as well as distinctions from, many of the larger issues at play in Islamic studies. This chapter explores the identity of Jewish studies as a field through the stories of its past, and asks what these stories might suggest about Islamic studies and its future.

Today, while places in undergraduate and, increasingly, graduate Jewish studies courses are filled by non-Jews, the probability that the professor at the front of the classroom is a Jew is extremely high. In 2008, an Association for Jewish Studies survey reported that 92% of its responding members identified as Jewish.[2] Funding and identity politics have both paved the road that has led to Jewish studies as it is today. Organizations like Tikvah and Posen, each with its own ideology, promote the academic study of Judaism, but the projects they fund tend to craft Jewish studies in their own image.[3] Identity politics, on the part of universities and Jewish communities, have also played a substantial role in shaping who are professors of Jewish studies. But here I want to highlight a different kind of identity: the identity of Jewish studies. And, I'll suggest, the identity of Jewish studies in the American academy is more closely related to the field of religious studies than the usual story of the development of Jewish studies explains.

Those who, like Aaron Hughes, have insisted on the importance of identity in Jewish studies have noted that scholars are implicated because we are always inventing the tradition we purport to study.[4]

---

2 Steven M. Cohen and Judith Veinstein, *The 2008 Association for Jewish Studies Membership Survey*, Association for Jewish Studies, Berman Jewish Policy Archive at NYU Wagner (April 27, 2008), p. 4. In 2012, Aaron Hughes estimated a similar 95%. Aaron Hughes, *The Study of Judaism: Authenticity, Identity, Scholarship* (Albany, NY: SUNY Press, 2013).

3 Zak Braiterman, "Conservative Money and Jewish Studies," *Zeek*, http://zeek.forward.com/articles/117374/ (September 6, 2011, accessed June 28, 2015).

4 In addition to Hughes, see Jacob Neusner, "From Private to Public Discourse 'Study of Torah' Becomes One of the Humanities," in *Judaism in the American Humanities – Second Series: Jewish Learning and the New*

There is no fixed thing in the world called "Judaism" or "Jewishness" just sitting and waiting to be described by scholars. The telling of stories, histories and biographies crafts identity in profound and essential ways. When scholars write about who Jews are, or what they have done in history, it is not merely description. They shape what Jewishness means. When they interpret texts they are not purely explaining the stable meaning of unchanging words, they are molding Judaism.

So too, when we tell the history of Jewish studies, we are also crafting a narrative: we're inventing an identity for the thing we call "Jewish studies." Beyond asking how Jewish studies creates the stories and identities of a people it calls Jews, how does Jewish studies create the story and identity of Jewish studies itself? Perhaps the most common version of this story emphasized *Wissenschaft des Judentums*, or the "science of Judaism," as the point of origin of Jewish studies.[5] *Wissenschaft*, as it is often abbreviated, began in the 19th century when German Jewish scholars applied scholarly, "scientific" inquiry to Jewish religious texts and culture. They proposed that the Bible, rabbinic literature and other religious texts be subjected to the same methodologies used to study non-religious material. Scholars such as Heinrich Graetz and Leopold Zunz, whose works are still read by Jewish historians today, campaigned for the study of Jews to take a respectable place in university curricula. There is an added complication to this story: *Wissenschaft* was ideologically, but not often explicitly, bound up with the contemporary struggle to get Jews accepted as professors in universities. Progress toward universities' acceptance of the study of Judaism, as well as the acceptance of

---

Humanities (Chico, CA: Scholars Press, 1983), pp. 61–102; J.Z. Smith, *Imagining Religion: From Babylon to Jonestown* (Chicago: University of Chicago Press, 1982), p. xi.

5 For just a few examples of *Wissenschaft* as the origin of Jewish studies, see Arnold J. Band, "Jewish Studies in American Liberal-Arts Colleges and Universities," *American Jewish Yearbook* 67 (1966): 1–30; Kristen Loveland, "The Association of Jewish Studies: A Brief History," *AJS Annual Conference* (2008), now available on AJS's home page: http://www.ajsnet.org/ajs.pdf

Jews themselves, was slow. Nevertheless, *Wissenschaft* undoubtedly helped open the academic door for Jews and Judaism.

Wissenschaft, then, was a significant moment, but casting it in the central role of the drama of the history of Jewish studies has molded a particular identity for the field. The founders of the Association for Jewish Studies (AJS) even marveled at their own accomplishment in creating a scholarly organization by invoking their *Wissenschaft* forefathers. Historian Leon Jick wrote of the AJS's founding: "Would Zunz, [Moritz] Steinschneider, or even Graetz have believed that in 1969 some fifty professors of Judaica, to a considerable degree American-born and trained, would gather at a major American university established by Jews to consider the status of their profession?"[6]

This *Wissenschaft*-influenced identity of Jewish studies is one that allows observers to look past the identities of individual scholars, and to classify concerns about scholarly identity as marginal to the academic project. In essence, when we position scholarly work as "scientific," as *Wissenschaft* has done, we've already suggested that the identity of the scientist is extraneous. It suggests that the knowledge produced is objective knowledge. A foundational part of the scientific method is that discoveries of knowledge should be repeatable by anyone with the same equipment and conditions. If the study of Judaism is a science, then its data would be the same whether Jews or non-Jews gathered them. This story allowed the early AJS meetings to give out *benchers* (books of blessings) with its logo on them and have participants say the *birkat hamazon* blessing at communal meals, all while insisting on the purely academic nature of its meeting. When Jewish studies tells the story of its own birth as one of the objective scientific study of Judaism, then it can assume that the religious and ethnic backgrounds of scholars are of marginal importance, if any. If the study of Judaism is objective, it matters little who does the studying.

When this is the creation story of Jewish studies, it becomes easy to overlook or dismiss interpretations that put causal or critical weight on the identity of scholars. It's certainly not inevitable, but the narrative themes of progress, goals of objective knowledge and growing

6 Leon Jick, "Introduction," *AJS Newsletter* 2 (1989): 3.

acceptance of Jews and Judaism in the academy are set. Turning our gaze away from these narrative themes is not impossible, but requires just that: a conscious turning away from the narrative, in a way that can make the observations seem marginal and not crucial to the identity of Jewish studies. I do not mean to suggest that a historical genealogy focused on *Wissenschaft* is wrong, but its hegemony has eclipsed other themes. What narratives, themes and identities for Jewish studies might we find if we told a different tale about how Jewish studies got to where it is today? How might the importance of the identity of individuals in Jewish studies appear to us, if Jewish studies itself appeared through a different story?

What if we moved our focus from 19th-century *Wissenschaft* to the 1960s as a focal point of Jewish studies' narrative and genealogy? Telling this different story offers both new themes and a compelling reason to consider the field of religious studies as a way to understand identity in Jewish studies. Of course, religious studies is only one field where Jewish studies takes place. In fact, a perusal of AJS materials and job listings shows that religious studies trains and employs a minority of Jewish studies scholars.[7] Nevertheless, analysis of religious studies shapes and contextualizes Jewish studies because Jewish studies in the American academy grew up at the same time as religious studies in the United States and Canada.[8] In the 1960s and early '70s both the fields "grew up" in two senses: they grew larger and also developed intellectually and institutionally to look something like they do today.

Religious studies in American academies grew immensely from the mid-1960s to the early '70s. Courses, departments and programs popped up across the US and Canada, funding for the academic study

---

7 As a discipline, history claims the most members of AJS, followed by religious studies. However, more AJS members belong to the American Academy of Religion than to any other scholarly organization (Cohen and Veinstein, see note 2 above).

8 As Crossley's analysis in the blog series that this essay is based on suggests, this is different in European contexts.
http://www.equinoxpub.com/blog/2014/04/taking-care-of-jesus-and-muhammad-reflections-on-islamic-studies/

of religion increased and a generically pro-religion Cold War attitude underwrote its political appeal.⁹ Confessional and theological studies had already begun to part ways with the academic study of religion; the "teaching religion" versus "teaching about religion" distinction became a widespread way to parse approaches. A popular creation myth in US religious studies attributes this growth to the 1963 Supreme Court decision *Abington School District v. Schempp*, but in truth, *Schempp* was merely a sign of its times.¹⁰ At the same time as these religious studies programs sprouted and grew, Jewish studies also began to grow. The number of Jewish studies courses offered more than doubled between 1965 and 1971, and the AJS was founded in 1969.¹¹

While others have noted the importance of the 1960s for Jewish studies, they tend to do so either by locating Jewish studies as simply one more instance of ethnic studies, or by offering sweeping generalizations of US American culture and American Jewry. It's true, the 1960s marked a turn toward particularism exemplified by the growth of ethnic and area studies, and Jewish studies participated in this trend in some ways. American Jews placed a greater emphasis on Jewish distinctiveness in the wake of the 1967 Six Day War and 1973 Yom Kippur War in Israel. And, yes, in some ways the 1960s marked the "coming into its own" of "the" American Jewish community, although this sort of generalization is far too simple to offer historical insight. Likewise, the idea that American universities kept both Jews and Jewish studies at bay until the sea change of the 1960s is far more a product of imagination than a reflection of historical

---

9 See Russell McCutcheon, "Just Follow the Money: The Cold War, the Humanistic Study of Religion, and the Fallacy of Insufficient Cynicism," *Culture and Religion* 5 (2004): 41–69.

10 One clear articulation of this myth appears in Nathan Schneider, "Why the World Needs Religious Studies," *Religion Dispatches* http://religiondispatches.org/why-the-world-needs-religious-studies/ (November 20, 2011, accessed June 28, 2015).

11 Paul Ritterband and Harold Wechsler, *Jewish Learning in American Universities* (Bloomington: Indiana University Press, 1994), p. 219; Loveland, p. 2 (see note 5 above).

reality.[12] Demographically American Jews already looked a lot like their neighbors by the mid-1950s. References to Protestantism, Catholicism and Judaism as the three American faiths reached their heyday before the 1960s.[13] In 1952 Eisenhower famously endorsed generic religion ("a deeply-felt religious faith – and I don't care what it is") as foundational for US democracy. Eisenhower, like the journalists and politicians around him, also used the newly coined "Judeo-Christian" to describe the character and tradition of their American nation.[14] All of these exemplified ways that Jewish inclusion in the United States was in continuity rather than a new development.

As the early years of many religious studies programs, and growth years for others, the 1960s saw a lot of discussion about what religious studies was, could become, and what its institutional arrangement within the university should look like. Some universities, both public and private, took their current faculty's course offerings and cobbled together classes that took religion as a topic of study, and which were already offered in various departments. Many religious studies programs – especially public universities, but also some private ones – started with what we might call the "zoo approach": they exhibited one of each animal. This often took the form of course offerings from a Protestant, a Catholic and a Jew, where each taught his (yes, overwhelmingly *his*) tradition. In this way, the presence of Jews alongside Christians lent legitimacy to the enterprise of teaching of religious studies in general.

Islam was not usually on the list. It did not appear as part of the "Judeo-Christian" or "tri-faith America," and it rarely appeared in religious studies departments. At mid-century, the American Academy

12 Frederick Greenspahn, "The Beginnings of Judaic Studies in American Universities," *Modern Judaism* 20(2), May 2000: 209–25.

13 For a recent historical work on this theme in American history, see Kevin Schulz, *Tri-Faith America: How Catholics and Jews Held Postwar America to Its Protestant Promise* (Oxford: Oxford University Press, 2011). For the classic analysis and critique of this culture, see Will Herberg, *Protestant, Catholic, Jew: An Essay in American Religious Sociology* (Chicago: University of Chicago Press, 1955).

14 Mark Silk, "Notes on the Judeo-Christian Tradition in America," *American Quarterly* 36 (Spring 1984): 65–85.

of Religion (AAR) didn't offer an Islam section – presenters appeared under the "History of Christianity" heading.[15] At the 1973 AAR conference, there was precisely one paper about Islam.[16] In the 1990s, only about one-tenth of the 1,200 US religious studies programs had a professor whose primary research was in Islam.[17] Though the study of Islam did not take place in many religious studies departments, it did happen elsewhere in the university. "Near Eastern" departments, home to textual scholars and Orientalists, frequently housed scholars of Islamic texts and histories. Anthropology, historically a discipline that saw itself as studying faraway or exotic cultures, often had scholars who studied Muslims in the contemporary world. Although a few religious studies departments felt they needed scholars of Islam in the 1960s, these other departments and burgeoning area studies programs were much more common institutional homes for scholars studying Muslims and Islam.

The story of Islamic studies begins in a similar time and place to the *Wissenschaft*-centered history of Jewish studies, but its cast of characters and their interests and motivations were quite different. Today's Islamic studies began with the study of a romanticized "Orient." Nurtured by 19th-century German romanticism, the academic field of Orientalism was born around the same time as *Wissenschaft*. In the 19th and 20th centuries, it too became a highly developed field focusing on textual studies. Unlike *Wissenschaft* with its Jewish scholars of Judaism, the Orientalist study of Islam began not primarily with scholars who identified as Muslims, but rather with Europeans who saw themselves as quite different from the Orient they conjured. (A significant number of them, including Moritz Steinschneider, were Jews.[18]) The first, most famous, and majority of Islamic studies

---

15 Carl Ernst and Richard Martin, *Rethinking Islamic Studies: From Orientalism to Cosmopolitanism* (Columbia, SC: University of South Carolina Press, 2010), p. 1.

16 Charles J. Adams, "The History of Religions and the Study of Islam," *ACLS Newsletter* 25(3–4), 1974: 1–10.

17 Ernst and Martin, p. 1 (see note 15 above).

18 For a short introduction to the literature on Jewish scholars of Orientalism, see John Efron, "Orientalism and the Jewish Historical Gaze,"

scholars were European and American men who saw Islam as part of cultures other than their own. Though Edward Said and other scholars critiqued the assumptions and interpretations of Orientalism and reoriented much of the study of Islam in the late 1970s and '80s, and some Muslims entered the field, the trend of a non-Muslim majority in the field of Islamic studies continued into the new millennium.[19]

So when religious studies programs were founded at American universities, they often had Christianity and Judaism, which were most often taught by Christians and Jews, respectively. They occasionally included Buddhism, usually taught by a non-Buddhist. The study of Islam, however, tended to happen outside of religious studies departments, and it was most often taught by non-Muslims.

As religious studies programs and departments flourished in the 1960s, university committees discussed the perceived benefits, concerns and liabilities of having or expanding these programs. While memos and meeting minutes rarely provide exciting histories, in this case, they do allow us to see what faculty and administrators thought was going on in religious studies.[20] "Indoctrination" recurred as an administrative worry in the discussions about Catholic and Protestant clergy, but not Jews teaching Judaism. Judaism, then, began its life as an academic subject in many American universities without undergoing the scrutiny of its instructors or their methods. Not one of the

---

in Ivan Davidson Kalmar and Derek Penslar, eds., *Orientalism and the Jews* (Lebanon, NH: Brandeis University Press, 2005), pp. 80–93.

19 Edward Said, *Orientalism* (New York: Vintage Books, 1978).

20 The information in this paragraph is based on archival research including, but not limited to, Danforth Foundation Archives, Philanthropy Archives, Indiana University – Purdue University Indianapolis; Indiana University Archives; Lilly Endowment Archives, Philanthropy Archives, Indiana University – Purdue University Indianapolis; Penn State University archives; University of Alabama archives; University of Illinois archives; University of Michigan archives; University of Tennessee Archives; York University archives. For a more in-depth analysis of this material in reference to the growth of religious studies, see Sarah Imhoff, "The Creation Story, or How We Learned to Stop Worrying and Love Schempp," *Journal of the American Academy of Religion* (June 2016).

1960s discussions I have found invoked a specific concern about the teaching of Judaism. Nor did a concerned faculty member or administrator use a hypothetical situation in which a Judaism course or its instructor would create legal or ethical problems for the university. By contrast, hypothetical examples using Catholicism and various Protestant denominations arose in most university discussions about the viability and wisdom of creating or expanding programs in religious studies. Would they use university time, resources and authority to train students to be religious? Put another way, a conversation about "critics" versus "caretakers" of religion in the university, to borrow Russell McCutcheon's typology,[21] took place in nascent form in the 1960s, but it never took on Jewish studies as its object of concern.

Why did Jewish studies, in the context of the growing field of religious studies, get a pass? It was not because it was located elsewhere in the university, nor that it was taught largely by non-practitioners, as was the case with the study of Islam. Rather, Jewish studies failed to raise red flags about "indoctrination" for other reasons. First, some faculty and administrators might have imagined the model of the scholar-rabbi, as opposed to, for instance, the stereotypical images of the confession-hearing and ritual-performing Catholic priest. But this sort of thinking cannot explain such a widespread trend. Second, as a minority religion, Judaism may have seemed less threatening: no biologist, literary critic or anthropologist was concerned that, by including a Jew or two teaching Judaism, their university would suddenly be mistaken for a Jewish seminary and thereby discredit the university's scholarly endeavors. Third, and most important, no one worried about instructors of Judaism as proselytizers. Perhaps classes on Judaism might make Jews more Jew-y, but no one seemed to mind. For better or for worse, these university discussions about religious studies never indicated any concern that rabbis, or PhDs in Jewish fields, would impart Judaism or Jewish identity to their students.

This lack of concern about Jews teaching Judaism has produced a legacy. The colloquium at which AJS was created did not include non-Jewish scholars of Judaism, and some argued that only committed

---

21 Russell McCutcheon, *Critics not Caretakers: Redescribing the Public Study of Religion* (Albany: SUNY Press, 2012).

Jews should teach Judaism in universities.[22] Almost thirty years later, in 1996, sociology professor Samuel Heilman protested the appointment of Yiddish literature professor Thomas Bird, a non-Jew, to direct the Queens College Jewish studies program. Heilman's rationale was that all "the other ethnic studies programs" were headed by scholars of their own ethnicities. The Jewish studies director should be both a scholar and a symbol "to the community." For the community, "the director is often a reflection of what they can be," Heilman wrote to the Jewish academic forum H-Judaic.[23] "Community," it went without saying, was the non-academic Jewish community. Any appointee also must know Hebrew, he argued, because it is "the essential language of the Jewish experience." I must confess that, even after many years in Jewish studies, I still don't know what "*the* Jewish experience" is. If knowing Hebrew is a requirement for having the Jewish experience, then a large majority of North American Jews haven't had it either.

The language of experience subtly moves the epistemological focus from the scholarly study of texts and social groups to that of "experience," traditionally a personal rather than academic way of knowing. Bird, as a non-Jew, could not have "the Jewish experience." An essential part of the directorship, Heilman continued, was "embodying what it means to take Jewish life and culture seriously." Without a Jewish body, how could Bird ever do this? It is also telling that when Bird resigned the appointment, Heilman called him "a good friend of the Jewish people." Heilman's letter suggested that the academic position of director of Jewish studies should understand "the Jewish experience," and so when the non-Jew stepped aside to let a Jew take the position, he showed himself to be a friend of the Jewish people. It is not the task of Jewish studies scholars to be "friends" of the Jews, but here Heilman suggested it was.

22 Loveland, p. 3 (see note 5 above); Harvie Branscomb, "A Note on Establishing Chairs of Jewish Studies," in *The Teaching of Judaica in American Universities* (New York: Ktav, 1970), p. 97.

23 Samuel Heilman, "Who Should Direct Jewish Studies at the University?" *H-Judaic*, http://h-net.msu.edu/cgi-bin/logbrowse.pl?trx=vx&list=h-judaic&month=9607&week=d&msg=owar/YAZ0rC9RYi2P3re1g&user=&pw= (July 21, 1996, accessed June 28, 2015).

There is a tangled logic here. The argument requires that we believe first that the identity of the scholar does not matter. "It is not about the person of Mr. Bird," Heilman wrote. In a spirit of *Wissenschaft*, Heilman's argument takes it for granted that the identity of the scholar will not be important for the scholarship he produces. Jews and non-Jews alike can scientifically study Judaism. Now, given that the identity of the scholar is immaterial for his scholarship, this thinking goes, we should have a Jew because he will more positively represent the university to the Jewish community and the Jewish community to the world.

In some ways, Heilman is correct: the identity of the director of Jewish studies does send a message to "the community." But he is wrong about what that message should be. Where non-Jewish scholars direct Jewish studies programs in universities, it says to "the community" that Jewish studies is the academic study of Jews and Judaism, and that that knowledge is produced and critiqued by both Jews and non-Jews. It does not imply that no Jews could be found who were up to the task, as Heilman worries some will think. If Jews alone direct Jewish studies programs, it suggests that Jewish studies in the university is merely an outpost for "the Jewish people," like a collection of mini-seminaries or Jewish federations.

Heilman is also correct in another respect: the kinds of human bodies we associate with scholarship are crucially important for our body of knowledge, for future generations of scholars, for students and for the broader community. I wholeheartedly disagree, however, about the criteria for deciding which scholarly bodies are more and less appropriate for the task. Who is teaching – Jews, non-Jews, men, women, people of color, those with disabilities – matters. Students see who is at the front of the class, and that sends a message about what kinds of people can be scholars of which subjects. This is, of course, an ongoing and high-profile issue for women in STEM disciplines, but it exists in the humanities and social sciences too. Many of my students assume they can't or shouldn't major in Jewish studies because they are not Jewish. What led them to think this? In part, it is because they see Jews teaching Jewish studies. Sometimes they even "see" Jews in the cases when their teachers are not Jewish. This is, of course, related to larger cultural assumptions about how we "see"

Muslims and Jews. Popular imagination codes Muslims as non-white and therefore identifiable, and Jews as white and less obviously visibly distinct. It is telling that when I teach about Judaism, many of my students assume I am Jewish, but when I teach about Islam, they rarely assume I am Muslim. They are accustomed to seeing non-Muslims teach about Islam, but they still assume that Jews teach about Judaism.

How does this story of Jewish studies help us think about Islamic studies? First, it highlights the issue of the persons doing the teaching and researching. Demographically, Jewish studies and Islamic studies are moving in opposite directions: Jewish studies has a growing, though still quite small, percentage of non-Jewish scholars, while Islamic studies has a growing percentage of Muslim scholars. Percentage-wise, Muslim professors were the minority in the early years of Orientalism, and then Islamic studies. But today's Islamic studies landscape looks quite different from the way it did in the 1960s, or even the 1980s. More and more Muslim scholars research, publish and teach in Islamic studies.

With this demographic shift, the status of authenticity, apology and the classic religious studies "insider-outsider" debates about epistemology and the identity of the scholar have all become highly relevant issues. Islamic studies has to wrestle with the same sorts of questions raised by Heilman's objection to Bird, or even those implicit in *Wissenschaft*: at one level, they argue that the identity of the scholar is irrelevant to his or her scholarship, but once that is accepted, they also suggest that there is particular value in having a scholar who embodies the tradition. Islamic studies need not (and, to my mind, should not) follow this path of argumentation; there are other ways to parse the insider-outsider question. Area studies models need not function as consolidators of ethnic or religious identity, in which those who teach must also embody the tradition and serve as a model for their students. But as more Muslim scholars, students and donors become involved in Islamic studies, these questions will only grow in intensity. Figuring out how to promote the best critical scholarship as well as a diversity of scholarly bodies will be central to the health of the field.

Second, thinking about Jewish studies shows the relevance of how we tell the history of an academic field. Here I am not suggesting that the received history of Islamic studies is inaccurate, or even that we need to reorient it, as I have suggested with Jewish studies. Rather, I'm suggesting that the Jewish studies example demonstrates that the way we tell the history of a field has profound effects on its current identity. When we tell the story of Islamic studies as a development from Orientalism to area studies, and then as a relative latecomer to religious studies, what facets are we emphasizing? That story claims that Islamic studies has its background in romanticism. And in the move to area studies, as well as the response to the Saidian critique, the story also claims that Islamic studies has – or at least should have – overcome its romantic roots. But has it? The large number of scholarly jobs focusing on the Qur'an in comparison to those focusing on medieval, modern or contemporary Muslim texts and cultures suggests that some currents in the scholarly study of Islam might still romanticize the past, though perhaps in non-Orientalist ways.[24] The newly-formed International Qur'anic Studies Association, which formed in part because some scholars found the AAR's Qur'an Group too apologetic, also suggests the continuing presence of such a romanticizing current. But the story of progress, with its move away from Orientalist beginnings, can obscure these currents. The story has so closely linked romanticism and Orientalism that it makes it difficult to see one without the other. When the story of Islamic studies emphasizes progress away from romantic and colonialist impulses, it may be hard to see where romantic impulses remain once they have been stripped of their colonialist aspects.

The tale of overcoming of romantic and colonial roots also has other implications. Taking seriously the critiques of Orientalism and

---

24 For instance, see Edward Said's post-9/11 review in *Harpers*. Although its main point is that Islam cannot be painted with a single brushstroke, it more subtly points to the continued presence of both Orientalist (Bernard Lewis) and less Orientalist, yet still romantic (Karen Armstrong) scholarship in Islamic studies. Edward Said, "Impossible Histories: Why the Many Islams Cannot Be Simplified," *Harper's Magazine* (July 2002): 69–74.

colonialism has rightly problematized the methods and assumptions typical of Islamic studies before the 1980s. But does this narrative create the conditions in which the field valorizes Muslim scholars' participation merely because they are Muslim, that is, as a sign of the field's (and American culture's) progress? In that case, Islamic studies could congratulate itself on moving beyond colonialism and letting the subaltern speak, as it were. Such a move, like the twinned *Wissenschaft* objectives of the study of Judaism and the entry of Jews into university teaching posts, would make conditions ripe for apology, from both Muslim and non-Muslim scholars. In both cases, liberal (and laudable) political motives aimed at greater inclusion of religious and ethnic minorities shaped both scholars and scholarship, but also enabled apologetics.[25]

Related to apologetics, and complex enough to deserve its own study beyond the cursory treatment I have given it here, is the issue of funding. When donors, whether individuals, communal organizations or even governmental bodies, fund research or professorships, they shape the field. This has long been an issue across the board in religious studies, but Jewish studies deals with this more than other fields because Jews have donated significant amounts of money for the study of Jews and Judaism in higher education. Though much of the impulse to hire scholars of Islam comes from current cultural relevance and liberal, inclusivist university administration, Islamic studies is swiftly moving toward more intimate involvement with donors. The American Muslim Alliance Foundation is currently fundraising toward an endowed chair at San Jose State University, with the ultimate goal of "a full fledged Islamic Studies Department."[26] The Saudi royal family endowed chairs at Harvard and UCSB. Endowed

---

25 The large number of white male converts to Islam in the academy, and the way white converts function as "fetish" objects for public Islam in North America, suggest this interpretation. See Mahdi Tourage, "Performing Belief and Reviving Islam: Prominent (White Male) Converts in Muslim Revival Conventions," *Performing Islam* 1(2), 2013: 207–26.

26 "American Muslim Alliance Foundation's Project for Endowed Chair for Islamic Studies at San Jose State University," http://sjsuislamicstudies.org (accessed May 10, 2015).

programs like the Abbasi Program in Islamic Studies at Stanford are already confronting the kinds of phenomenological questions posed to Jewish studies programs: Who is representing Islam? Are they "authentic"? Are they portraying Islam positively? Donors want to know. As American Muslim populations grow, and as Muslim philanthropists from abroad see American universities as crucial locations for the study (and perhaps perception) of Islam, Islamic studies is now facing the complicated questions of funding and the identity of scholars.

I do not purport to have the solutions to these problems with Jewish studies, nor to tell Islamic studies precisely how to implement any lessons learned from them. But I do think that if we shift our focus in the narrative of Jewish studies, we can see the issues more clearly. The usual *Wissenschaft*-focused genealogical narrative about Jewish studies can still tell us about the history of Jewish studies, but it has led us to look past its formative moments in the 1960s, where the rise of religious studies as an academic field facilitated teaching about Jews and Judaism in the university. Because faculty and administrative concerns about religion's entry into the university focused on various stripes of Protestantism and Catholicism, the teaching of Judaism largely escaped the scrutiny of the academic camps critical of the idea of religious studies. Judaism, at the same time, was not sufficiently exotic or demographically rare to be taught largely by scholars who did not identify with it ethnically, as Hinduism was, for example. Nor did it find its home elsewhere in the university, as Islam did. Judaism, then, was taught by Jews, and religious studies had other battles to fight (an ongoing one about separating religion and theology was brewing from the late '60s on, for instance.) Is religious studies to blame for Jewish studies' "Jewish problem," then? No, but their intertwined histories have combined with the narrative emphasis on *Wissenschaft* in Jewish studies' biography to allow a Jewish studies which is full of Jews, and which doesn't yet know how to be otherwise. Perhaps Islamic studies can learn the lessons that Jewish studies is still struggling with?

Sarah Imhoff is Associate Professor in the Department of Religious Studies and the Borns Jewish Studies Program at Indiana University. She writes about religion and the body with a particular interest in gender, sexuality and American religion. She is author of *Masculinity and the Making of American Judaism* (Indiana University Press, 2017). Her current book project considers the question of what it means when our embodied lives do not match our religious and political ideals, largely by considering the life of a queer disabled American Zionist woman named Jessie Sampter.

6. The Quest for the Historical

Can Biblical Studies Lead Qur'anic Studies away from Theology?

James Crossley

The debate sparked by Aaron Hughes's response (Hughes 2014) to Omid Safi's article (Safi 2014) on the state of Islamic studies in North America has once again prompted discussion of emic-etic tensions in the study of religion. We might put it another way: are scholars of religion "critics" or "caretakers" (to use terms from McCutcheon 2001), and should the field of the study of religion make room for both? In the articles and in the comments sections responding to Hughes, questions about the impact of September 11 on Islamic studies were raised alongside contentious issues of labelling those undertaking the quest for the historical Muhammad as "Islamophobe," "racist," or "colonial invader." Carl Stoneham's response to Hughes's article suggested that such categorizations of those "whose sole 'mistake' is to approach Muhammad as Albert Schweitzer" (Stoneham 2014) were unfair. But, commenting on Hughes's 2014 post, he argued that this "should certainly not be unexpected (we can 'thank' Edward Said for this). As such, the tension here is not simply religious, but political as well (if, indeed, the two are not, in reality, one)." The assessment of such familiar claims might be better served by scholars with expertise in the study of Muhammad than by a biblical scholar. However, what I want to do here is to provide a point of comparison from biblical studies and, in particular, the study of the historical Jesus brought up as a point of analogy by Stoneham. I will suggest that approaching Jesus broadly in the manner of Schweitzer is still a largely theological discourse and I will unravel some examples of this. I will then move on to suggest some ways in which the critical historian of pre-modern figures might develop their own discourse in distinction from that of the caretaker or theologian.

Scholarship Post-September 11

Certainly, historical Jesus studies has its own histories and peculiarities, but there are also some notable points of comparison with what has happened in the Hughes-Safi debate, including issues relating to post-September 11 discourses and the role of theological caretaking (Crossley 2006, 2008, 2012). Despite the long history of common debates along the lines of "did it really happen or not?" or "did Jesus say it or not?," post-September 11 has seen the emergence of intensified polarized mainstream debates where scholars have identified, or been identified, as "conservatives," "evangelicals," "agnostics," "atheists" and "secularists" (Crossley 2012: 133–66). Biblical studies, and areas close to the quest for the historical Jesus, have seen mainstream and much-discussed books claiming it is possible to establish the historicity of the resurrection of Jesus (Wright 2003), that the Gospels were eyewitness accounts of the historical Jesus (Bauckham 2006) and that "high" Christology was especially early (e.g., Hurtado 2003). Perhaps as part of a reaction to the prominence of such books, there has also been the emergence close to the mainstream of "mythicist" arguments that have suggested, or at least toyed with the idea, that Jesus did not exist (e.g., Hoffmann 2010). More recently still, the "mythicist" Richard Carrier (2014) has published a lengthy book arguing for the likelihood that Jesus did not exist, though it is probably too early to see if it will be discussed in mainstream historical Jesus circles. The emergence of "mythicism" so close to the mainstream has in turn provoked lengthy rebuttals from mainstream historical Jesus scholars, notably Bart Erhman and Maurice Casey, both of whom (significantly?) identify or identified themselves as nonbelievers (Erhman 2013; Casey 2014). Irrespective of whether any of these arguments are right or wrong they remain connected with the kinds of intensified "culture wars" after September 11 and, in certain cases, there are some fairly clear Orientalist discourses present in constructions of Jewish and Mediterranean, and even Arab and Muslim,

Others (Crossley 2008). In one sense, we could be more positive in our "thanks" to Said: it is possible to imagine that post-September 11 discourses have generated controversial interests in reconstructing Muhammad or Jesus which cohere with broader Orientalist or "New Atheist" agendas (the two can overlap, as the comment on Hughes's article suggested, albeit slightly differently).

Providing historical and ideological contexts for scholarship is one thing; it is not so easy to provide an answer to what can be done in terms of (say) historical research. The quest for a given historical figure does not *necessarily* have to be part of such agendas and the relationship between scholarly intentions and cultural context is not straightforward, even if historical reconstructions cannot escape contemporary politicized discourses. Indeed, cultural contexts we may not like can generate questions we might find interesting and may have otherwise missed. I personally dislike a lot of New Atheist discourse, particularly as it seems to me to have strong idealist, ahistorical, apologetic and Orientalist tendencies, but its prominence also provides an opportunity to raise questions about the dominance of theology in the field that might not have been so easy ten to fifteen years ago. And explaining the interrelationship of scholarly and cultural tendencies hardly means giving up the enterprise of (say) historical research. Issues surrounding the "historical Muhammad" or the "historical Jesus" are obviously (or theoretically should be) still open to assessment, evidence and argument (as Hughes stresses).

I do not have a satisfactory answer to how we deal with this tension between scholarly contexts and historical reconstruction, other than an ideal of an anarchic "anything goes" attitude – that is, accepting that any question, no matter how uncomfortable, can be raised in academia, or at least should be allowed (compare the similar comment in Stoneham 2014). The further suggestion raised by Stoneham on Hughes's post, namely that we take advantage of such scholarly flashpoints to study the tensions between the "confusing morass of theologians and Humanities scholars," seems worth pursuing, if only to understand the peculiarity of the fields of religious studies and biblical studies. One of the functions of an academic society like the American Academy of Religion can be, and presumably is, to provide a venue for such controversies; and academics have enough control and privilege to promote and engage in such debate. We may do something similar with reference to the dominance of theology across the study of religion, but more precisely in New Testament studies and the quest for the historical Jesus.

Theology and the Study of the New Testament

The responses by Hughes and Stoneham focused primarily on typical notions (for the critical historian) of evidence and argument. What this does not mean, of course, is that behaving like Schweitzer will produce a field where it is so easy to think that scholars can be freed from confessional, apologetic and theological dominance. Obviously, the situation is different in biblical studies as compared to Islamic studies, at least in terms of potentially sensitive reconstructions of historical figures such as Jesus. In academic biblical studies, at least, the quest for the historical Jesus is a topic that has been domesticated in the sense that it is no longer especially shocking to argue that Jesus made mistakes, even if some scholars will still try anything to suggest he did not. However, it remains that the quest for the historical Jesus is hardly a-theological and we should not forget that Schweitzer himself had his own theological and philosophical agendas and constructed heroic figures like Jesus and Paul to help come to terms with the trauma of modernity (Blanton 2007).

We can go further. It is fairly clear that certain kinds of caretaking have dominated agendas in biblical studies, and certainly in historical Jesus studies. The history of New Testament studies (very much tied to the quest for the historical Jesus) may be noted for its historic break from theological and ecclesiastical authorities, and it may have prominent traditions of "liberal" attitudes towards the historicity and the development of texts, but we might suggest that it originated in part as a reaction against its previous theological masters in order to carry out a different kind of theology. This is still a field whose history has been dominated by, or felt the influence of, theological figures such as Schleiermacher, Bultmann, Käsemann, Wright, Crossan or Funk, and we might add figures from the canon of theologians, such as Barth and Pannenberg. Indeed, we might even add the influence of the previous pope, Joseph Ratzinger, who published overtly theological approaches to the study of the historical Jesus (e.g., Ratzinger 2007) and was assessed (typically positively) in a book containing some mainstream New Testament scholars (Pabst and Paddison 2010).

We might likewise look at the major debates in historical Jesus studies which are still framed by theological questions or anxieties and repeated time and time again: whether Jesus mistakenly predicted end times or not, whether he really did say x, y or z, whether he was a social reformer or Cynic, what his views about salvation were, his attitude towards women (very rarely men), how he viewed his death, what the Christological titles might really mean, how unique he must have been, and, in one of the more confused debates in the history of scholarship, how Jewish Jesus might have seemed. Whatever the future may hold for "the quest for the historical Muhammad," if pursued as Hughes and Stoneham might want, historical Jesus studies over the past two hundred years have seen endless retellings of theologically-inspired debates to the extent that it would not be unreasonable to suggest that the quest for the historical Jesus remains a sub-branch of theology. And look at any number of historical Jesus books and you will still find concluding sections telling us about the relevance of the reconstructed historical Jesus for our lives today or how the historical Jesus project relates to theology, even by some of the most prominent critical scholars who are most open about how different the historical Jesus was from contemporary Christianity.

Compare, for instance, the following examples from some of the most lauded, critical historical Jesus scholarship:

> The central message of the parables may be reduced to three radical points .... They all reflect, as may be expected, the simple and profound eschatological piety of Jesus the Jew .... Christianity still possesses fundamental elements of the piety of Jesus, such as his emphasis on purity of intention and generosity of heart, exemplified by Francis of Assisi who relinquished wealth to serve the poor, and even in our own century, an Albert Schweitzer, who abandoned fame to heal the sick in God-forsaken Lambaréné, and a Mother Teresa who, age-old, cares for the dying in the filthy streets of Calcutta. ... the magnetic appeal of the teaching and example of Jesus holds out hope

and guidance to those outside the fold of organised religion, the stray sheep of mankind, who yearn for a world of mercy, justice and peace lived in as children of God. (Vermes 1993: 117, 214–15)

He [Jesus] could distinguish between what was important and unimportant ... he abrogates a maxim of the Torah by an even more important (implicit) axiom, which has the relationship to God governed by the will of God and human beings and not by reified qualities .... Confrontation with this tremendous ethical energy in the words of Jesus in real life immediately raises the questions: Can this ethic be practised at all? Does it not ask too much of people? ... If we regard Jesus and his disciples as a group with socially deviant behaviour which went through Palestine without ties and limitations of everyday professional and family life, the radical nature of Jesus' ethic seems capable of being lived out .... It becomes irrelevant today only if one thinks that minorities with deviant behaviour are "irrelevant" to society as a whole .... Thus in its radical nature, but also in its combination of radicalism with a readiness for reconciliation, the ethic of Jesus remains one of the ethical "basic texts" of human culture ... the Jesus tradition as a chance to keep beginning the dialogue with God all over again. (Theissen and Merz 1999: 394–400, 572)

It is not that the historical Jesus is theologically neither here nor there. The quest has, as a matter of modern theological history, had far-reaching consequences. Still, my take is that it is, by nature, primarily negative. Its chief function has been to discourage many of us from believing some of the things that we were taught in our youth or have heard in churches. We should be grateful, then, that the so-called historical Jesus is only one of numerous theological resources, and far from the most important ... while I am proudly a historian, I must confess that history is not what matters most. If my deathbed finds me alert and not overly racked with pain, I will then be preoccupied with how I have witnessed and embodied faith, hope and charity. I will not be fretting over the historicity of this or that part of the Bible. (Allison 2010: 461–2)

We might observe that in the final quotation, even when the quest's theological significance is downplayed, the importance of the best sort of theology still has a haunting presence.

None of this should be a surprise when we think more about the history of biblical studies. How many debates in historical Jesus studies, and biblical studies more broadly, are effectively debates between theological "liberals" and theological "traditionalists," or the heterodox versus the orthodox (cf. Tite 2014)? Even the social-scientific contextualization of New Testament texts has historically been used to illuminate further these sorts of ideas, and such approaches are still not widely employed in distinction from theology. This too has long been an issue. Between (approximately) the 1930s and the '70s, social-scientific approaches to Christian origins were largely absent because they were so closely associated with Marxism, which was influential in history departments and faculties but not so in the study of the New Testament due to its perceived association with atheism. A range of factors heralded the return of the social sciences in New Testament studies but such interdisciplinary scholarship became theologically domesticated to a sufficient degree for the needs of New Testament scholarship (Crossley 2006). We might note, for instance, that one of the leading social-scientific critics of the New Testament today, Philip Esler, published a prominent book, *New Testament Theology: Communion and Community* (2005).

One thing is thus clear: New Testament studies and historical Jesus studies – certainly in Europe and North America – have typically been a branch of theology and theological concerns continue to frame the debates. While there are different academic histories and different contemporary problems, the issue of caretakers and critics is not entirely different in biblical studies and Islamic studies, at least in the broad theological sense. Theology unites us more than it divides us. The common rhetorical move of "Islam needs a reformation," or "needs to become more critical of its own tradition," may well find its way into the rhetoric of any future quests for the historical Muhammad. But, if the quest for the historical Jesus is any sort of analogy, the influence of such rhetoric of reform does not necessarily mean that the results will be removed from theology. As the language of "Islam needs a reformation" already suggests, this is playing the game on the terms of the caretaker, is it not? Just as we get countless Jesuses repacked and updated for our age, we could see the same (theological) phenomenon happening with reconstructions of Muhammad. Taken on their own terms, one big question for Hughes and Stoneham, it seems to me, is this: Can alternative discourses concerning the quest for Muhammad be free from the dominance of theology? It has certainly not happened yet in historical Jesus studies, at least not in any thoroughgoing way.

The Anxiety of Theology

But there are signs that things are starting to change, at least in the UK. My degree, like most of those of my generation and older, was, tellingly, in "Theology." I remember when questions were raised in the 1990s about changing the degree and/or departmental title to "Religious Studies," the suggestion was shouted down very quickly and no one realistically thought change was possible. Yet within only about three years, most degree programs and departments in the UK (including my old department) became "Theology and Religious Studies/Religion" or just "Religious Studies." It is not that the critic/caretaker debate has necessarily changed dramatically but it is an indication that the dominance of Christian theology and theological biblical studies does not have quite the same hold it once did.

We might also compare the comments of that "caretaker" extraordinaire, N.T. Wright, who reflects some of the anxiety felt by those with most at stake in identifying as "theologians." In his recent mammoth work on Paul, he tacitly and sarcastically defends the seemingly threatened theologian ("they even pray before studying their texts – as if that were not a recipe for falsifying the evidence before you start!") while attempting to ease any worries that the work of the historian and theologian might be mutually exclusive. On the contrary:

> Paul will reassure both sides that they are full partners in his work. As we shall see when we examine his worldview, the symbols, praxis and stories which contribute to it are none of them simply about "ideas" and "beliefs." They are about the

creator God, his world and his people – and this world and these people are creatures of space, time and matter, open by definition to historical enquiry, living life in public without shame, modelling a way of life which is precisely in and for the world, affirming the goodness of the creator's universe and of human beings within it. Yes, says Paul to the suspicious slave-master History: I am your partner! You and I belong together! (Wright 2013: 72)

It would, of course, be difficult to imagine (say) a classicist or ancient historian with such concerns in a mainstream academic publication. Yet there are more nuanced assumptions at play. This is not just theology in dialogue with history, but *Christian* (or, perhaps better for Wright, *Judeo-Christian*) theology. Wright has also expressed a view against those non-Christian traditions which are deemed to be challenging the Christian or theological dominance of the field:

But these things shift over time. All it takes is one or two people to move on, retire, or whatever. Sadly Oxford has just lost a NT scholar and they've replaced him with two people teaching Buddhism. And I have no idea what the Oxford faculty thinks it's doing, but it's like, excuse me, Oxford used to be the place where you studied the primary texts of the Christian tradition. (Wright 2014)

I think there is a lesson to be learned from Wright's comments but not the one he would want us to learn. There is increasing and influential hostility in the UK to this kind of rhetoric of the superiority of biblical studies and Christian origins. This is understandable. Biblical studies has no right (or "divine right"?) to being given pride of place in a religious studies program and defending it in such terms will not (and should not) convince colleagues outside.

But taking advantage of this subtle but important shift should provide an opportunity for behaving more like "critics" and might help the field and subfield engage with issues not guided by specific theological presuppositions, including the avoidance of the language and ideas of assumed theological superiority. Behaving more like critics, and at least trying to share a common critical discourse, would open up different questions from those framed by theological caretakers and lead them to have two-way discussions with (say) historians. To return to historical Jesus studies, there are all sorts of different questions that might be posed which look at human engagements with social contexts and historical change, and without the endless focus on Jesus the Great Man or without framing the questions in terms of how the earliest Jesus movement was somehow "superior" to, or "unique" in, its context (Crossley 2015: 3–34). None of this necessarily excludes some of those questions which have been posed by a history of theological dominance, but locating such discussions more in non-theological contexts and settings can help further understand them in ways of interest beyond the confessional and for those working more broadly in the field of religion and in the humanities. The potential parallels with how scholarship on Muhammad might likewise progress should be clear enough.

This might sound obvious but it is not – at least in historical Jesus studies. Maybe historical Jesus studies, or the Society of Biblical Literature, need their own interventions to hammer out these problems. Equally obvious is that I also know what I have done in recent years, though whether it was the right move, I do not know. I have found myself moving to academic areas where the critic/caretaker problem is less of an issue, namely the reception of biblical texts and the construction of "the Bible." More specifically, I found spending a few years working on the use of the Bible in English political discourse enjoyable (and the potential for enjoyment should never be underestimated in academia – Graeber 2014; Sutton 2014) and a relief, partly because I realized that I did not have to be as defensive or concerned about acting as an outsider or "critic." This is an area that has not received anything like the attention the use of the Bible has in its ancient contexts and one where "insider" and (implicitly or explicitly) theological concerns are less likely to dominate for obvious reasons, even if the somewhat Protestant assumption tends to be that "historical criticism" ends around the 3rd century CE and the rest of time ("reception") then begins (see below). One of the great eye-openers to me was to be able to talk to colleagues in different fields and disciplines about economic and social contexts of political rhetoric and not to be involved in some of the typical (theological) battles of traditional biblical studies, such as the all-too-common charges of "reductionism," "Pelagianism," or "denying the resurrection," for carrying out such analyses. As with certain readers working on "problematizing religion," including those scholars associated with the North American Association for the Study of Religion (NAASR), I have also found that being involved with relatively new seminars, sessions, journals and conferences with like-minded people provides (obviously enough) contexts where ideas of the "critic" can be developed with greater ease. While this sort of behavior may potentially contribute to the fragmentation of the field, it may also potentially contribute to new ideas being more widely discussed in the longer term – a common enough phenomenon in the history of academia – and specific contexts whereby the "critic" can flourish.

Critics, the Historical Jesus Needs You!

But does this not mean intensifying the problems for the isolated "critics" active in historical studies of Jesus or Muhammad? Hopefully not. I still feel drawn back to engaging with more traditional biblical studies, partly because I struggle with intentional or unintentional exclusion of ideas. This is also because I would still want to convince people, no matter how much they will not listen, of ideas that might be troubling to them. This is further because I do not like the attitude of some colleagues outside religious studies and biblical studies who believe their subject is more "valuable" because it generates more income (or is less embarrassing). But this is also because there is a clear advantage for the caretaker to dominate (ancient) historical criticism for the foreseeable future on account of there being more resources and a bigger market and audience for caretakers in biblical studies, especially in areas such as historical Jesus studies and ancient historical-critical contextualization of biblical texts. In fear of being misunderstood, this is emphatically not to say that voices should be silenced. But, equally, do we want discrete periods of history such as the "time of Jesus" to forever be largely caretaker fields? Would not a retreat of those more strongly identifying as critics potentially facilitate an overall victory for caretakers? As Hughes and Stoneham might appreciate: critics, historical Jesus studies need you!

What this further suggests is that there are topics where being a critic is easy enough and topics where being a critic can be problematic. I have never had a problem teaching on contemporary constructions of "religion and terror" or the Bible and contemporary politics. However, teaching on Paul, the Gospels or the historical Jesus is different and confessional commitments do come to the fore and are very difficult to avoid in debate, try though some of us might to navigate around them. Let us take a hypothetical example: the resurrection. It might even be possible for certain critics and caretakers to lie down and profess agreement that supernatural causes are beyond the scope of the historian, but what if the critic argues that the empty tomb was a fictional story created years after Jesus's death? And what if there is good reason to believe that the bodily resurrection itself was a later fictional creation? This is not, of course, to say that these are right or wrong arguments but the resurrection is one notable area that would be a potential problem in the classroom or academic seminar in a way that talking about media or political constructions of "Christianity," "Islam," or "religion" probably would not. Presumably the main reason for something like the resurrection (or indeed a reading of a text that goes against certain denominational readings) being problematic is what we have seen throughout: that the discourse of origins – whether the "historical Muhammad" or the "historical Jesus" – continues to hold its power in academic as well as confessional circles and it is where the tension between caretakers and critics is at its most acute.

But what this also shows, in biblical studies at least, is that the assumptions of a Protestant construction of time remain even for those who avoid the fraught debates of Christian origins: the sacred time of the "biblical world" and the less relevant time – i.e., the rest of history – that follows. This is, again, the distinction between "historical criticism" (which *really* matters and is "historical") and "reception history" (snidely deemed, among other things, as biblical studies "on holiday" – Lyons 2015). Such (implicit?) theological constraints are part of the very structure of academic biblical studies. But by promoting alternative seminars, societies, publications and conferences this can be, and is being, challenged. Again, this might not just be the promotion of other periods of history as being just as legitimate or worthy of analysis as the so-called "biblical period," but also that the so-called "biblical period" needs populating with more critics. If we want to push forward with arguments about standards of evidence and argument – rhetoric that cuts across critics and caretakers – then should we not push an agenda across the fields of religion and biblical studies that requires all students and all academics (caretakers and critics alike) to realize that there will be engagement with lots of ideas and arguments they do not like, particularly if they wish to work in a university setting and play by its rules? This is not an earth-shattering conclusion but it is one that I do not think is reflected widely in practice in mainstream academic societies that certainly do remain a "confusing" – and I would add fragmented and ghettoized – "morass of theologians and Humanities scholars."

Theses for the Critical Historian

In light of the above, I would like to finish by giving some (often obvious) suggestions – and only suggestions – about how the critical historian of Jesus or Muhammad might go about their task:

- Collectively, critical historians will inevitably think in interdisciplinary terms. Economics, social anthropology, philology, archaeology and so on, will be mainstays of the field, even if individuals prefer to have their subspecialities. They need not be used for greater theological profundity.
- The critical historian might explain how a movement in the name of a given figure emerged when and where it did and the ways in which it survived, giving attention to the role of both structure and agency. Suspicion should be cast on an over-reliance on ideas of an individual genius or geniuses causing and creating everything, as this will typically be the explanation of the apologist and theologian.
- The critical historian might want to avoid strict theories of origins, inevitable though the rhetoric may be at times. Instead, the historical figure and associated movements are part of

ever-changing, contingent and overlapping genealogies. Critical historians may want to prioritize the importance of hindsight and supply a range of reasons explaining how things ended up the way they were or are. History may at times be predictable but it is never inevitable.
- In the case of pre-modern figures, it is unlikely that the critical historian can establish any serious degree of certainty about whether a figure really did say or do x, y or z. The critical historian might want to prioritize an approximate chronology of ideas in discourses and perceptions about such a historical figure and look at the range of ideological issues present in such discourses, irrespective of whether they are consistent or inconsistent with one another. For instance, a range of gendered perceptions among audiences about a figure like Jesus could be present simultaneously.
- This has the advantage of avoiding apologetic questions about whether miracles really did or did not happen. Discourses and perceptions about such a historical figure might include miraculous narratives that could, theoretically, have been told during the lifetime of the historical actor. But the critical historian may not wish to spend time assessing the validity of supernatural claims.
- Indeed, the critical historian may want to leave positivist claims about establishing the actuality of supernatural events to the apologist and the theologian. Likewise, claims that a scholarly argument is a "denial of the supernatural" or dismissals of a scholarly reading as "heretical" are debates for the apologist or theologian. This would not mean, of course, that reconstructing the theology of the historical Jesus or the historical Muhammad is unimportant for the critical historian but rather it would leave the theological assessments of their theology to the theologian.
- Having said that, the critical historian may not wish to shy away from meta-critical analyses of the field. If nothing else, these can show if theological assessment is implicitly taking priority over critical historical practice. Moreover, thinking about the present can open up new ways in thinking about the past.

- If a theologian in a university setting wishes to shut down debate and outlaw certain views in the critical study of "scripture," it would not be unreasonable to ask them why they wish to work in a university and not a seminary.

To repeat, these are only some suggestions about how a critical historian might proceed and plenty more could no doubt be added. While classroom and conference scandal might still not be entirely avoided, these are a set of relatively uncontroversial approaches to the history of more uncontroversial periods. And, for the historical critic, there should be no inherent reason why one period is better or worse than another for the object of analysis. All the above approaches are, or should be, obvious to the humanities scholar. But I am yet not convinced they are obvious to, for instance, the scholar of the historical Jesus.

Concluding Remarks

I probably do not see myself quite as ascetic as my "theses" might suggest. Perhaps my political concerns for linking the ancient and modern may violate my own guidelines. I also am less anxious about the presence of theology and theologians in the field, departments and faculties than some of my intellectual kindred spirits in the study of religion. For what it might be worth, my own views on these things involve a radical acceptance of most participants, or the right for any questions to be asked, no matter how bizarre or uncomfortable I may find them. Nevertheless, my experience of the quest for the historical Jesus is that it is dominated by the agendas of caretakers and I am more interested in the questions and answers of the critic. To appropriate what some might see as the language of the caretaker, the role of the critic in this discourse might be a light to the nations, an example of how historical criticism might progress. In this respect, a number of the principles apply to the questions of Hughes and Stoneham. The grass may not, after all, be quite as green on the historical Jesus side of the fence, and theology is a dominant presence on both sides. Nevertheless, we (critics) are close to playing the same game in both fields and if we actively pursue the agenda of the critical historian we might even attract more converts from among the caretakers. At the very least, we should leave a legacy for the next generation of critics.

References

Allison, Dale C. 2010. *Constructing Jesus: Memory, Imagination and History*. London: SPCK.

Bauckham, Richard. 2006. *Jesus and the Eyewitnesses: The Gospels as Eyewitness Testimony*. Grand Rapids: Eerdmans.

Blanton, Ward. 2007. *Displacing Christian Origins: Philosophy, Secularity, and the New Testament*. Chicago: University of Chicago Press.
https://doi.org/10.7208/chicago/9780226056883.001.0001

Carrier, Richard. 2014. *On the Historicity of Jesus: Why We Might Have Reason for Doubt*. Sheffield: Sheffield Phoenix Press.

Casey, Maurice. 2014. *Jesus: Evidence and Argument or Mythicist Myths?* London and New York: T&T Clark.

Crossley, James. 2006. *Why Christianity Happened. A Sociohistorical Explanation of Christian Origins 26–50 CE*. Louisville: WJK.

— 2008. *Jesus in an Age of Terror: Projects for a New American Century*. London: Equinox.

— 2012. *Jesus in an Age of Neoliberalism: Quests, Scholarship, Ideology*. London and New York: Routledge.

— 2015. *Jesus and the Chaos of History: Redirecting the Quest for the Historical Jesus*. Oxford: OUP.
https://doi.org/10.1093/acprof:oso/9780199570577.001.0001

Erhman, Bart D. 2013. *Did Jesus Exist? The Historical Argument for Jesus of Nazareth*. New York: HarperCollins.

Esler, Philip F. 2005. *New Testament Theology: Communion and Community*. Minneapolis: Fortress.

Graeber, David. 2014. "What's the Point if We Can't Have Fun?" *The Baffler*.
http://www.thebaffler.com/articles/whats-the-point-if-we-cant-have-fun

Hoffmann, R.J., ed. 2010. *Sources of the Jesus Tradition: Separating History from Myth*. Amherst, NY: Prometheus.

Hughes, Aaron W. 2014. "When Bad Scholarship Is Just Bad Scholarship: A Response to Omid Safi." *Religion Bulletin*.
http://www.equinoxpub.com/blog/2014/02/when-bad-scholarship-is-just-bad-scholarship-a-response-to-omid-safi/

Hurtado, Larry W. 2003. *Lord Jesus Christ: Devotion to Jesus in Earliest Christianity*. Grand Rapids: Eerdmans.

Lyons, William John. 2015. "Some Thoughts on Defining Reception History and the Future of Biblical Studies." *Bible and Interpretation.* http://bibleinterp.com/articles/2015/08/lyo398005.shtml

McCutcheon, Russell T. 2001. *Critics Not Caretakers: Redescribing the Public Study of Religion.* Albany, NY: SUNY Press.

Pabst, Adrian, and Angus Paddison, eds. 2010. *The Pope and Jesus of Nazareth: Christ, Scripture and the Church.* London: SCM in association with The Centre of Theology and Philosophy, University of Nottingham.

Ratzinger, Joseph. 2007. *Jesus of Nazareth: From the Baptism in the Jordan to the Transfiguration.* London: Bloomsbury.

Safi, Omid. 2014. "Reflections on the State of Islamic Studies." *Jadaliyya.* http://www.jadaliyya.com/pages/index/16269/reflections-on-the-state-of-islamic-studies

Stoneham, Carl. 2014. "Will It Ever Be 'Just about Bad Scholarship?': A Response to Aaron Hughes and Omid Safi." *Religion Bulletin.* http://bulletin.equinoxpub.com/2014/02/will-it-ever-be-just-about-bad-scholarship-a-response-to-aaron-hughes-and-omid-safi/

Sutton, Ed. 2014. "Fun with David Graeber." *Antidote.* http://antidotezine.com/2014/02/08/fun-with-graeber/

Theissen, Gerd, and Annette Merz. 1999. *The Historical Jesus: A Comprehensive Guide.* London: SCM.

Tite, Philip L. 2014. "Rethinking Gnostic Intellectuals? Categories as Weapons and History as Construct," *Religion Bulletin.* http://www.equinoxpub.com/blog/2014/03/rethinking-gnostic-intellectuals-categories-as-weapons-and-history-as-construct/

Vermes, Geza. 1993. *The Religion of Jesus the Jew.* London: SCM.

Wright, N.T. 2003. *Resurrection of the Son of God.* London: SPCK.

— 2013. *Paul and the Faithfulness of God.* London: SPCK.

— 2014. "N.T. Wright ranks the top places for New Testament Studies." *The Jesus Blog.* http://historicaljesusresearch.blogspot.co.uk/2014/03/nt-wright-ranks-top-new-testament.html [no longer available].

James Crossley is Professor of Bible, Culture and Politics in the Centre for the Social-Scientific Study of the Bible, St Mary's University, Twickenham, London. He is author of numerous books and articles on Christian origins, reception histories of the Bible, and religion in contemporary English political discourses. His latest book is *Cults, Martyrs and Good Samaritans: Religion in Contemporary English Political Discourse* (Pluto, 2018).

Part IV
A Critical Appraisal

7. A Modest Proposal for Islamic Studies

Devin J. Stewart

Aaron Hughes's *Theorizing Islam: Disciplinary Deconstruction and Reconstruction* published in 2012 denounces the Study of Islam Section of the American Academy of Religion (AAR) as an institutional haven for bad scholarship, critiquing what is in fact a small corner of Western Islamic studies, and ends with a list of theses to guide Islamic studies research in the future in hopes of reforming this section of the academy.[1] In presenting his criticisms, Hughes incorrectly maps the current divide in Islamic studies between unrepentant empiricists and radically skeptical revisionists onto a quite different divide between naïve, apologetic work and serious, critical investigation. Many of Hughes's assessments of particular works' shortcomings are justified, but the type of writing he condemns is highly promoted by university presses and found in scholarship on all other religious traditions and in many other fields throughout academia; this is an endemic, and not a local, problem.

The main conclusion that one rightly ought to draw from this debate is that most scholars in Islamic studies are trained in narrow subfields and tend to falter when they write on general topics. This is a situation that is unlikely to change: the demand for such general works is so high that specialists and other even less qualified authors will not refrain from writing them before they have educated themselves sufficiently to ensure quality and accuracy. I would, however, thoroughly reject Hughes's suggestion that improved scholarship

---

1 Aaron W. Hughes, *Theorizing Islam: Disciplinary Deconstruction and Reconstruction* (Sheffield, UK: Equinox, 2012).

on Islam would result from more rigorous engagement with recent theories in religious studies. It seems appropriate to mount a modest defense, if only to put Hughes's critique in perspective within the larger field of Islamic studies, to correct some of his misperceptions regarding it and to promote awareness of some of its contours. In the following, I propose an alternative set of theses to guide research and writing on Islamic studies in the future.

The roots of this debate lie in Hughes's *Theorizing Islam*, so it seems expedient to address that work in particular. I have participated in the annual conference of the AAR several times and, having read Hughes's book, I know that would be enough to include me among his targets; luckily, hard-earned obscurity has protected me in this instance. I know many of the people involved in the Islamic studies section of the AAR, though I do not distinguish them as a group hermetically sealed off from other scholars of Islamic studies. I am acquainted with most of the scholars on both sides of the ideological divide that Hughes has constructed, and many are friends. The following remarks will undoubtedly be blunter than those of more circumspect respondents. Colleagues know that I do not sugarcoat my opinions, so I trust they will understand these remarks as a normal feature of scholarly exchange, for "Learning lives through refutation and critique" (*ḥayāt al-ᶜilm bi'l-radd wa'l-naqd*).

Despite the expansive title, *Theorizing Islam* is a narrow work. Broad titles are in vogue, so this is not surprising, and often they are the fault of the publisher rather than the author. (However, as Hughes accuses Carl Ernst and Richard Martin of just this fault for their collection *Rethinking Islam*, one might have expected him at least to be sensitive to the issue of exaggerated advertising.) The restricted focus is not in itself a problem, but despite Hughes's disclaimer that he is not treating Islamic studies in general, the rhetoric slips on many occasions into general statements. The title indicates a discussion of Islamic studies in general, and many passages in the book refer to "scholars of Islamic studies," but Hughes limits his discussion to North America, to the years 2001–12, and, within that fairly narrow category, to scholars who work in religion departments and are members of the Study of Islam Section of the AAR. In short, he is referring to a group of "over 50 people." This number must be restricted further, to *some* of those "over 50 people," and then again, to *some* of those scholars' published works. Neither a general discussion of Islam nor a guide to the study of that faith's tradition, Hughes's work could be more accurately titled *A Number of Semi-Scholarly Books I Don't Like That Address Islamic Topics, by Authors Somehow Associated with the American Academy of Religion.*

Hughes's argument raises questions about what sorts of books get published and how the academy responds to them. He suggests that if a work is written by a scholar and presented as scholarly, then it should be held to the highest standards, expected to be a cutting-edge critical investigation and evaluated as such. As will become apparent below, his own 2013 volume *Muslim Identities: An Introduction to Islam* does not live up to this concept of scholarship.[2] Hughes is, moreover, overlooking current practices that produce works along a spectrum from not-so-serious to very serious, usually weighted towards the former end. University presses are giving scholar-authors the exact opposite message and, unfortunately, are in a position to impose their own advice. Such authors as Karen Armstrong and Reza Aslan publish widely-read books on religious topics. Their advantage is that they write in simpler, more accessible prose than most scholars in the academy and are not overly concerned with footnotes or attribution. They reach more people in the public sphere than most academics do, and some scholars recognize this as a valuable service. Their works are not serious scholarship because they paraphrase others' results and present no significant discoveries or advances of their own. Between their works and scholarly tomes of the most serious type, packed with massive footnotes, dense prose, technical terms, hundreds of names and dates, and diacritical marks, there is a wide spectrum, within which fall many books and articles.

In addition, the same scholars may write different sorts of books, with different audiences in mind. University presses clamor for scholarly submissions that will also be accessible to a wide audience or could be used as undergraduate textbooks; their practice thus places under the same banner original, cutting-edge investigations with

---

2   Aaron W. Hughes, *Muslim Identities: An Introduction to Islam* (New York: Columbia University Press, 2013).

unoriginal digests and lighter reading aimed at a larger reading public. One might take this further: university presses force authors to fill out questionnaires, virtual contracts with the devil, including prompts that cajole them into claiming that, in fact, their books will have a general audience and will be suitable for use as undergraduate textbooks in a plea to get their work accepted for publication. In the age of email, text messaging and constant cell-phone use, when the average attention span of an undergraduate is a few minutes and the public definition of research is cutting and pasting paragraphs from the internet, that is setting the bar rather low. Textbooks cannot be too complicated or encumbered with erudite baggage or else they will not get used. Where to draw the line, to determine the exact point at which one leaves the area of "work for popular consumption" and enters "*real* scholarship" is difficult to decide, even on the individual level, and once a large group of scholars is involved, a consensus is unlikely to arise.

I am narrow-minded on this issue, and I would characterize a large swath of the spectrum as "scholarship-lite™." Many colleagues may disagree with my assessments. I would consign Omid Safi's book on Muhammad to this category, but not his book on intellectual history during the Seljuk period. I would put all of Karen Armstrong's books in this category, all of Reza Aslan's works and both of Hughes's books on Islam. *Theorizing Islam* is 132 pages, contains a handful of Arabic words, has a tiny number of footnotes, refers only to sources in English, is fairly accessible, and does not show evidence of profound knowledge of the history of Islamic studies. *Muslim Identities*, even if judged as an undergraduate textbook, similarly fails to impress.

Hughes criticizes the Study of Islam group for presenting Islam in an uncritical and positive manner. But he seems to forget that in many fields scholars end up saying nice things about the traditions they study; professors who study Islam do not have a monopoly in this regard. Professors of Christianity, Judaism, Hinduism and Buddhism often write laudatory comments about these religious traditions, the high ideals they embody, the inspiration they can provide, the great ideas they have fostered and their unique genius. Many scholars, and not just believers, claim that love, justice, the desire for peace, and egalitarian tendencies are important features of this or that religious

A Modest Proposal for Islamic Studies 161

tradition. Biblical studies and Christian studies in general are replete with such ideas. Similar remarks could be made of French professors who gush about the wonders of French culture or comparative literature scholars who fetishize Foucault and Derrida.

Why should scholars make the effort to study a tradition unless they have some fascination with it? I would like French teachers to have reverence for the French language and literature, and math teachers to extol the genius of Euclid, Leibniz and Newton. I would probably refuse to take a course on Shakespeare with a professor who did not have reverence for the Bard. Many scholars of religion have reverence for the religions they study, but this does not prevent them from producing useful and even critical scholarship. Louis Massignon, who, no matter how you slice him, was a great scholar of Islamic studies, wore his reverence on his sleeve, as did Annemarie Schimmel.

Many scholars, and not just Islamic studies scholars, do not adopt a radically skeptical view of the traditions they study, and they often bring into relief the positive aspects of the material they investigate. Great scholars of the Bible have written about Abraham and the binding of Isaac without addressing the evident suggestion that the Israelites used to sacrifice their firstborn children on analogy with the tithing of crops. Should we complain that biblical scholars have covered up the embarrassing truths and the macabre underbelly of ancient Judaism? As another example, any scholarly study of Maimonides (d. 1204) will describe him as a highly educated polymath and consummate scholar, and celebratory sentences are bound to punctuate the text every so often. If, however, as Hughes suggests, one is obligated to take a highly skeptical and critical stance toward one's subject of inquiry, one might end up writing the following:

> Maimonides was a jurist and theologian highly admired in subsequent Jewish tradition. Born in Cordoba, he converted to Islam to escape persecution in Spain and Morocco, something which probably facilitated his access to Islamic legal education, but he later returned to Judaism and hid his former conversion when he settled in Egypt. He wrote one major work in Hebrew, *Mishneh ha-Torah*, but all his other works were written in Arabic. His main accomplishments consisted in borrowing the conventions

of Islamic legal scholarship and applying them to Jewish law. ʿAbd al-Laṭīf al-Baghdādī (d. 1231), a Muslim philosopher and polymath who met him in Cairo c. 1191, reported that he was indeed learned but too involved in currying favor with the rich and powerful to be a serious scholar.

Nor do introductory works on Christianity or the New Testament usually begin as follows:

> John the Baptist started a heretical Jewish religious movement in the Galilee, and one of his relatives, another Jew named Jesus, joined the movement. When John was killed as a heretic, Jesus assumed leadership of the group and, predictably, got killed as well. Somehow, the account of this series of events was later adopted as the foundational myth of Christianity. Of course, we aren't sure exactly when or how it happened, but it is nevertheless an interesting story, and Jesus may actually have existed.

Should we really expect works on Muhammad or Islam to begin in a similar manner?

Hughes criticizes Islamic studies scholars for making theological arguments, but theology involves the use of sacred texts and elements of tradition to justify, critique or seek to modify doctrine, attitudes, politics and institutions in the modern world. I would hesitate to call some of it scholarship, considering such work as activism, wishful thinking, creative writing or sermonizing. Some of it is erudite, well-documented and well-written; some of it is none of those. Nevertheless, it is written by professors, published in university presses, and evaluated and recognized as scholarship in the academy. Entire PhD programs are based on it. Many works on Islam present reductive, essentialist, political, uncritically laudatory and apologetic arguments, but then so do many works in Latin American Studies, Women's Studies, any subfield called Critical ... Studies, and most other fields one might care to shake a stick at. Scholars of Islam at the AAR do not have a monopoly on this type of writing. Hughes must criticize a much larger sector of the academy as well. In the AAR itself I would hazard a guess that truckloads of such works in Christian studies dwarf the production of the Study of Islam Section by several orders of magnitude. One might want to exile the authors of such works from the academy, but they are not going anywhere soon. After all, most established academic institutions in the United States, with the exception of state colleges, began as seminaries, and theology formed the backbone of American higher education from the colonial period until recent times.

I agree with many of Hughes's assessments of a number of particular issues. The ubiquitous claims after 9/11 that Islam really means "peace" (*salām*) and that *jihād* means an internal spiritual struggle and not holy war were misleading, and either simple-minded or incompetent. On another part of the spectrum, the works of Amina Wadud, Asma Barlas and others on the Qur'an engage in feminist, constructive theology. It is wonderful if this work can inspire Muslim women and help reform Islamic tradition, but it does not qualify as scholarship in my view. Many of their interpretations of the Qur'an are creative riffs on the sacred text that tell more about their political and intellectual goals and commitments than they do about the Qur'an.

Nevertheless, this mode of writing is not a strange development: Sufis do the same thing, rabbis do the same thing with the Hebrew Bible, and Christian scholars have produced reams and reams of such writing. Some of John Esposito's works present typical Islamic apologetics in English, along with some level-headed analyses of Islamic doctrine and the portrayal of Islam in the West. In my view, Tariq Ramadan is a not a critical scholar but a religious leader and preacher on a par with Joel Osteen. Why Oxford University Press publishes his books would be a mystery, if it were not for the fact that they also publish such groundbreaking studies as *Making Your Case: Using R for Program Evaluation*, by Charles Auerbach and Wendy Zeitlin, which is every bit as riveting and intellectually substantial as the manual for the programming language C, or *Moonpaths: Ethics and Emptiness – The Cowherds*, an edited volume which, the catalog announces, is "the first book to take seriously the problem of the conventional status of reality in Mahayana Buddhist philosophy for ethics" and which "combines careful textual analysis and doctrinal exposition with philosophical reconstruction and reflection." Already somewhat suspicious of what they call "philosophical reconstruction and reflection," I note that the catalog avers that the work is intended not only for scholars of Buddhist studies but also for Buddhist practitioners. For all my willingness to weigh in on such matters, Oxford University Press is not obliged to consult me before giving any book submitted its imprimatur.

If Hughes wants to criticize his colleagues who study Islam for engaging in "soft" scholarship, he should look around some more. Almost all fields, including entire subfields of sociology, American studies, history, literature and other fields, include studies and textbooks of a comparable nature, and even much "softer." I would put perhaps 50% of the production of university presses in the same category. The best-selling works of the University of North Carolina Press include their *Savor the South* cookbooks, for cryin' out loud, and even those contain about fifty recipes a-piece, compared to thousands in Betty Crocker. Religious guidance, interfaith dialogue, conflict resolution, twelve-step programs – all of these are areas that promote their own particular ideologies and work to describe things as they should or could be, drawing on religious traditions in a selective, presentist, goal-oriented and skewed manner in order to promote specific understandings and outcomes. It seems arbitrary and odd for Hughes to single out professors of Islamic studies as the chief culprits.

In contrast, as an example of solid scholarship by members of the group Hughes criticizes, and which he does not mention, one might cite Walid Saleh's book *The Formation of the Classical Tafsīr Tradition*.[3] This work objectively breaks new ground by investigating the *tafsīr* of al-Thaʿlabī (d. 427/1035), a major figure whose commentary on the Qur'an was influential but had not been studied in depth. It is not only an insightful analysis of his commentary but also an important contribution to the history of Qur'anic commentary in general. Other works worthy of mention are Kecia Ali's *Marriage and Slavery in Early Islam*, which analyzes key texts in the Islamic legal tradition from a feminist perspective,[4] and Karen Bauer's *Gender*

---

3   Walid Saleh, *The Formation of the Classical Tafsīr Tradition* (Leiden: Brill, 2004).

4   Kecia Ali, *Marriage and Slavery in Early Islam* (Cambridge, MA: Harvard University Press, 2010).

Hierarchy in the Qur'ān, which presents an excellent overview of the ways in which scholars throughout Islamic history have dealt with passages in the Qur'an related to women's rights.[5] Neither is facile or ignores historical or linguistic specifics in the service of a manifestly political interpretation. Another excellent work is Vincent Cornell's *The Realm of the Saint*, which deftly treats hagiography, religious authority and sainthood in specific cases in Moroccan history but in a way that answers general questions about the workings of sainthood.[6]

Other cases, such as Carl Ernst's book *Following Muhammad*, which Hughes does rail against, fall somewhere in between.[7] Ernst has written scores of excellent studies on the Sufi tradition, including his article "From Hagiography to Martyrology: Conflicting Testimonies to a Sufi Martyr of the Delhi Sultanate," which investigates the hagiography of Mas'ud Bakk, a Central Asian Sufi who was martyred in 1387.[8] In my view it is exemplary scholarship, presenting an insightful analysis of a particular Sufi hagiography and a cogent discussion of Islamic hagiography and martyrology. *Following Muhammad* does not belong to the same category. But should the reader expect it to?

Following Muhammad is a readable, well-written and engaging introduction to Islam through the figure of Muhammad. It presents a portrayal of Muhammad as he is understood in the tradition, and the book could be used quite successfully as the main text in an introductory class on Islam. In particular, the work brings out aspects of devotion to the Prophet that are not included in other introductory works. Hughes judges it as one would a highly scientific investigation into Muhammad as a historical entity, which is not really the point of the work. The work is not based on groundbreaking research, does not present any new discoveries, and makes several general claims that

5 Karen Bauer, *Gender Hierarchy in the Qur'ān: Medieval Interpretations, Modern Responses* (Cambridge: Cambridge University Press, 2015).

6 Vincent Cornell, *The Realm of the Saint: Power and Authority in Moroccan Sufism* (Austin: University of Texas Press, 1998).

7 Carl Ernst, *Following Muhammad: Rethinking Islam in the Contemporary World* (Chapel Hill: University of North Carolina Press, 2004).

8 *History of Religions* 24(4), 1985: 308–27.

are incorrect and misleading. Ernst characterizes *jihād* as "struggle for truth" and not "holy war," and claims that it only means a military struggle against evil opponents *secondarily* (pp. 31, 117–18). This is blatantly incorrect and adopts the argument of apologists uncritically, flying in the face of the use of the term *jihād* and its derivatives in the Qur'an, in the legal tradition and in Muslim societies all over the world.

Almost every Islamic legal manual from the 9th century to the present includes a chapter devoted to *jihād* that discusses the rules of war against non-Muslims, and it is worth keeping in mind in this regard the relative hegemony of legal discourse in most Islamic societies. Historically, in West Asia *jihād* referred most often to the conflict with the Byzantines in northern Syria, Iraq and eastern Anatolia up until the Crusades, then to the effort to topple the Crusader States of Outremer. In the West it referred to fighting against the Reconquista in Iberia, the conquest of Sicily, fighting against Portuguese in Morocco and so on. The primacy of this usage has continued into modern times. Reference to a moral struggle, *jihād al-nafs* "the struggle against one's lower instincts," *al-jihād al-akbar* "the greater (moral) struggle," etc. is certainly part of the tradition, but this cannot be construed as the *dominant* meaning of *jihād* in Islamic tradition by any stretch of the imagination. Based primarily on a hadith frequently cited in ethical literature, *jihād al-nafs* is decidedly the secondary concept, and the commonly understood meaning of *jihād* is war, just war, holy war or some equivalent.

Ernst also links *jihād* with *ijtihād*, an unusual move that may explain where he gets the "truth" in the definition "the struggle for truth." The relationship between the two terms, based on their shared root consonants, is only incidental. *Ijtihād* derives ultimately from the phrase *ijtihād al-raʿy* "the exercise of judgment," which is a technical term used in legal hermeneutics to mean the expenditure of effort on the part of a jurist in order to arrive at the best estimate of a correct legal ruling on a particular issue. The idea of "effort" (*juhd*) is included in both terms, but they generally appear in disparate contexts, and the connection is tenuous at best. It is such inaccuracies in Ernst's work that are the real issue.

Another passage in *Following Muhammad* plays down the gravity of the Crusades from the Muslims' point of view. Ernst writes, "... the ultimately unsuccessful Crusader attacks had much less significance in the Near East, where they were often viewed as one more series of raids by northern barbarians" (p. 17). This is simply wrong. The Crusades, like the campaigns of Byzantine generals Nicephorus and John Tzimesces in the mid-10th century, were a shock throughout West Asia, since they showed that the relatively stable border between Islamic states and the Byzantines could shift dramatically to the Muslims' detriment. The forces of the First Crusade won back large territories that had been conquered by the Seljuk forces in Anatolia after the Battle of Manzikert in 1071, thus shoring up the Byzantine empire and allowing it to survive for three-and-a-half more centuries. In a concentrated campaign beginning in 1096, the Crusaders rapidly conquered territory all along the Syrian littoral, creating the four states of Outremer – the County of Edessa, the Principality of Antioch, the County of Tripoli and the Kingdom of Jerusalem – building impregnable fortresses and securing ports, which would ensure continual access to supplies and reinforcements. The counter-Crusade, the *jihād* mounted against the Frankish conquerors, was a long and massive effort at political mobilization that affected all levels of society and eventually led to the re-conquest of Jerusalem in 1187 and the expulsion of the Crusaders from Acre, their last stronghold on the coast, in 1291.

Both the Crusader occupation and the counter-campaigns had a number of long-term effects in West Asia and North Africa. Strong ties were created between Levantine and Western Christians, including the Catholic popes and the kings of France. The Maronite Church owes its existence – as formerly Syrian Orthodox Christians who became a Uniate Church affiliated with Rome – to the Crusades. Anti-Crusading propaganda produced a large number of religious works extolling *jihād* and the religious merits of Jerusalem and Syria. The Zengid ruler Nur al-Dīn promoted a "unified *jihād*" that was continued by his successors, the Ayyubids and Mamluks, and which linked resistance to the Crusader kingdoms with the suppression of

Islamic religious diversity.⁹ This policy involved strong anti-Shiite rhetoric and the active persecution of Shiites in Syria and Egypt on the grounds that they weakened Muslim unity from within. The population of Shiites dwindled in many regions, including Egypt, where they either converted or emigrated, and Aleppo, which had been half-Shiite, became an entirely Sunni town by the Ottoman period. Muslim societies in Egypt and Syria became less tolerant of diversity; the status of local Christians, who were viewed as potential allies of the foreign invaders, deteriorated and their numbers dwindled.

However, beyond those two ideas, which I consider very wrong, the book has only minor problems. Ernst mentions H.A.R. Gibb's *Mohammedanism* (1947) as setting the pattern for subsequent textbooks on Islam (p. 47). The pattern was set earlier, by D.S. Margoliouth's 1912 work of the same title, to which Gibb's work is heavily indebted, or earlier still, by Duncan Black MacDonald's *Development of Muslim Theology, Jurisprudence, and Constitutional Theory* (1903) and Goldziher's *Vorlesungen über den Islam* (1910).¹⁰ *Muẓlim* does not mean "tyrant" (p. 63); *ẓālim* does – *muẓlim* means

---

9   On the counter-Crusade, see Nikita Elisséeff, *Nūr ad-Dīn, un grand prince musulman de Syrie au temps des Croisades (511–569 h./1118–1174)*, 3 vols. (Damascus: Institut Français de Damas, 1967); Emmanuel Sivan, *L'Islam et la Croisade: Idéologie et Propagande dans les Réactions Musulmanes aux Croisades* (Paris: Librairie d'Amérique et d'Orient, 1968); Carole Hillenbrand, *The Crusades: Islamic Perspectives* (Edinburgh: Edinburgh University Press, 1999); Devin J. Stewart, "The Maqāmāt of Aḥmad b. Abī Bakr al-Rāzī al-Ḥanafī and the Ideology of the Counter-Crusade in Twelfth-Century Syria," *Middle Eastern Literatures* 11(2), 2008: 211–32.

10 Duncan Black MacDonald, *Development of Muslim Theology, Jurisprudence, and Constitutional Theory* (New York: Charles Scribner's Sons, 1903); Ignaz Goldziher, *Vorlesungen über den Islam* (Heidelberg: Carl Winter, 1910), 2nd ed., reworked by Franz Babinger (Heidelberg: Carl Winter, 1925), translated by Andras and Ruth Hamori as *Introduction to Islamic Theology and Law* (Princeton, NJ: Princeton University Press, 1981); D.S. Margoliouth, *Mohammedanism*, revised ed. (London: Thornton Butterworth, 1912). The first edition of Margoliouth's work was published in 1911.

"dark." Ernst cites Q 53:13–18 as a reference to the *Isrā'* and *Mi‘rāj*, the legend of the Prophet's night journey to Jerusalem and ascension to heaven (p. 87), when the *Isrā'* is attached by commentators most directly to Q 17:1, which contains the verb *asrā* from which the term *isrā‘* derives. The passage Q 53:13–18, which mentions neither a journey nor an ascension, apparently refers to a vision of the Prophet near the very beginning of his mission. There are a few other errors of detail and translation.

Overall, then, the work contains several sweeping statements that are misleading and some additional, smaller errors, but it still stands as a decent introduction to Islam in general. Does that make it deserve a prize? I don't think so. If I had the wherewithal to give out prizes, I would give one to Nasser Rabat for his brilliant article on al-Maqrīzī, his allegiances and his fascination with the Fatimids, which was due in part to the fact that he claimed descent from the Fatimid Caliph al-Mu‘izz li-Dīn Allāh.[11] The truth is that the Saudi prize committee did not contact me before they chose to commend *Following Muhammad.* But again, neither the AAR nor the Saudis have a monopoly on questionable book awards. The 2015 Christian Book of the Year™ is *The Daniel Plan: 40 Days to a Healthier Life*, by Rick Warren, Daniel Amen and Mark Hyman, which looks something like *The Miami Beach Diet* interlarded with Bible quotations.[12]

In the course of his argument, Hughes makes a number of statements that strike me as odd. At one point he critiques Carl Ernst for claiming that the Prophet Muhammad was an important historical figure. Except for a tiny group who deny Muhammad's existence and claim that we can know nothing about him, almost no one, including the Evangelists who are bent on preventing "creeping Shari'a" and the Islamic invasion of the USA, would deny this.[13] Hughes also decries

---

11 Nasser Rabbat, "Who Was al-Maqrīzī? A Biographical Sketch," *Mamluk Studies Review* 7(2), 2003: 1–19.

12 http://christianbookexpo.com/christianbookawards/winners2015.php

13 There is, we should admit, a dedicated group of such deniers in Germany who have been publishing anthologies since 2007. They adopt the thoroughly skeptical stance towards early Islamic sources, presenting some interesting critiques and speculations along with many patently false

Esposito's use of the term "Abrahamic" faiths as a convenient label for Judaism, Christianity and Islam. Yes, it is in part a modern construct. Yes, one could criticize it as covering over distinctions. And yes, it serves a blatant political purpose: to include Muslims as part of the normal religious landscape that characterizes the public culture of Europe and North America. Many people, including scholars, consider this an admirable goal that might have positive consequences, and they would not agree that such views should be strictly segregated from "real" scholarship. Of course, the term "Judeo-Christian tradition" is similarly contrived and serves a similar political purpose, yet we don't see scholars batting an eyelash when it is used. One could make similar claims against scholars who argue that an understanding – whether "true," "authentic," "revisionist" or "modern" – of this or that religious tradition gives proper recognition and space to adherents who are women, minorities or gay, or who have disabilities, cross-dress, handle snakes and so on.

Hughes's critique implies that the group he is attacking, or the specific books he mentions, somehow represent the center of gravity of Islamic studies writ large in the West and thus deserve an enormous amount of focused attention. The modern, critical study of Islam is a large field with many subfields, each with its complex history and present constitution. The Study of Islam Section in the AAR is part of it, but it is a relatively small part. The project of the study of Islam involves dozens of nations, hundreds of universities, scores of learned societies and thousands of individual scholars. Modern Islamic studies has a long history, going back long before 9/11. One could set the beginning c. 1600 with the work of the talented Dutch Arabist Thomas Erpenius (van Erpe) (1584–1624), c. 1700 with the publication of d'Herbelot's *Bibliothèque orientale* (1697) and the Latin Qur'an (1698) of Ludovico Marracci (1612–1700), or c. 1800 with

---

claims. The group includes Christoph Luxenberg, Karl-Heinz Ohlig, Markus Gross, Volker Popp and others, who publish under the auspices of INARAH (Institute for Research on Early Islamic History and the Koran). One of their recent publications is *Early Islam: A Historical-Critical Reconstruction on the Basis of Contemporary Sources*, ed. Karl-Heinz Ohlig (Amherst, NY: Prometheus Books, 2013).

the work of Antoine Isaac Sylvestre de Sacy (1758–1838) and the foundation of the École des Langues Orientales in Paris.

With a history of at least two hundred years, Islamic studies is an international project conducted in France, Germany, England, Spain, Italy, Russia, the Netherlands, and now in many countries in the Islamic world. It has required the documentation, analysis and acquisition of expertise in Arabic, Persian, Turkish and many other languages of West Asia and elsewhere, and in many other technical topics besides. It has involved the acquisition and cataloging of Oriental books in libraries throughout Europe. It has been conducted in many languages, and it boasts a number of outstanding accomplishments. Hughes seems to be innocently unaware of most of this tradition. It is surprising to me that a work with the title *Theorizing Islam* does not include any works in Arabic, Persian, Turkish, French, Spanish, Italian or German; that Hughes's knowledge of Islam seems to stem entirely from general works written in English; and that a journey through 132 pages in search of the secret key that would unlock the mysteries of Islamic studies reveals little new information about Islam and only a bit more about Islamic studies.

The AAR is only one piece of the puzzle, and not nearly the most important. If the AAR were to drop off the face of the planet tomorrow, it would create a tiny blip in the history of Islamic studies as a discipline, which has seen major disruptions before, such as those caused by the Second World War. After the hypothetical apocalyptic annihilation of the AAR, the Islamicists involved in that learned society would find other associations and networks to support their work – most already attend other conferences – and the field would carry on. I imagine the same might not be said so easily for the study of Christianity. Hughes's efforts are thus somewhat misplaced, if he is truly concerned about the future of Islamic studies. Why focus on this particular group of scholars when he could be attempting to solve some of the major outstanding puzzles in Islamic religious thought?

Addressing the works that Hughes holds up as real scholarship in Islamic studies, and which he criticizes the "softies" for rejecting, is a more complex task. There are better examples of less disputed, undeniably major contributions to Islamic studies, such as Fuat Sezgin's *Buhari'nin Kaynakları Hakkında Araştırmalar*

(Investigations regarding Bukhārī's Sources, 1956), which focuses on the *Ṣaḥīḥ* (Sound Traditions) of al-Bukhārī (d. 256/870), the most prominent compilation of the oral traditions attributed to the Prophet Muhammad. In this work Sezgin shows that al-Bukhārī systematically cut and pasted the entire content of the *Muwaṭṭa'* (The Well-Trodden Path) of Mālik b. Anas (d. 179/795) and other earlier works into his own compilation. Before Sezgin's work, scholars had generally taken at face value the traditional accounts that portrayed al-Bukhārī traveling throughout West and Central Asia, painstakingly recording traditions one by one from thousands of individuals, relying on oral transmission. This was despite the conviction since the work of Goldziher that earlier generations of Muslim scholars had forged many of these individual reports. Unfortunately, Sezgin wrote his work in Turkish, and it has never been translated, and this has led to widespread neglect.[14] Another example of a fundamental contribution is Josef Van Ess's magnum opus *Theologie und Gesellschaft* (*Theology and Society*) (1991–97) a masterful survey of theology in the 8th and 9th Islamic centuries, based mainly on fragments quoted in later works.[15] No matter one's ideological stances in the field, one cannot deny that it is truly groundbreaking.

A number of the works Hughes cites as examples of true scholarship are more contested in the field of Islamic studies today because they are highly *skeptical*, which does not equate directly with *critical* or *sound* scholarship. There is a divide in the field between studies that adopt a radically skeptical approach and those that do not, though both sides merit consideration. Hughes mentions *Hagarism*, by Patricia Crone and Michael Cook, both excellent scholars. That work is erudite and ingenious but, in my view, a type of thought-experiment and not a straight critical historical inquiry. The premise of the work is that, since the earliest Islamic sources are late and present various problems of interpretation, it might be interesting to

---

14 Fuat Sezgin, *Buhari'nin Kaynakları Hakkında Araştırmalar* (Ankara: Ankara Üniversitesi İlahiyat Fakültesi, 1956).

15 Josef Van Ess, *Theologie und Gesellschaft im 2. und 3. Jahrhundert Hidschra: Eine Geschichte des religiösen Denkens im frühen Islam*, 6 vols. (Berlin: Walter De Gruyter, 1991–97).

see what early Islamic history would look like if one ignored Islamic sources *in toto* and used only sources from outside the tradition. The result is highly surprising, and most scholars in the field would now reject the concrete results. One must understand that this experiment is something like writing the history of Christianity using only Jewish sources, or the history of the papacy using only Protestant sources. Indeed, in her later years, Crone herself referred to the work as an exercise in youthful iconoclasm and rejected its results. Hughes could have cited other, later works that are less controversial, such as Crone's *God's Rule: Government and Islam*, a masterful survey of theories of government in the first six centuries of Islamic history that draws on a wide array of sources, or Michael Cook's *Commanding Right and Forbidding Wrong in Islamic Thought*, which covers an enormous amount of material and presents the myriad interpretations and social, historical and political ramifications of an Islamic legal injunction.[16]

Another example Hughes cites is Wansbrough's *Quranic Studies* (1977), an erudite but cryptic work that remains poorly understood, even by Wansbrough's supporters. Scholars in the field found the work, together with its companion volume *The Sectarian Milieu* (1978), extremely difficult to follow.[17] Reviewers complained most about the dense prose bristling with undefined terms in Latin, Greek, Hebrew and German, but the real stumbling block was Wansbrough's practice of not writing introductions or conclusions, either to the work as a whole or to the individual chapters, a recipe for puzzlement on the part of the audience. From what readers did understand, they were upset mainly by his radical suggestion that the Qur'an was

16 Patricia Crone and Michael Cook, *Hagarism* (Cambridge: Cambridge University Press, 1977); Patricia Crone, *God's Rule: Government and Islam – Six Centuries of Medieval Islamic Political Thought* (New York: Columbia University Press, 2004); Michael Cook, *Commanding Right and Forbidding Wrong in Islamic Thought* (Cambridge: Cambridge University Press, 2000).

17 John Wansbrough, *Quranic Studies: Sources and Methods of Scriptural Interpretation* (Oxford: Oxford University Press, 1977); idem, *The Sectarian Milieu: Content and Composition of Islamic Salvation History* (Oxford: Oxford University Press, 1978).

probably not produced in Arabia at all and only canonized later, as much as two centuries after the Prophet's death, probably in Iraq. In his studies, Wansbrough makes many insightful and brilliant points about the Qur'an, Qur'anic commentary and related matters, but there are legitimate reasons to question his results, which he appears in many instances to pull out of a hat. For one thing, recent research on Qur'anic manuscripts has proved his late dating untenable by showing that there was an established text of the Qur'an at a very early date, so that canonization probably occurred much earlier than he suggests. This does not mean that the traditional account of the Qur'an's redaction by a committee appointed by the Caliph ʿUthmān is proved correct, but the chronological window during which the Qur'an coalesced and was canonized is shrinking and moving closer to the date proposed in Islamic sources.

Wansbrough's works also deny something that Hughes accepts as fact: the significant presence of Judaism and Christianity in Arabia before Islam. Wansbrough's main reason for supposing that the Qur'an was produced outside Arabia is that the text shows too intimate an understanding of Judaism and Christianity, which could not have been the case in Arabia, in his view. Other scholars, even critically demanding ones, do not agree. In addition, scholars have not sufficiently realized that Wansbrough's work is based on the assumption – which he nowhere discusses or justifies – that the collection, redaction and canonization of the Qur'an recapitulates those of the synoptic Gospels. This assumption is plausible but certainly open to question. While Hughes criticizes other scholars for rejecting the views of Crone, Cook, Wansbrough and others on the grounds that they are engaging in knee-jerk reactions to critical scholars who dare to question Islamic doctrinal views, the true story is not so simple. The main problem is that the authors of such skeptical studies are extremely demanding when evaluating and rejecting the traditional evidence but then much less critical when building up counter-narratives.[18]

18 A number of later scholars have been continuing scholarship in a similar vein. Among the most reasonable of such works is Gerald Hawting, *The Idea of Idolatry and the Emergence of Islam: From Polemic to History* (Cambridge: Cambridge University Press, 2002). Less reasonable are such

Hughes's statements on the place of Judaism and Christianity as the background to Islam also miss the mark. He writes that Islamic studies scholars, relying on the traditional account, try to claim that Arabia was a remote area, uninfluenced by Judaism and Christianity, in order to stress the uniqueness of Islam, and he wants to correct this view by insisting on their presence. Hughes seems to be unaware that his "correction" actually matches the traditional account and the version of the story adopted by the uncritical anti-skeptics that he denounces, whereas the view he critiques is actually promoted by a number of the skeptics he admires. Islam presents itself as a continuation of Judaism and Christianity, and that is the main background for the story of the rise of Islam.

Most scholars are in agreement that Islam's roots derive from Judaism and Christianity and that they were essential background for the rise of Islam. Judaism and Christianity also figure in the opening chapter of dozens of introductions to Islam and the Qur'an, and only the radical skeptics, including Wansbrough, Crone and others, have disputed their strong presence in and around Arabia and their influence on nascent Islam. Traditional accounts of the Prophet's mission such as the *Sīrah* of Ibn Hisham (d. 212/828) include many examples of a close relationship: the legend of Baḥīrah, the Christian monk in Syria who foretold Muhammad's prophecy, the Prophet's consultation of Khadijah's uncle, Waraqah ibn Nawfal, who was a Christian, about the episodes of revelation he had experienced, the sending of a group of Meccan Muslims to Ethiopia to escape persecution at the hands of the Meccan pagans, the Prophet's reception of the delegation of Christians from Najran, the close contacts with Jews in Medina, and so on. A number of Islamic texts report that among the Kaʿbah's decorations were paintings of Abraham and Mary and Jesus. All these elements are fully accepted in Islamic tradition.

Though the Jewish and Christian influence on Islam is well known, its particulars are not well understood, and more work needs to be done to investigate them fully. A structural problem in academia

---

works as Yehuda D. Nevo and Judith Koren, *Crossroads to Islam: The Origins of the Arab Religion and the Arab State* (Amherst, NY: Prometheus Books, 2003).

176 *Identity, Politics and the Study of Islam*

that has slowed progress in this particular area is the treatment of the rise of Islam as a sharp dividing line. Scholars trained as Islamic historians generally do not focus on the preceding period. Scholars trained as ancient historians often stop at Alexander the Great. The intervening period, over nine centuries, is something of a no-man's land, and few study that period seriously along with the rise of Islam. Individual exceptions are Gordon Newby's book on the Jews of Arabia, G.W. Bowersock's studies of Ethiopia and its relation to the Arabian Peninsula, and Irfan Shahid's works on the history of Byzantine relations with the Arabs leading up to the Islamic period. In recent years, scholars have made an effort to overcome this divide in a programmatic way by convening conferences and publishing collected volumes with the term "late antiquity" in the title, and this has led to the publication of such works as Garth Fowden's *From Empire to Commonwealth*.[19]

In my view, in general accounts of the rise of Islam there are two great omissions, neither of which appears on Hughes's radar screen. The first is attention to the pre-Islamic pagan tradition, which clearly had important effects on the Qur'an and Islam but which Muslim tradition generally denigrated and suppressed, leaving only hints such as the Arabic term for "rainbow," *qaws Quzaḥ* "the bow of Quzaḥ (the thunder god)," or the term for "genius," *ᶜabqarī*, meaning from ᶜAbqar, a valley known as a favorite haunt of genies. Unlike the Greeks and the Romans, who were rehabilitated in the Renaissance, the pre-Islamic Arabs were never similarly recuperated, and they have got

---

19 G.D. Newby, *A History of the Jews of Arabia: From Ancient Times to Their Eclipse under Islam* (Columbia: University of South Carolina Press, 1988); G. W. Bowersock, *The Throne of Adulis: Red Sea Wars on the Eve of Islam* (Oxford: Oxford University Press, 2013); Irfan Shahid, *Rome and the Arabs: A Prolegomenon to the Study of Byzantium and the Arabs* (Washington, DC: Dumbarton Oaks, 1984); idem, *Byzantium and the Arabs in the Fourth Century* (Washington, DC: Dumbarton Oaks, 1984); *Byzantium and the Arabs in the Fifth Century* (Washington, DC: Dumbarton Oaks, 1989); *Byzantium and the Arabs in the Sixth Century*, 2 vols. (Washington, DC: Dumbarton Oaks, 1995–2010); Garth Fowden, *From Empire to Commonwealth: Consequences of Monotheism in Late Antiquity* (Princeton, NJ: Princeton University Press, 1993).

bad press ever since, especially with regard to religion. While the Arabian pagans clearly had a complex pantheon of gods, an extensive mythology and a wide variety of religious practices, their religion is regularly dismissed and deprecated in Islamic tradition – not surprisingly, given that the Qur'an calls their rituals "clapping and whistling." A well-known story reports that the Banū Ḥanīfah tribe of Yamāmah ate their god, an idol made out of dried yogurt, during a time of famine.[20] The 9th-century pundit Ibn Qutaybah, though an expert on Arab lore, reports that the pre-Islamic Arabs were such clods when it came to religion that when they had been traveling all day in the desert and wanted to stop and rest, they would look for a place with four nice stones. On three of them they would set their pot to cook dinner, and the fourth, they would worship.[21] Such views are contradicted by the Qur'an itself, for the pagan opponents of the prophets of earlier salvation history resist conversion because of their reverence for and devotion to the religion of their forefathers.

In this, Western scholarship on Islam and on the Qur'an has for the most part followed the traditional view. Montgomery Watt denies that the pre-Islamic Arabs had a real religion, calling their belief system "tribal humanism." Western Qur'anic studies, when they have examined sources of the Qur'an, have paid attention primarily to Judaism and Christianity, with only a handful of exceptions such as Julius Wellhausen's *Reste arabische Heidentums*, Toufic Fahd's *La Divination arabe* and *Le Panthéon de l'Arabie central à la veille de l'Hégire* and Jaroslav Stetkevytch's *Muhammad and the Golden Bough*.[22] Most introductions to Islam neglect the pagan religious tradition altogether.

20 Ṣāᶜid al-Andalusī, *Kitāb Ṭabaqāt al-umam*, ed. Louis Cheikho (Beirut: al-Maṭbaʿah al-Kāthūlīkiyyah, 1912), p. 43.
21 Hishām b. al-Kalbī, *Kitāb al-Aṣnām*, ed. Aḥmad Zakī (Cairo: Maṭbaᶜat Dār al-Kutub al-Miṣriyyah, 1924), p. 19; idem, *The Book of Idols*, trans. Nabih Amin Faris (Princeton, NJ: Princeton University Press, 1952), p. 28.
22 Julius Wellhausen, *Reste arabischen Heidentums*, 2nd ed. (Berlin: Verlag von Georg Reimer, 1897); Toufic Fahd, *La Divination arabe: études religieuses, sociologiques, et folkloriques sur le lieu natif de l'Islam* (Leiden: Brill, 1966); idem, *Le Panthéon de l'Arabie central à la veille de l'Hégire* (Paris: P. Geuthner, 1968); Jaroslav Stetkevytch, *Muhammad and the Golden*

The pre-Islamic pagan religion also included a tradition of prophecy, something that does not appear in any introduction to Islam of which I am aware. Muhammad was not the only prophet in Arabia during his time: Maslamah (Musaylimah) b. Ḥabīb was the prophet of the Banū Ḥanīfah tribe in Yamāmah, Sajāḥ was the prophetess of the Banū Tamīm tribe in central Arabia, al-Aswad al-ᶜAnsī was the prophet of the Madhḥij tribe in Yemen, and Ṭulayḥah b. Khuwaylid was the prophet of the Banū Asad tribe. No introduction to Islam reports that during the 7th century Arabia was home to several active prophets, each leading his or her own religious movement, and that Muhammad's movement grew to be the strongest, overcoming and suppressing the other movements, including the next-most successful one, that of Maslamah, who became known in Islamic tradition as "Musaylimah the Liar."[23] Hughes, despite his arguments for a critical approach, simply has followed the typical introductions in ignoring these prophets, thus unwittingly bolstering the idea that Islam was a unique development.

The second great omission is the ideological shift that occurred after the rise of Islam, during the first three Islamic centuries, to distinguish and separate Islam from Judaism and Christianity. Later Islamic orthodox doctrine modified and suppressed fundamental ideas found in the Qur'an, moving away from original tenets that portrayed Islam as quite close to its predecessor faiths. As an emblematic example one

---

Bough: Reconstructing Arabian Myth (Bloomington: Indiana University Press, 1996).

23 Dale F. Eickelmann, "Musaylima: An Approach to the Social Anthropology of Seventh-Century Arabia," *Journal of the Economic and Social History of the Orient* 10 (1967), pp. 17–52; Marilyn Waldman and Robert M. Baum, "Innovation as Renovation: The 'Prophet' as an Agent of Change" in Michael A. Williams, Collett Cox and Martin Jaffee, eds., *Innovation in Religious Traditions: Essays in the Interpretation of Religious Change* (Berlin: Mouton de Gruyter, 1992), pp. 241–84; M.J. Kister, "The Struggle against Musaylima and the Conquest of Yamāma," *Jerusalem Studies in Arabic and Islam* 27 (2002), pp. 1–56; Al Makin, *Representing the Enemy: Musaylima in Muslim Literature* (Frankfurt am Main: Peter Lang, 2010); Asᶜad Muḥammad al-Ṭayyib, *al-Mutanabbi'ūn: nash'atuhum, uṣūluhum, nihāyatuhum* (Beirut: Dār Ibn Ḥazm, 1996–97).

may cite the fact, pointed out by Reuven Firestone, that half of the authorities cited by al-Ṭabarī claim that Isaac was the son Abraham intended to sacrifice, while half claim that Ishmael was the one.[24] Later commentators utterly rejected the interpretation that the son involved was Isaac, thus setting a clear barrier between the Qur'an and the Bible. Donner's work *Muhammad and the Believers* grapples with this issue, and so do a number of other studies, but many of the particular developments are highly contested and poorly understood, and few have made it into introductory works.[25]

Elements of this grand theological shift include a large complex of interrelated ideas. The illiteracy of the Prophet was stressed in order to obviate the accusation that the revelations of the Qur'an were in any way influenced by the Prophet's personal knowledge of the Bible. Any similarities between the Qur'an and the Jewish and Christian sacred texts could not be explained by shared background but only by the shared source, God. The miraculous nature of the Qur'an (*iʿjāz al-Qurʿān*) was stressed, thus setting the Qur'an apart, not only from mundane texts such as poetry and oratory but also from other scriptures, which were not accorded the same miraculous status. This doctrine counters a decided theme in the Qur'an, which is to identify the Qur'an not as a text sui generis but as an equal member in the category of Scripture (*kitāb*). God revealed to mankind several scriptures that are mutually corroborating and present an essentially unified message. The Qur'anic claim that the sacred texts of the Jews and Christians have been tampered with, termed *taḥrīf*, probably meant in the original context that the Torah and the Gospels that are in the hands of the Jews and Christians have been altered in some matters of detail, in order to explain apparent small discrepancies, but the concept later came to be used to disqualify resort to the Bible in attempts to explain Qur'anic material and, in its most extreme form, to support a moratorium on reading the Bible for Muslims. Related to this was

---

24 Reuven Firestone, *Journeys in Holy Lands: The Evolution of the Abraham-Ishmael Legends in Islamic Exegesis* (Albany: State University of New York Press, 1990), pp. 135–51.

25 Fred M. Donner, *Muhammad and the Believers at the Origins of Islam* (Cambridge, Massachusetts: The Belknap Press, 2010).

the rejection of "*Isrā'īliyyāt*," accounts of Biblical lore from Jewish tradition, as a proper source for commentary on the Qur'an.

The designation of the Prophet as the final and universal prophet, sent to all of mankind, renders his mission categorically different from that of earlier prophets, while many passages of the Qur'an suggest that every nation is entitled to receive a prophet of its own who presents God's message in that nation's tongue, just as several Qur'anic passages designate the Prophet Muhammad as sent to the members of his tribe or to Mecca and the surrounding region.

Already in the *Risālah* of al-Shāfiʿī (d. 204/820) it is clear that Arabic is viewed as the sacred language par excellence, while a careful reading of the Qur'anic references to Arabic suggests that it is not the default sacred language but actually the exception. The Qur'an has been couched in Arabic so that the Biblical message, ordinarily presented in other languages, might be intelligible to the Arabs in particular and so demand their serious attention.

All these doctrinal shifts worked to widen the gap between the Qur'an and Islam on the one hand and the Bible and Jewish and Christian traditions on the other, but they were not inherent in the Qur'an.

In *Theorizing Islam,* for all his insistence on a "critical" approach, Hughes also accepts the standard Islamic doctrine of the *Isrā'* and *Miʿrāj*, the legend of the Prophet's miraculous night journey to Jerusalem and his ascension to heaven on the mythical steed Burāq, including the claim that it is mentioned unambiguously in the Qur'an. In fact, he suggests that it was cited early on as a major proof of the Prophet Muhammad's mission despite the fact that it has been contested in a series of discussions going back to the 19th century. In *Historisch-kritische Einleitung in den Koran,* Gustav Weil argued that the verse to which the *Isrā'* is attached, 17:1, was fabricated after the death of the Prophet and erroneously included in the Qur'an.[26] Q 17:1 does not rhyme with the following verses, and Nöldeke for one considered it blatantly obvious that the verse was out of place. He suggests either that intervening verses, between vv. 1 and 2, had

---

26 Gustav Weil, *Historisch-kritische Einleitung in den Koran*, 2nd ed. (Bielefeld: Belhagen & Klasing, 1878), p. 74.

somehow dropped out, or that an original introduction to the surah had been lost, and v. 1 intentionally substituted for the lost section. Against Weil, however, Nöldeke accepted v. 1 as an "original" part of the Qur'an.[27] I side with Weil here in thinking that the Q 17:1 is a later interpolation, while Hughes has sided unwittingly with the naïve traditionalists, and he seems to be unaware of the entire debate.

The point is not that Hughes has contradicted his announced principles; rather, it is that scholars will find it difficult to be aware of *all* of the critical issues in the field about which they are writing unless they have engaged in long and serious preparation and have read the relevant secondary literature, which in some fields is large, and in others, such as Qur'anic studies, difficult to collect.

Overall, *Theorizing Islam* is a critical assessment of several recent works in Islamic studies, many of which were written for a popular, non-specialist audience. This critique resembles a condemnation of the American novel's literary merits by examining a selection of the bestsellers in the airport bookstore, and many of the authors involved have written other more serious and substantial contributions to the field. Even with his disclaimers, though, Hughes's remarks come off not as a series of quibbles with particular works but as a wide condemnation of certain scholars on the basis of one work, and an entire sector of Islamic studies scholarship on the basis of a selection of recent work.

My own view is that a great deal of scholarship in the academy is shoddy work. Professors in departments of religion produce some of it, but so do psychologists, specialists in language and literature, historians, anthropologists and others. Half of the papers at any large conference are not worth attending, and many published works are disappointing. One general rule that a concerned reader might arrive at in the course of this debate is that scholars who are perfectly reasonable when writing on their particular area of expertise become little better than rank amateurs when they try to write general, more popular works, or write on an area outside the main focus of their training. Experts on Sufism who venture into general works on Islam

---

27 Theodor Nöldeke et al., *The History of the Qur'an*, trans. Wolfgang H. Behn (Leiden: Brill, 2013), pp. 110–12.

make large blunders because they are not versed in Islamic legal tradition, anthropologists make silly claims about Islam in general because they are not versed in Islamic religious literature, and so on.

In Hughes's textbook *Muslim Identities*, he sets out to practice what he preaches. The book is actually quite interesting, for it attempts to give room both to the traditional doctrinal views of Islamic history and thought and to critical views from the vantage point of religious studies. It must be admitted, though, that Hughes falls into the same traps as other textbook authors do, mainly because limited expertise does not allow him to write an original and informed account of many of the aspects of Islam addressed in the work. Inevitably, he ends up repeating many of the old saws found in earlier textbooks, including ones that are flat-out wrong. Building on earlier introductions' distinction between Sunni caliphs and the Shiite imams, he describes the difference between the Shiite and Sunni senses of the term "imam":

> In Shiʿi Islam, it is used to refer explicitly to one of the Twelve Imams, who are believed to be direct descendants of Muhammad. There currently exists no Imam on earth because he is in occultation, abiding in such a state until the time arises when he will return as the Mahdi (Guide). In Sunni Islam, however, there are plenty of imams. The word imam in Arabic is a preposition that means "in front of" and traditionally refers to the person who leads the daily prayers.[28]

There are a number of problems with this statement in addition to the major flaw that it suggests a complete divide between Shiite and Sunni Islam with regard to the term imam.

First, *imām* is not a preposition but rather a noun that means, at base, "leader." (The related preposition is *amāma* "in front of," which looks the same in Arabic script but is a distinct word.) The term is used both by Sunnis and by Shiites to refer to the leader of prayer, even an ad hoc one, as well as an official leader of prayer attached to a particular mosque, or a local religious leader. It also may be used in other circumstances to mean a commander or leader of some other group, including the jurists after whom the Islamic legal schools are named,

---

28 Hughes, *Muslim Identities*, p. 126.

Khomeini, military commanders, and so on. However, Imam is also a title used for the ruler of the Muslim community, and both Shiite and Sunni theologians use the term in this fashion. Nevertheless, it has been common in textbooks on Islam to distinguish between the Sunni Caliphs, who are said to have held political power but do not have religious authority, and Shiite Imams, who were religious leaders but did not generally wield political power. Hughes has merely followed the works of predecessors in presenting this view.

The truth is that the dichotomy is false. The terms Caliph and Imam refer to the same office. Crone and Hinds have shown that the Caliphs of the Umayyad and early Abbasid periods viewed themselves as both political and religious leaders of the community, and the Abbasid Caliphs continued to claim religious authority in various ways until the Mongol conquest of Baghdad in 1258. Both the Sunnis and the Shiites understood that they supported rival claimants to the same position, that of the leadership of the Muslim community, and not that they envisaged a categorically different type of leader. Shiites sought to overthrow the Umayyad and Abbasid Caliphs not because they thought that the Caliphate should be abolished but rather because they desired to remove illegitimate usurpers and replace them with the legitimate claimant to the established office.

There are additional problems with this short statement. Hughes implies that there is some doubt about the Twelve Imams' descent from the Prophet. There is no doubt about their pedigree; the only questions have to do with the existence of the Twelfth Imam. Hughes's description of the Occultation is true only for the Twelver Shiites, whom he treats as if they were the only Shiites in the Islamic world, ignoring the Zaydis, who had Imams in Yemen until 1962, the Mustaᶜlī Ismāᶜīlīs, or Bohras, who have living representatives of a hidden Imam, and the Nizārī Ismāᶜīlīs, who have a living Imam in the person of the Aga Khan. Even for the Twelvers, the statement that the Imam is not in the world is incorrect. According to Twelver Shiite doctrine, the Twelfth Imam is not in limbo, since he is a physical man, circulating among the believers, his life having been miraculously prolonged. He therefore definitely exists on earth, contrary to Hughes's statement, but he is incognito; one does not generally know where he is or how to contact him.

Muslim Identities contains a number of other errors. Hughes refers to the Arabian pagan gods and goddesses mentioned in the Qur'an as al-Qaum, Wadd, Nasr and Nuha (p. 24). Wadd and Nasr actually appear in Q 71:23, the verse he cites, but the other gods mentioned there are Yaghūth, Yaᶜūq and Suwāᶜ. There are references elsewhere to al-Lāt, al-Manāt and al-ᶜUzzā, the "daughters of Allāh," in Surat al-Najm (Q 53), and the people of Sheba are said to be worshippers of the sun, al-Shams, in Surat al-Naml (Q 27). Neither Nuha nor Qaum appear in the Qur'an, but rather are known from Nabatean and North Arabian inscriptions. When Hughes remarks, "the Quran is *inexplicably* bound up with the personality of Muhammad," I believe he means *inextricably*; *wa* "and" is not a separate word in Arabic (p. 68); surah 114 has 6 verses, not 5 (p. 68); *fuquha* "jurists" (pp. 135, 141, 277) should be *fuqahā'*; the abrogation of a Qur'anic verse refers to the cancelation of its legal implications, but Hughes states that it means making the verse "more specific" (p. 142). He reports that the legal term *ijmāᶜ* "refers solely to the consensus of male scholars" (p. 145), when a more accurate definition would be "the consensus of fully qualified jurists" – women are not excluded, for legal Islamic theorists across the board hold that they may indeed become fully qualified jurists. Most jurists, with the exception of Muḥammad b. Jarīr al-Ṭabarī (d. 310/923), would bar women from serving as judges, but that is a different issue. Abū Ḥāmid al-Ghazāli is introduced as a legal scholar and philosopher (p. 170), when he was above all a theologian. It is claimed that the Saudis destroyed the tomb of the Prophet Muhammad along with all shrines devoted to saints (p. 175). While they did remove gold ornaments from the Prophet's tomb early in the 20th century, they left it standing, and so too the great dome built over it. Only recently has a Saudi committee recommended that the dome be dismantled and the tomb removed and reduced to a flat, ordinary marker, but this plan has not been carried out. The magazine *Nid'ul Islam* (p. 175) should be *Nidā' al-Islām* ("The Call of Islam"). A grave sinner is equated with a murderer (p. 186), when it could refer as well to someone who has committed other infractions such as adultery. The term *bilā kayf*, literally "without how," is rendered "without knowing how or what" (p. 193) – there is no reference to "what." The 10th-century theologian al-Māturīdī is called al-Maturdi four times (pp. 193–4). The beginnings of Islamic philosophy are dated to the 10th century and the works of al-Fārābī (p. 194), which ignores the prolific philosopher Yaʿqūb b. Isḥāq al-Kindī (d. c. 870) in the 9th century, whose works presented nearly the entire corpus of Aristotle's writings in Arabic versions. Hughes reports that Avicenna's great medical work, *The Canon of Medicine*, comprises fourteen volumes (p. 196). Avicenna divided the work into five "books," and *The Canon* was usually published in editions varying from two to five volumes; the more voluminous work was his *Shifāʾ* (The Cure), on philosophy, which has been published in over twenty volumes. Hughes reports that female circumcision is popular in many Muslim countries, including Saudi Arabia, Jordan and some countries in Africa. (p. 219). The truth is that it is rare in Jordan, though prevalent in Saudi Arabia, Egypt, Sudan, Ethiopia, Somalia and other sub-Saharan African countries. Hughes gives the modern Shiite term *vilayat-i faqihi* and translates it as "guardianship of the religious scholars" (p. 245); it should be *vilāyat-i faqīh*, and a better translation would be "the comprehensive authority of the jurist," in the singular. The Baʿath Party ("Resurrection Party," pp. 246, 248, 249) should be *Baʿth*; Allahu Akhbar (p. 246) should be Allāhu Akbar. The term *takfīr* is defined as "apostasy" (p. 279), but apostasy would be *irtidād*, while *takfīr* means "declaring someone an unbeliever."

Overall, then, while the textbook has some positive points, it reproduces a number of the problems of its predecessors and is not any more precise or accurate than the average. Columbia University Press seems to have done little to edit or review the work or guarantee its quality.

Specialists in various subfields of Islamic studies have biases that make it difficult for them to write objectively and insightfully about other subfields. Edward Said failed to understand that scholars in Islamic studies often have deep-set biases that derive not from the imperial power structures from within which they work, but rather from the Muslim scholars they study and the Muslim authors whose works they read. Louis Massignon's sympathy for al-Ḥallāj colored his view of mystics and their opponents. Marshall Hodgson clearly sided with the Sufis against their main enemies, the jurists, whom he termed "the *sharīʿah*-minded." George Makdisi viewed the jurists as the most important scholars of Islamic history and the Ḥanbalīs in particular as the leaders of the jurists, a position that Ḥanafīs and Shāfiʿīs would have found surprising. Until the late 20th century, most Islamicists had a decidedly negative view of Shiites simply because they only knew about them through their enemies' descriptions of them as extremist heretics. The list goes on.

All of these factors contribute to a scholarly environment in which it is difficult for specialists to write excellent general works. One cannot straightforwardly rely on the opinions expressed by one's colleagues, expecting them to be free of scholarly bias. They are producing their own narratives based on limited areas of specialization, rationalizing only the material that they themselves have read and digested. But this is referring to disputed and perhaps arcane matters. A large percentage of the errors in Hughes's textbook and other similar general works could be cleared up easily by scholars who have strong training in Islamic studies and good control of Islamic languages. Unfortunately, it is not cost-effective for the presses to pay the best scholars to edit all of their publications – and obviously not necessary, since they sell anyway – and it may not make sense to make the most knowledgeable scholars in the field invest their time in improving the hasty, general works of others rather than working on resolving difficult problems in specific areas of Islamic studies.

At the end of *Theorizing Islam*, Hughes presents a plan for "New Islamic Studies" containing ten theses. It appears that this plan is a modified version of a plan proposed by Bruce Lincoln about religious studies in general. The proposals are well-intended but unrelentingly vague, and they focus on method rather than substance. Most are acceptable as general sentiments: scholars of religious studies should not engage in apologetics for the tradition they study, and the like.

The nearest to a concrete suggestion is the assertion that history might be an antidote to some of the ills that plague scholarship on Islam. I agree, but this is insufficient to solve many of the problems in the field, and particularly the ones with which Hughes is concerned. Training in the broad sweep of Islamic history would most benefit the modernists, who tend to use pre-modern history as a foil for their own claims without knowing what actually took place. So, scholars writing about women in the modern region of West Asia and North

Africa often assume that the women of this region in the pre-modern period were not wealthy, powerful or educated and that they had few or no rights to speak of because of the dominance of the patriarchy – ideas that do not reflect historical reality and are based on mere supposition.[29] It would also benefit anthropologists, sociologists and political scientists, many of whom have a shallow knowledge of history. Historical awareness might help them to see the connections of the phenomena they are studying with long-term processes and lead them to find parallel cases from other times, in addition to providing fundamental background knowledge, including knowledge of the Islamic world outside their chosen regions of focus.

However, attention to history will do little to solve the problems with which Hughes is concerned. Both the empiricists and the radical revisionists pay attention to history, particularly with regard to the rise of Islam and the first few Islamic centuries; they do not need to be told to attend to it. The issue is that they have widely divergent views regarding proper sources and their interpretation. Those differences are mainly theoretical and ideological, and to claim that an unproblematic historical understanding will somehow settle their debates is misunderstanding a fundamental feature of the present state of Islamic studies. The same may be said for the scholars in Hughes's dichotomy between scholars who adopt the apologetic mode and those who adopt the critical mode. A historical understanding will not in itself resolve their differences and create a unifying reform in the field; fundamental ideological differences will remain, no matter how much historical detail is added to the picture.

When Hughes states that scholars should not have "reverence" for the tradition, however, I cannot help thinking that this rule would be

---

29 Such views are being countered by a growing body of scholarship focused on women in pre-modern societies, such as Ruth Roded, *Women in Islamic Biographical Collections: From Ibn Saʿd to Who's Who* (Boulder, CO: Lynne Rienner Publishers, 1994); Yosef Rapaport, *Marriage, Money, and Divorce in Medieval Islamic Society* (Cambridge: Cambridge University Press, 2005); Devin J. Stewart, "Women's Biographies in Islamic Societies: Mīrzā ʿAbd Allāh al-Iṣfahānī's *Riyāḍ al-Ulamāʾ*," in Louise Marlowe, ed., *The Rhetoric of Biography: Narrating Lives in Persianate Societies* (Cambridge, MA: Harvard University Press, 2011), pp. 106–39.

hard to police, and that it may be undesirable as well as impractical. What might help matters, though, is if scholars make it clear in their publications what type of work they are trying to write, clearly and honestly presenting their goals and indicating to what degree they intend their works to be descriptive or prescriptive, revisionist or otherwise.

Most importantly, I have a hard time believing that any of Hughes's suggested points is likely to lead to new, improved work in Islamic studies, because method with no content, like critical thinking with no knowledge, cannot produce results. I present an alternative set of directives below.

Theses for the Improvement of Islamic Studies

I. For God's sake, learn Arabic. This is fundamental and, even for someone who wants to study Islam outside the Arab world, unavoidable. The sacred text is in Arabic, prayer is in Arabic, and most introductory and advanced texts on any of the religious sciences are in Arabic. Arabic, just as Latin was in Christendom, was and remains the language not only of religion but also of learned discourse in the Islamic world. Almost all learned traditions in other Islamic languages, such as Persian or Turkish, are heavily indebted to Arabic models. Arabic vocabulary and turns of phrase permeate the language use of Muslims all over the globe, whether in Persian, Turkish, Malay or Urdu, and this includes popular speech as well as learned discourse. In practical terms, this means undertaking 4–6 years of dedicated study to become competent, since, for English speakers, Arabic is objectively several times more difficult than French, Spanish or Hebrew. (For native speakers of Hebrew or Amharic, Arabic is much easier.) In all honesty, the main weakness of most scholars in the field is their limited knowledge of Arabic. Many textualists are familiar with only one genre or a small set of genres in Arabic letters, and they would be better scholars if they read more widely. A structural problem in the academy is that many doctoral programs do not provide the time for rigorous Arabic training and do not promote language learning as a high priority. Area studies departments are better in this respect than others such as religion or anthropology.

II. If you have time, learn Persian as well. Persian is Islam's second language of learned discourse, and in certain contexts, the most important. It is crucial for the study of Islam in Turkey, Central Asia, Pakistan and India, in addition to Iran and Afghanistan. Persian is easier than Arabic, and a general competence may be acquired more quickly, perhaps in three years. However, expertise in particular genres such as historical chronicles or poetry requires additional study.

III. Learn another Islamic language, if necessary. Whoever is studying Malaysia should become an expert in Malay, and whoever studies contemporary Morocco needs to learn the Moroccan dialect of Arabic well. It is becoming less difficult to acquire a high degree of competence in the Arabic dialects because better dictionaries and more pedagogical materials are available and because the internet has made access to material in the dialects much easier.

IV. Study the European languages that are necessary for knowledge of research in your field. Traditionally these have been French and German, but the relevant languages vary by subfield. German is fundamental for Qur'anic studies and Arabic linguistics. French is crucial for the study of North Africa. Spanish is important for the study of medieval Iberia and North Africa as well.

V. Become versed in grammar. It is difficult to learn foreign languages and remain innocent of grammar, yet a number of writers out there manage to do it. It never happened when anyone attending the university had years of training in Latin and Greek, whose grammars make Arabic look relatively simple. It is important to acquire the technical terms of grammar in Arabic, which differ quite a bit from their counterparts in English or other European

languages. They appear in nearly every Islamic discourse imaginable, including commentaries of all kinds, and even jokes.
VI. Become competent in the main religious sciences of Islam. These are:
   A. Qur'an and the Qur'anic sciences.
   B. *Tafsir* [exegesis of the Qur'an].
   C. Hadith and hadith criticism.
   D. Law and legal theory.
   E. Theology and doxography.
   F. Religious philosophy.
   G. Sufism.
   H. Minority Islamic traditions: Zaydi, Ismaʿili and Twelver Shiites, Kharijis and others.

This is a tall order. Most scholars in Islamic studies are only versed in one or two of these subfields. While it is nearly impossible to become an expert in all these fields, a basic familiarity is advisable for anyone who wants to write on Islamic studies. This would prevent many of the most egregious errors. It is also important to know the main studies in these fields in the history of Islamic studies scholarship.

VII. Know the basic rituals:
   A. Prayer.
   B. Friday prayer.
   C. The fast of Ramaḍān.
   D. The Feast of Sacrifice (ʿĪd al-Aḍḥā).
   E. The Prophet's birthday celebration (*al-Mawlid*)
   F. The pilgrimage to Mecca and visitation of the Prophet's mosque.
   G. Other pilgrimages, to the Shiite Imams' tombs, to saints' tombs, etc.
   H. Naming rituals, usually seven days after the birth.
   I. Circumcision rituals.
   J. Marriage rituals.
   K. Funeral rituals.
   L. ʿĀshūrā' rituals.

A Modest Proposal for Islamic Studies 191

VIII. Read some fundamental religious texts:
   A. The Qur'an.
   B. *The Life of the Prophet* by Ibn Hishām
   C. The *Shifā* by Ibn Qāḍī ʿIyāḍ (d. 544/1149) on the miracles of the Prophet.
   D. *The Forty Hadiths*, compiled by al-Nawawī (d. 676/1277).
   E. One of the main hadith compilations, either the *Ṣaḥīḥ* of al-Bukhari or the *Ṣaḥīḥ* of Muslim (d. 261/875).
   F. One of the basic creeds, such as that of al-Ṭaḥāwī (d. 321/933).
   G. A basic manual of law, such as the *Risālah* of Ibn Abī Zayd al-Qayrawānī (d. 386/996) or *Minhāj al-Ṭālibīn* by al-Nawawī.

   These have all been translated into English and other languages, which may help speed up the process. Most anthropologists and most modernists fail in this category. As a consequence, when they run into a contemporary practice, concept, term or phrase they cannot identify its origin in Islamic religious tradition.

   Read *Iḥyā' ʿulūm al-dīn* (The Revival of the Religious Sciences) by al-Ghazālī (d. 505/1111). This book, four volumes in most editions, is Islamic literature's most widely plagiarized work for a reason. Going through it will provide the reader an education in Islamic religious thought writ large, especially in theology and ethics. While it is important to realize that al-Ghazālī's views are by no means representative of Islamic orthodoxy, reading this single book would do more to raise the bar in Islamic studies scholarship than fifty Bruce Lincolns and J.Z. Smiths put together. Several sections of this work have appeared in translation, of uneven quality, but many have yet to be translated.

IX. Acquire a basic knowledge of Judaism and Christianity, including the Bible and biblical history. This is important not only because of their role in the Qur'an and the beginnings of Islam, but also because of Islamdom's constant contact and negotiation with Jewish and Christian tradition ever since. Modern scholars in the Islamic world have significant problems in acquiring this knowledge because access is more difficult and in many cases frowned upon.

X. Study biography. Most scholars of Islamic studies of any period before the 20th century will have to make extensive use of at least the particular genre that is their focus of study – such as law digests, philosophical works, manuals of hadith criticism – and, in addition, biographical sources that give information about the lives and works of particular scholars and other figures. Consequently, a strong understanding of biographical works is a common denominator and should figure prominently in the formation of all Islamic studies scholars. The biographical notice (*tarjamah*), a common form found in biographical dictionaries, historical chronicles and other types of collections from the 9th century until the present and throughout the Islamic world, has specific conventions and is carefully constructed for particular purposes. Understanding these conventions, in addition to acquiring the particular language skills required, is an important part of general competence in Islamic studies.

XI. Work on translation as a skill. Being able to translate accurately takes years of training and practice, particularly when there is a wide gap between the cultural frameworks of the original language and the target language. It is a crucial part of explaining and presenting material from Islamic tradition in scholarship. Bad translations riddle the field. They are not just a nuisance but lead to serious misunderstandings and misinterpretations of the material, some of which are perpetuated by subsequent scholarship. They also prevent scholars from other disciplines from learning and engaging with Islamic material. Do not fill your translations with transliterated words in Arabic that are completely unnecessary. (This is a prevalent disease in many subfields of Islamic studies.) I present one paragraph of a typical translation, followed by my own translation, as an example.

> The Creator of the universe must be an existent (*mawjūd*), for existence and non-existence are polar opposites (*mutaqābilan*) between which there is no intermediate mode of being (*wāsiṭa*). Since it has been established that things must have a cause (*fāʿil*), it is necessary that it be both existent (*mawjūd*) and eternal (*qadīm*), for a [first] cause must be antecedent to what is caused, necessary to its existence, and without beginning, for if it had a beginning in time it would itself require a cause (*muhdith*) and thus for a *regressus ad infinitum* (*tasalsul*). Since [God] is eternally existent, non-being may not be predicated of Him, for He whose eternal pre-existence (*qidam*) is established cannot be conceived as non-existent. If His non-existence were possible, He would be dependent on a cause. However, He is one whose existence is uncaused, hence there can be no cause for His non-existence.

In my view, this should read as follows:

> The Creator of the universe exists, for existence and non-existence are opposites between which there is no middle term, and since it has been established that He causes things, one must necessarily conclude that He exists. He is also pre-eternal, because the agent precedes that which is done. He is necessarily existent, without a beginning to his existence, because, had He been contingent, He would have required an originator, and this would lead to an infinite regression. He is also everlasting and cannot cease to exist, because it is impossible for something to become non-existent when its pre-eternal existence has been established. If His non-existence were possible, then it would be dependent on a cause, but there cannot be a cause for the nonexistence of One whose existence is uncaused.[30]

30 Devin J. Stewart, Review of Merlin Swarz, *A Medieval Critique of Anthropomorphism: Ibn al-Jawzi's* Kitāb Akhbar aṣ-Ṣifāt: *A Critical Edition of the Arabic Text* (Leiden: Brill, 2002) in *Journal of the American Oriental Society* 124(3), 2004: 616–19.

XII. Learn how to transliterate properly. Transliteration seems tedious and boring, but it is important for the accurate transmission of information. Linguists are usually careful about this, and anthropologists and modernists the worst offenders. The most common error across the board is probably failure to represent doubled letters. Among those who ought to know better, the most stubborn errors are of the following type: *tarbiyyah* for *tarbiyah* "education," which follows the pattern *tafʿilah*, and *shāfiyyah* for *shāfiyah* "curing," which follows the pattern *fāʿilah*. I have just been reading Francis Robinson's *The ʿUlama of Farangi Mahall and Islamic Culture in South Asia*, in which these last mistakes are made with frightening regularity.[31]

XIII. Pay attention to dates. Know when the figures you are studying lived. Include dates in your writing whenever possible. Know the Islamic calendar thoroughly, and know the technicalities involved in reading dates in Islamic texts. *Laylat al-ithnayn* is the eve of Monday, not Monday night – as in Judaism, the day begins at sundown the previous evening. The term *ghurrah* refers to the 1st of the month; *niṣf* refers to the 15th of the month; *salkh* refers to the last day of the month. The months have typical epithets. There is much more.

XIV. Use theories when they are useful and help to produce a tangible result that would remain standing if the jargon were paraphrased or removed. Do not use a theory because it is the latest fad in religious studies, history or comparative literature. Theories are tools; use the right tool for the right job. Don't try to force a theory into a topic that it does not fit. This thesis opposes Hughes's directives, since he criticizes scholars for applying theories *selectively* (they should!). For example, Erving Goffman's *Stigma* and James Scott's *Hidden Transcripts* are helpful for the analysis of the behaviors of stigmatized minorities,

---

31 Francis Robinson, *The ʿUlama of Farangi Mahall and Islamic Culture in South Asia* (London: C. Hurst, 2001).

and Goffman's *The Presentation of Self in Everyday Life* is useful more widely. Bakhtin's "The Problem of Speech Genres" and Dell Hymes's *The Ethnography of Speaking* are useful for analysis of many types of oral discourse. Derrida's works are useful as an object lesson in how not to write in English.

XV. Know your field. If you are writing about Shiism, that is your field, even if you are an anthropologist. You should know what has been written about Shiism, and not only what anthropologists have written about Shiism.

XVI. Avoid fads. This also contradicts the advice Hughes gives when he urges scholars of Islamic studies to apply the latest religious studies theories in their work. Do not follow, propagate or advocate for the latest theoretical fad, and above all, do not treat it as an orthodoxy that must be forced on others and on account of which dissenters must be persecuted or pooh-poohed. If it really adds something to your work to use the term "cosmopolitanism," go ahead, but if, when you take away the word, there is no *there* there, or if adding it does not provide any additional results, desist.

XVII. Avoid jargon. Technical terms and shorthand may be necessary for scholarly exchange, but do not use the latest chic terms when the old ones were perfectly good and comprehensible, and do not overburden your prose with them unless they serve a tangible purpose in the argument. Use nuts-and-bolts language whenever possible. Don't say "methodology" when you mean "method." Don't say "unpack" when you can say "analyze." Don't call something "emerging" unless you are describing a gopher coming out of his hole. Feel free to add to this list.

XVIII. Do not make secondary literature the basis of your scholarship. Even if you set out to critique secondary scholarship, you can only do so well if you know the material those studies are arguing about. In most cases, original ideas do not come from reading someone else's summary that filters out the odd details and includes only those points that support a particular argument. Original ideas most often come from making an unexpected connection, and this occurs when one is reading the raw, unfiltered data.

XIX. Do not reinvent the wheel, if you can avoid it. Try to consult all relevant earlier studies before you publish your argument. This is getting more difficult to do as works in Islamic studies are growing in number and it has become impossible to keep up with all the subfields of Islamic studies. But do not assume that because it hasn't been written about in English your search is over. Communication barriers remain, even in the era of globalization, and it may take an extra effort to get around them. There is a great deal of scholarship in Russia, Turkey, Israel, Iran, the Arab countries and elsewhere that is not on the radar screens of Islamic studies specialists in the US, and it is sometimes quite difficult to gain access to it. Seek out learned informants who can check for you.

XX. Think about what will last. One hundred years from now, will this study remain valid? *Theorizing Islam* is concerned with a fleeting situation that will shortly pass over. It is a few rounds of a debate in the editorial column, when what we need in the field is the *OED*. (No such historical dictionary exists in Arabic; it would be quite massive. There is one for Persian, Dihkhudā's *Lughatnāmah*.) Sezgin's work on al-Bukhārī's sources will remain a solid contribution five hundred years from now.

XXI. Which Islam are you addressing? I tell my students that statements about Islam often conflate several levels that need to be teased apart for a serious analysis: (1) the ideals of Islam; (2) what the Qur'an actually says; (3) what Islamic law says; (4) what my grandfather/grandmother, the ideal Muslim, does; and (5) what run-of-the-mill Muslims actually do. One can of course generate more categories, but the important point is to understand that the Islam of these categories is potentially different and distinct and that conflating them can lead to serious misunderstandings. Another category that causes misinterpretations in the field is *ʿulamāʾ* "religious scholars," which are often viewed as one, undifferentiated category. Even when texts use this general term, the intended meaning is often a particular type of scholar, since the categories of scholar were divided by professional or academic category. Always try to determine whether *ʿulamāʾ* means jurists, theologians, philosophers, *ḥadīth* experts, or all of the above.

XXII. Give each study you write a title that fits the contents and reveals what they are. If others press you to make your title too broad, resist, especially when the gap between the title's implications and the contents of your study widens. The numbers of titles throughout the academy that violate this principle are legion. An example that I find amusing is Lawrence Rosen's *The Anthropology of Justice: Law as Culture in Islamic Society*.[32] The first half of the title encompasses all mankind, all cultures and all manifestations of law, while the second narrows it down to law in all of Islamdom, still a breathtaking expanse. The book is actually about several sessions of one court devoted to family law such as marriage, divorce, and so on, presided over by one judge in the Moroccan town of Sefrou.

XXIII. Solve a problem. Present a thesis that unravels a puzzle or reveals something *that was not obvious*. The number of works in academia that have weak theses or prove something that was obvious to begin with is astounding. Thousands of studies prove that poverty is miserable, that violence is evil, that abuse is unfair, that women did not have the same rights as men in this or that place and time – the list goes on. Do not follow suit. Avoid writing something to which the appropriate response is, "Didn't we know that already?"

---

32 Lawrence Rosen, *The Anthropology of Justice: Law as Culture in Islamic Society (Lewis Henry Morgan Lectures)* (Cambridge: Cambridge University Press, 1989).

XXIV. Study abroad. This is crucial for three purposes: to acquire language skills, to learn about a particular culture firsthand, and to be confronted with a culture that has a set of rules and assumptions that differ radically from one's own. The experience will make one a better scholar.

XXV. Translate book titles. Many scholars do not think to translate the titles of books they mention in their studies, but a title often reveals something important about the work or the thought of the author.

XXVI. Consult an expert. Admit ignorance when necessary, but whatever you do, show your work to someone who knows the field and the necessary languages and technicalities before you publish it. Scholars have a collective responsibility to reduce the number of embarrassing and incompetent statements published in their fields. However, the process requires you to be a good judge of who is competent enough to catch your slips; there are too many cases of the blind leading the blind. Unfortunately, some mistakes and typos will escape detection no matter how much you try; that's just how it is. In the old days, the great Orientalists would review new works in the field as they appeared, and after three or four reviews had been written, the main problems of the work had all been corrected and revised. The sheer number of publications makes this impossible at present.

XXVII. Due diligence is obligatory, especially when you plan to write outside your main area of training and scholarly focus. When you step into unfamiliar territory, expend the time and effort to produce responsible scholarship. Some scholars believe in sticking to one specialty or subfield, and many important scholars in the history of Islamic studies followed this rule. Louis Massignon wrote on mysticism, M.J. Kister wrote on hadith, and so on. There seems to be a gentlemen's agreement in Israel, for example, according to which scholars of Arabic and Islamic studies divide up the field into distinct furrows, each one sticking to his own furrow lest he disturb that of his neighbor. I don't know how this is enforced, or what pressures or discomforts it creates from the point of view of those on the inside, but from the outside it seems to work quite well, because experts tend to stick to the areas in which they are best prepared.

In my view it is not necessary for scholars in Islamic studies to stick to one subfield, particularly since there is so much to do and relatively few hands that are capable of doing serious work. A number of great scholars in the history of Islamic studies, such as Theodor Nöldeke (1836–1930) and Ignaz Goldziher (1850–1921), wrote on many different topics and excelled in many subfields. Gaping holes riddle many facets of Islamic religious history, which covers fourteen centuries and a geographical area larger than all the European countries combined. In addition, rigid separation between subfields can lead to a sort of ossification in some of them, in which the current orthodoxy is never challenged.

The first tactic, specialization, obviates the need to review all scholarship to date in a new field. If you opt for the second tactic, writing on several fields, you should become familiar with the relevant primary sources and the relevant tradition of secondary studies in that subfield in order to ensure that you make an original argument and write highly competent contributions. Scholars who write on the Qur'an often fail miserably in this regard. Scores of books on the market at present have been written by scholars who have a rudimentary knowledge of Arabic and have not read the most important works on Qur'anic studies in medieval Arabic or in German. The process of gaining mastery of the secondary scholarship is extremely time-consuming, and if one aspires to be the next Martin E. Marty, publishing a book every year, simply impossible. The problem is not that these scholars do not have the proper critical attitude or acumen, or are surreptitious propagandists for Islam, as Hughes seems to think, but rather that they have not done enough preparation to do a better job when they write on topics outside their expertise. To solve this problem, one should not rail against their apologetic tendencies but rather point out their identifiable omissions, mistakes and shortcomings.

I could go on to list additional technical skills such as paleography, but I believe that the theses presented above cover the main requirements for responsible Islamic studies. I have purposely provided specifics where I saw that Hughes's suggestions were vague. While Hughes insists that his theses are designed only for Islamic religious studies, I would claim the opposite: my theses apply not just to scholars in West Asia/Middle Eastern studies who are writing on Islam but rather to *anyone* who writes on Islam. Being an anthropologist, sociologist, literary critic, philosopher or religious studies specialist does not give one a pass, and background in any body of theory in those fields does not make up for incompetence in the areas listed above. I have faith in the long run – everything can be fixed, and even professors can remedy the gaps in their education. Finally, I would like to apologize to all those friends whose writings I have passed over in silence and so did not get their fair share of criticism. Your day will come.

Devin J. Stewart earned a BA magna cum laude in Near Eastern Studies from Princeton University in 1984 and a PhD with distinction in Arabic and Islamic Studies from the University of Pennsylvania in 1991. He now teaches in the Department of Middle Eastern and South Asian Studies at Emory University in Atlanta, Georgia. His areas of scholarly interest include Shiite Islam, the Qur'an, Islamic legal scholarship, biography and autobiography, Arabic speech genres, and other topics in Arabic and Islamic studies. He is the author of *Islamic Legal Orthodoxy* (Utah University Press, 1998) and *Disagreements of the Jurists* (NYU Press, 2015) and a co-author of *Interpreting the Self* (University of California Press, 2002).

Afterword

The Meaning and End of Scholarship on Religion[1]

Russell T. McCutcheon

> My own view is that a great deal of scholarship in the academy is shoddy work.
>
> – Devin Stewart in this volume

On February 21, 2016, Robert Jones (onetime Missouri State University faculty member and now founder and CEO of the Public Religion Research Institute[2]) appeared on MSNBC, to try to help explain the early support that then Republican candidate Donald Trump was receiving from so-called evangelical voters (80% of whom, according to exit polls on election day, voted for him).[3] For how can someone who, as described in a February 27, 2016 article in *The New York Times*, is "[a] twice-divorced candidate who has flaunted his adultery, praised Planned Parenthood and admitted to

---

1   Given the prominent place the work of Wilfred Cantwell Smith still plays for some in the field of Islamic studies, let alone the study of religion itself, I thought it was fitting to opt for a title related to one of his own but in an essay that called into question the approach represented by his work. (An earlier version of this chapter was published in *Culture and Religion* 18(1), 2017: 34–48.)

2   As described on its website, the PRRI "is a nonprofit, nonpartisan organization dedicated to research at the intersection of religion, values, and public life" (see: publicreligion.org/about/ [accessed February 25, 2016]).

3   See https://www.washingtonpost.com/news/acts-of-faith/wp/2016/11/09/exit-polls-show-white-evangelicals-voted-overwhelmingly-for-donald-trump/ (accessed March 5, 2017).

never asking for God's forgiveness,"[4] be so successfully courting this group of voters in the primaries? For although he seems not to possess their "values," they nonetheless support him inasmuch as – or so Jones claimed in his MSNBC interview – he successfully appeals to their sense of a bygone time in American history when their interests were dominant and unquestioned. (But is this a memory or a myth? – *that's the key question*, of course.) As Jones phrased it during the primaries (an analysis that proved prescient, given what happened in the November 2016 election): "White evangelical voters are showing themselves in this cycle not to be values voters, the way many of us have kind of been trained to think of them, but really to be what I call nostalgia voters." Elaborating, he made clear that, contrary to how many scholars usually think, those whom we call evangelical Christians in the US may not vote merely based on their supposedly single-minded attention to a small number of so-called religious issues (e.g., same sex marriage, abortion rights, etc.); instead, the interest among this subgroup in a candidate who repeatedly focused on illegal immigration and the ever-present danger of "others" (e.g., the promised "Muslim ban" that, once elected, his administration has had trouble making good on), building walls, saying it "like it is" and longing for the "good old days" (i.e., his campaign slogan: Make American Great Again) – to name but a few topics repeatedly highlighted at his rallies – suggested early on to Jones that these supporters might be better re-described as a "disaffected group of voters ... who feel their kind of cultural world in many ways is passing from the scene."

Whether Jones's analysis was persuasive or not at the time (he proved correct, by the way), what I found particularly interesting about that interview was the host's response. For, as soon as he finished his initial comment, NBC reporter Tamron Hall commented as follows:

> And a cynical person, Dr Jones, would say, then, what you're just saying, in a more harsh way, is that religion, perhaps, does

---

4 See the opening paragraph to: http://www.nytimes.com/2016/02/28/us/politics/donald-trump-despite-impieties-wins-hearts-of-evangelical-voters.html (accessed February 28, 2016).

not matter but the white culture and the preservation of what they saw as a nationalist attitude, or nativist attitude, is what matters more, and so they're looking for a guy who can win it for them, and putting religion and faith aside. That's what a cynical person would say about what you're describing here.[5]

Jones's reply to her rephrasing?

Well, I think these things are wrapped together; and so if you believe that the best thing for America is for a kind of conservative, Christian moral outlook to be, to kind of rule the day and kind of be dominant in the culture, then this is not cynical at all; this is actually, in a kind of roundabout way, it's pushing for values.

This exchange is instructive, I think – if we can even call it an exchange, since, in a way, they strike me as talking past each other, or at least the reporter spins his comments to suit her own narrative about race supplanting the importance of religion (a narrative that, evidenced in his reply, Jones thinks is far more complex). It's instructive because we see here two models of how we often talk about religion (whether in academia, as per the preceding chapters, or in non-technical public discourses, as per the MSNBC interview): while Jones adopts one in which items that we classify as religious are but always and already part of a hybrid cultural, historical, racial, economic, gendered, etc., situation (and so they inevitably mix and blend with innumerable other items, possibly gaining or losing significance, let alone gaining or losing the designation "religious" or "sacred," at almost any point along the way), Hall – exemplifying a classic and strictly binary logic that reflects a commonsense use of the term employed by many scholars, no less than anyone else – seems to understand religion to be a distinct and separate identity that one either does or does not possess (i.e., issues either are or are not religious). And so the puzzle for those adopting this latter approach is why religious voters are interested

---

5 These quotations were transcribed from the web version of the four-and-a-half minute interview at: http://www.msnbc.com/tamron-hall/watch/why-did-white-evangelical-voters-choose-trump-627694659803 (accessed February 25, 2016).

in what some might see as an irreligious politician. ("Surely their support of him would lessen after his 'grab them by the pussy' comment aired during the election campaign – no?" such a person might ask.) But for the scholar who assumes the former position – the one adopted by Jones – there is no puzzle to self-described evangelicals (i.e., members of what we once called the Moral Majority) supporting Trump, for their so-called religious identity is presumed to intersect at a variety of points with, say, their economic and political, even nationalist and, yes, racial, interests. Which interest is operationalized at which moment is then the key issue to examine.

Or, to rephrase, the media and pundits only had a problem to solve concerning why evangelicals were apparently so supportive (aka forgiving?) of Trump's supposed indiscretions if they assumed certain things about this designator religion that they used to name this group of voters in the first place. Had they instead seen them as self-interested and strategic social agents working with what was at hand to attain shared, practical interests within their subgroup, and in competition with other subgroups (as the so-called Moral Majority also had been doing, like any group), then perhaps there would have been no problem to solve.

I open this Afterword by referencing this interview (from a primary season that, by now, likely seems to be ancient history for readers in the US), not to preoccupy us with the sport known as American politics or to exemplify the challenges that face any academic with dreams of becoming a public intellectual (and thus dealing with the supposed price of making accessible generalities, as described in an early chapter or two); instead, I cite the reporter either missing or just talking past an approach that takes seriously classificatory ambiguity and multiple social interests – a reporter who apparently sees (and dismisses?) such a more nuanced starting point as "cynical" – as an example of an attitude that is just as present within the academy as anywhere else. Yet while possibly being understandable when coming from a television news reporter – whose training hardly touches upon things with which the historically-oriented and, ideally, critically self-conscious scholar of religion is often said to be concerned – seeing scholars reject as cynical, overly critical, reductionistic, dismissive and disrespectful, etc., any approach that fails to reproduce and thereby sanction a people's own commonsense view of the world is troubling, to say the least. Yet today, in a variety of the study of religion's subfields (as more than one contributor in this volume has pointed out – none more vehemently than Devin Stewart), the stance of this reporter remains far more widespread than the stance of this scholar; it is therefore not difficult to find claims that scholarship that rigorously historicizes what we could term the folk or commonsense way people talk about their own worlds when queried about them – i.e., their understanding of their goals, their understanding of their past and their sense that they and not others constitute a specific sort of "we" – is inappropriate, even disrespectful, because (as that old adage went) it fails to take religious people *seriously*.

What's lamentable to me, then, is that aiming simply to describe (aka summarize) the meanings some people claim to be making and experiencing (and, in the process, failing to realize that people talk about their goals, their past and their meanings when we, the outsiders, ask them about them) sometimes passes as the end of scholarship, thereby curtailing any form of higher-order analysis (or redescription, in the language of theory).

Among the many subfields in which this happens I have in mind, for the sake of this volume, Islamic studies – at least as it is often practiced in the academic study of religion; I should repeat, however, so that this critique is not misread as unfairly focusing on this one area, that, yes, it is hardly unique (despite some claiming this to be the case[6]) in being an area where scholarly advocacy for normalizing a specific sort of discursive object (variously known, using a nomenclature found in other subfields as well, as authentic Islam, lived Islam, embodied Islam, progressive Islam, orthodox Islam, classical Islam or Islam on the ground) is portrayed as not just one acceptable model among others but is, instead, generally seen as the only legitimate way to study how people known as Muslims actually talk, act, think and organize. That few who carry out such work would likely see it as advocacy (calling it, instead, engaged, serious

---

6   I think here of Juliane Hammer's recent reference to what some refer to as "Islamic studies exceptionalism" (2016a: 26) in a set of *JAAR* papers to be discussed below – an assumption contested by Brockopp (2016).

or rigorous scholarship) also deserves to be noted, of course; for they might portray their work as a species of postcolonial ethnography, one that finally allows the Other to speak for him- or herself. That such work fails to treat all Others comparably, however, and that it fails to engage in any sort of explanatory analysis and, instead, is deeply invested in documenting just some participants' views of the world either as the people might talk about it themselves or, better yet, as the scholars themselves wish to talk about it (after all, as already noted, it's the scholars who arrive and ask all the questions, for their own purposes), is something that we cannot overlook if, appealing to that earlier word, we're actually *serious* about the so-called reflexive turn in the field. Over the years I've discussed these problems at a variety of sites across the study of religion, to be sure (e.g., consider how scholars often dehistoricize and spiritualize almost anything to do with what we know as Buddhism [see McCutcheon 1997: 167 ff.]), and with regard to the study of Islam in particular it is something I've explicitly addressed at least twice before (i.e., all throughout McCutcheon 2005 [a book written out of frustration for the sort of dehistoricizing discourse on Islam that arose in much of the academy post-9/11] and also in McCutcheon 2012 [which focused explicitly on the controversy around Hughes's recent work on Islam]).[7] Inasmuch as the problems have not gone away – and, moreover, in light of the fact that, in my reading, some of the previous chapters strike me as exemplifying them – this Afterword provides an occasion to revisit the topic yet again.

Now, what makes Hughes's work controversial to some – traits present in almost all of his recent work on Islam (e.g., Hughes 2007, 2012c, 2015, and I would also include his critique of the concept

7   McCutcheon 2012 is an introduction to a set of papers; it details the story behind the appearance in *MTSR* of one of Hughes's earlier essays on the current state of Islamic studies within the study of religion (it was published along with responses solicited by the journal); it was an essay originally submitted to and then rejected by the *Journal of the American Academy of Religion* (for which I had served as one of its outside readers – part of the backstory I disclose in the introduction). His essay instead appeared in *MTSR* because, as Hughes was told when it was rejected by the AAR's journal, one of *JAAR*'s anonymous reviewers thought that it was too controversial.

Abrahamic religions [2012a]) – is that he refuses to play favorites (to borrow an apt phrase from Hughes's co-editor at *Method & Theory in the Study of Religion* [Ramey 2015][8]). Instead, derivation and difference play a leading role throughout his work – a role we would reasonably expect of any scholar who, to use that word once again, takes the historical details (i.e., the contingent, the happenstance, the situated, along with competing human interests and unintended consequence) *seriously*. But this is hardly everyone's approach; for instance, as Jonathan Brockopp has mostly recently (and rightly, I think) observed, at least in the case of class resources on the study of Islam, "[m]any ... writers follow ... [the] lead" of popular writers on Islam who often "aim to present a clear story without getting bogged down in details" (2016: 29). Case in point: consider the opening to no less than Jane McAuliffe's section on Islam in volume 2 of *The Norton Anthology of World Religions* (Miles 2015 – though certainly *not* a textbook, it strikes me as a book pitched at the introductory reader all the same). Predictably, it adopts an exclusively descriptive voice, telling readers how various (though mostly authoritative) Muslim actors understood their own worlds. While this is not unimportant at the level of data, failing to move a reader to any sort of analysis (what Hughes, I believe, means by recommending we engage with theories of religion in doing work on Islam, let alone any other group) is a severe shortcoming.

As an example, consider McAuliffe's section entitled "The History of the Qur'anic Text," which begins as follows:

> Conventional accounts of the history of the qur'anic text ordinarily begin with its oral conveyance in the Prophet's initial preaching. Then they move to the period after his death, the decades of the early caliphs. During this era, the Qur'an was "collected" from the memories of its first recipients and from whatever written fragments could be found. A small team of

---

8 Ramey's term is not unrelated to what Jonathan Brockopp refers to as "incidental normativity" – such as the often unarticulated scholarly "presumption that Islam is unique among the world's religions" (2016: 28–9). "This view," he then goes on to comment, "is a parallel to the apologetic claim that Islam was perfect and complete in Muhammad's lifetime ...."

> scribes set down the collected portions in an assemblage of chapters, or suras, arranging them roughly from the longest to the shortest .... (Miles 2015: 1379)

You will find in her text no other account of the Qur'an's origins; for, contrary to how one might read her opening line ("Conventional accounts ... ordinarily begin with..."), as if it sets up an eventual description of, for lack of a better term, an alternative and thus unconventional or unordinary (i.e., analytic or scholarly) account, *no redescription is offered* and thus there is no change in authorial voice – simply put, the other shoe never drops. Sadly, in the case of much work in our field, there is no other shoe to be dropped. Instead, readers learn what influential participants think of their own text and that's all. Interestingly, David Biale's introduction to his section on Judaism, in the same Norton volume, is careful to distinguish the presumption of some participants for how the Tanakh was produced from how scholars discuss it: "it is the product of many hands, including even the Torah, which tradition holds to have been written by Moses," he writes (Miles 2015: 56). In fact, he proceeds to inform his readers that the Book of Deuteronomy, for example, "written most probably at the end of the seventh century BCE ... [w]as composed *in the form of* a speech by Moses before his death..." (57; emphasis added), giving a significant nod to a few centuries' worth of scholarly work on the compositional history of a text (a viewpoint significantly different from those who yet maintain that, in the case of those early Hebrew texts, Moses actually wrote them). And Lawrence Cunningham's introduction to the same anthology's section on Christianity (notably the shorter introduction to his initial sub-section, entitled "The Apostolic Era [4 BCE–100 CE]"), presupposes the Markan priority thesis, thereby giving a nod of his own to no less serious scholarship on the compositional history of the New Testament (as a body of literature that, in this volume, Crossley rightly recommends as offering a few lessons of use in the study of Islam) and, in particular, the first three Gospels – an approach that produces a story rather different from the conventional view of many Christians whom we might interview about their book (let alone from those scholars who still prioritize the text of Matthew).

But unlike Hughes's work, which ensures readers are familiar with, as he phrases it in his own introductory book, "a very different account of the emergence of Islam" (2013: 34) – i.e., the work of such scholars as Patricia Crone, John Wansbrough, Michael Cook, etc. – and not just, as he puts it, "[t]he customary presentation" (2013: 20), McAuliffe's text never entertains that a scholarly apparatus is needed to make sense of how participants themselves talk about their worlds. Instead, inasmuch as these origins stories – "[l]ike the myths of Moses receiving the commandments on Sinai and the death and resurrection of Jesus" (Hughes 2013: 34) – are just that, *origins narratives*, as scholars we should likely presume that they represent the interests of later generations (their "backward projections," as Hughes phrases it [2013: 23]), developed in their effort to define themselves and, by means of a discourse on the past, authorize that self-understanding (on the politics of origins see McCutcheon 2015a). The tales are therefore not just to be reported on; but this shift in the camera angle, one that allows us to see the local account as itself being curious and deserving of study for reasons not necessarily shared by those who tell the tales, is a shift that McAuliffe (like many others) fails to make.

That Hughes more than acknowledges the temptation for scholars not to make this critical shift can't be overlooked; in fact, he consistently tips his hat at the conundrum. So, with this in mind, he makes plain from the outset that his intro book, *Muslim Identities*, is written for those who "are unused to or uncomfortable with speaking about religion using terms and categories normally relegated to explicating more mundane phenomena" (2013: xi). So, he ironically (at least for his detractors) aims to reach what he characterizes as a middle ground by not only offering careful description of how some (maybe even many) participants themselves might discuss a topic (his minor errors, as some reviewers have pointed out, notwithstanding) – e.g., recounting a traditional tale of the Prophet's migration from Mecca to Medina, etc. – but then also moving on to the sort of analysis that we would undoubtedly expect of scholarship on virtually any other human act or organization, i.e., work that presses beyond certain insider views of homogeneous or monolithic social life developing along a linear path and, instead, recovers evidence from the archive (as we *happen* to have it) of what the social theorist might characterize as a more meandering historical trail of debate, disagreement, compromise, unanticipated result, etc.

And that's what sets Hughes's work apart, in my reading, from that of many of his peers – e.g., that technical, social theory terminology, such as the category myth (defined as something other than a lie, of course), social formation, inheritance, innovation, anachronism, not to mention origins and authenticity (both seen as contestable claims made by situated social actors rather than as descriptive realities[9]), along with the names of such theorists as Benedict Anderson, Jean-François Bayart, Pierre Bourdieu and Bruce Lincoln, regularly appear in his work, nearly as frequently as do an insider discourse of transliterated Arabic terms and the names of various theologians thought by many to be important to this thing called "the tradition." And it is the fact that both are present – not just a recapitulation of the emic discourse but also an accompanying etic, comparative and explanatory analysis – that, although making Hughes provocative to some, ensures that, from where I sit, his work is essential reading. In fact, although his 2013 book is an introduction to the study of Islam alone we would do well to have a comparable volume for each of those groups studied in the typical world religions class. For example, where is the introduction that did not just tell us about antique cross-legged carvings along with stories of ancient peoples living along the Indus River Valley (as if they lead irresistibly to modern-day Hindus) but which, as well, made plain the role played by colonial-era bureaucrats and scholars (the ones who came up with that tale of the Indo-Europeans that we today tell as if it was historical fact [see Arvidsson 2006]), all of which ensured that we today feel confident in talking so casually about some supposedly unified thing in the world called Hinduism. For while the latter thesis is now hardly controversial for some scholars (case in point: consider Josephson's book on the invention of the notion of religion in modern Japan [2012]), it has yet to fully make

---

9   For example: "Accounts of Islamic origins, like the accounts of religious origins more generally, are largely projections by later groups attempting to read their own agendas into or onto the earliest period with an eye toward legitimation" (Hughes 2013: 36).

its way into the classroom – a place where students all across the disciplines are still generally told the (admittedly, appealing) story of pristine origins and linear development (a point documented in McCutcheon 1997: ch. 4).

But, as noted above, and as stated somewhat provocatively in my epigraph, the trouble is that simplistic narratives are not only present in textbooks. As another example of the endemic nature of this problem in our field's study of Islam, I'd like to consider some of the papers published at the start of 2016 in the *Journal of the American Academy of Religion* (our field's widest circulating scholarly, peer-review periodical). Originating at a session at the 2013 annual AAR meeting (held in Baltimore that year – a panel to which, as I recall, Hughes was originally asked to respond, though he did not attend the session; no response from him appears with the subsequently published AAR papers[10]), the papers assess the current state of normativity in Islamic studies, as carried out in our field. Despite his absence from this set of papers, what's curious is that almost all of the contributors at least implicitly situate themselves in relation to Hughes's work – so it's not only that without his unremitting critique I doubt such a panel would have been organized, but several of the papers cite his programmatic *MTSR* essay (2012b) while one goes to lengths to critique it.[11]

The tone of the *JAAR* collection of essays is set from the start in Juliane Hammer's introduction, where the papers' overall theme is described as involving a discussion of "the elusive boundary between theology and the study of religion" (2016a: 26).[12] As might

---

10 Instead, Anna Gade (2016) responds; described as a scholar of eco-Islam, she is a Chicago-trained historian of religions who is professor at the Nelson Institute for Environmental Studies at the University of Wisconsin – Madison.

11 I have in mind Zareena Grewal's essay, which makes the interesting move to characterize Hughes's critique of the field as an emotional reflex characteristic of defensive posturing prompted by anxiety (2016: 46; see Gade's response to this set of papers for a similar characterization about this "old anxiety in religious studies" [2016: 113]).

12 In her own paper in the set Hammer elaborates: "The position of the objective scholar as free of positionality and/or religious commitment has

be evident to readers, for Hughes and other vocal critics in the field there is nothing "elusive" about this boundary and to claim as much already skews the conversation away from his position significantly, as if the starting point is that these two pursuits (i.e., the articulation and defense of, for lack of a better term, the faith as opposed to studying those who articulate and defend it) are somehow easily (or productively?) conflated. This skewing of the issue is further accomplished in Hammer's opening paragraph where she claims that the debate is between normative and prescriptive studies, at the one end of the spectrum, and "*supposedly* more critical scholarship" at the other (2016a: 25; emphasis added). This qualifier, "supposedly," does much work, of course, for the seemingly broad spectrum has just been flattened considerably, inasmuch as, upon closer look, critical scholarship may not be so critical after all, and thus akin to the very thing it tries to disallow from admission to the academy. (This too is the point argued in Bazzano's paper in the same set).

It's a key move, this flattening, when scholars are intent not just on studying religion but (as was Eliade when he described his "new humanism" back in 1961's inaugural issue of *History of Religions*) also on normalizing and authorizing specific social worlds by means of the information they create and control as scholars – something Hammer herself engages in, I'd argue, when, as she phrases it in her introduction, she asserts that "all scholarship is based on normative claims and assumptions" – an assertion that she then describes as "an important step in reclaiming the humanities as a tool for change in contemporary society" (2016a: 26–7). While I have no idea from whom she wishes to "reclaim" the Humanities (as if it has been hijacked?) or, at this point, what sort of societal changes she wishes to enact (this becomes more evident in her own paper in the set), a strategic move is being made here, one also made by Zareena Grewal

---

been thoroughly debunked as a patriarchal as well as white normative construction that restricts access to the secular academic" (2016b: 99). That her project for "making societal change both a moral and intellectual imperative for scholarship" (100) is anchored in a quote from the work of a bearded white male (i.e., Karl Marx) is either ironic or demonstrates the hegemonic nature of the good toward which she thinks her work moves us.

(in her own *JAAR* paper) when she conjectures: "If we understand normativity to mean any and all claims directing people to ways they ought to act or think, then *all* scholarly activity is inevitably normative and interested" (2016: 45). But what if this is *not* how we understand normativity? In other words, such a move vacates this term "normative" of specificity by universalizing it, such that now *everyone is normative* – and thus no one is normative, thereby opening the proverbial big tent of our field to any and all approaches, since they're apparently all no less normative.[13]

To rephrase: seeing normative claims about how, for example, society *ought* to work or concerning the existence and features of powerful, invisible beings as indistinguishable from, say, claims concerning how to go about doing comparison in the university classroom (what Thomas Lewis, appreciatively cited by Grewal, calls the "norms for scholarship itself" [2011: 171]) is the first step to allow such a flawed project to get off the ground. And I say it is flawed because those offering such critiques fail to understand what I would characterize as the difference between what others before me termed methodological reductionism and metaphysical reductionism. As I phrased it in an earlier work:

> [B]ecause I presume this natural world to be a complex place of competing judgments and interests, I also presume that no human community knows what is *really* going on in it. (2003: 151)

"Metaphysical reductionism," I then concluded, "simply makes no sense to me as an explanatory option." Instead, our conclusions – as

---

13 It's an amateurish move, to be honest, akin to saying that because my syllabus makes claims on students (e.g., specifying due dates, required style of submitted essays, policies on missed tests, etc.) then I'm being no less normative than the things that I study in my classes, thus eliminating, or at least blurring, the line between insider and outsider. That my syllabus makes no claim about the point of human existence or what happens after death – to name but two domains where the stakes are rather higher than needing one-inch margins and 12-point font – strikes me as so obvious a distinction in types or zones of normativity that it actually seems to be just a little silly to address such criticisms.

evidenced in the indented quote above – are premised on assumptions, on shared scholarly conventions, etc., always forming a conditional "if/then" argument: if you grant me X then I'm able to say Y about the world. We are therefore careful to note that our claims are not anchored in a correspondence to the real world (i.e., we are not competing with the people whom we study when it comes to the claims we make about the world, for we are playing entirely different games); instead, they are a function of *our* interests, assumptions, tools, theories, rubrics, etc., and, for instance, should you share those interests, then you may find the claims that I make to be helpful in going about your own work (and thus we arrive at scholarly research traditions, schools of thought, departments, disciplines, etc.). In the case of the academic study of religion, this is a game suited to be played within the public university and within any domain where we work toward making rational claims about a world that we presume to be inter-subjectively available (i.e., our claims can be empirically applied and tested/critiqued, such that my claim about this or that ritual can be contested by you). Nothing is premised on an ontology and so, contrary to Lewis, who notes in that set of journal papers that "we make normative claims whenever we try to identify '*what is really going on here*'" (2011: 175; emphasis added), scholars of religions whom I have in mind as models for the profession – Hughes among them – never aim to make such a metaphysical (i.e., normative) statement about *what is really going on anywhere*; and thus, strictly speaking, they are *not* normative in the way that those whom they study are (i.e., those making claims about, say, the origins of the universe, it's ultimate meaning, etc.). It's therefore not news to us that our claims are always partial and limited – of course they are. How could it be otherwise?[14]

14 I have in mind here Gade's reply to the *JAAR* set: "the discipline of the academic study of religion offers tools that are useful, but, ones that are nevertheless limited and acquired only with some effort" (2016: 114). In the hands of some this limitation is a way to, in turn, argue for the need to supplement such tools by those which offer a bigger or the whole picture. This secondary move is one that I would resist for it conflates to two reductions mentioned in my main text. Scholars of religion whom I have in mind do not set out to offer the whole picture because they (i) own their questions,

What is ironic to me, then, is that the flattening of our understanding of normativity that this flawed project requires doesn't, as Hammer sees it, "expand the boundaries of the debate" at all; for, as with that set of *JAAR* papers completely lacking the explicit voice of someone like Hughes to counter and thereby contest their authors' claims, it ensures that the boundary (dare I refer to it as a bubble?) around this one subfield is shrunk and policed all the more tightly and thus effectively – for it's not that all approaches are now possible (as these writers maintain, Hughes's absence notwithstanding) but, instead, approaches once ruled to be significantly out of bounds (inasmuch as they were engaged in what we once termed theologically constructive projects internal to one or more religions and not interested in the empirical, historical, cross-cultural study of religion) are now admitted and those who engage in what we once called *Religionswissenschaft* are marginalized in what they once considered to be their own field (their work is characterized in this one set of papers as old, ill-considered, unprincipled, etc. – simply put, appealing again to that word, it fails to take religion *seriously*). Case in point: consider the entire issue of *JAAR* that starts off 2016 and in which the above-mentioned papers appear. We not only find there a series of articles advocating for the admission of theologically normative approaches to the study of Islam (e.g., among them is also Bazzano's paper on furthering interreligious dialogue by means of comparative studies of Qur'anic exegesis [2016]) along with the new editor oddly, to my way of thinking, characterizing the field as "our effort to divine what marks humankind's adventure with mystery, meaning, and community" (Eller 2016: 2 – "mystery" seems a curious code word to appease those among us who see the field as being about more than just studying human beings), but also the issue includes the immediate past AAR President discussing a scholar of religion's specific duties to help solve global warming (Zoloth 2016)[15] along with an

---

methods, and thus findings while (ii) seeing rhetorics of the whole as being just that – socially efficacious *rhetorics* rather than descriptions of actual states of affairs.

15 See ch. 8 of McCutcheon 2015b – "And That's Why No One Takes the Humanities Seriously" – for my own thoughts on Zoloth's overly ambitious

article that offers lessons from Christian missiological studies and other "theological and religious ways knowing" to assist the study of religion in grappling with issues of self and other (Lybarger 2016).

Given these contents, no doubt put in place by the immediate past editor (given that this issue is the new editor's first and responsible editors usually pass along a pipeline filled with articles to their successors), if anyone is going to argue for a field being hijacked it might be those who worked so hard, over the past generations, to establish the academic study of religion ....

And this is where I return explicitly to my opening; for the gap between these two ways of approaching our material ensures that those who wish to do something other than *study* Islam (or Judaism, Buddhism, Hinduism, Christianity, etc.) as, for lack of a better term, a variegated socio-historical identity or a rhetoric used by actors to carve out a place in the world (i.e., the never-ending work of social formation) – nothing more and nothing less – are seen by others as cynical, to recall that MSNBC reporter's words, or as "debunking ... Muslim normative beliefs and claims" (Grewal 2016: 46). Grewal elaborates:

> To adopt a definition of criticism and reflexivity that is so narrow as to require a scholar to have a skeptical and perhaps even hostile relationship to the normative beliefs of Muslims is to posit religion as beyond the realm of reason, as that which cannot be argued about .... Furthermore, Hughes' position elides the fact that all scholars of religion have normative investments of their own by unnecessarily resurrecting the perennial religious studies debate about insiders/outsiders, or believers/nonbelievers. (46)

At this point I feel I've sufficiently addressed, here and elsewhere, the spurious moves made in such a critique and can therefore simply add that it seems to me that, not unlike my opening's reporter talking past the scholar, such writers are – as we say in politics (especially during

---

presumption that scholars of religion, inasmuch as we study religion, have "a role specific duty" (as she phrased it in her call to AAR program unit chairs, in advance of the 2014 meeting) to help solve the global warming crisis.

Presidential elections here in the US) – simply playing to their base, with no interest in a substantive engagement with scholarly interlocutors who may question the merits of their arguments. (What's more, Grewal's claim that "Hughes himself remains committed to the possibility of 'real' scholarship about 'real' Islam," an approach that reifies the category belief" [2016: 47], prompts me to wonder how carefully critics have even read him over the years.[16]) For only if one thinks that a scholar of religion's task is to nurture the object of study would one refer to Hughes's careful efforts to pay attention to the historical details as aiming to debunk Islam or be hostile to it. (Yet if one is working to limit what legitimately counts as Islam – or Christianity, or Taoism, etc. – in order to highlight a particular strand, then I could indeed see Hughes's interest to pay attention to a broad range of Islamic argumentation and social organization as undermining one's ends.) This sort of thin-skinned rhetoric, to my way of thinking, is an indictment of those who use it, for it betrays a bit of a scorched-earth policy whereby one's aim is to cast all adversaries beyond the pale – hardly the sort of move one would expect from a field that revels in, as Hammer phrased it above, "expand[ing] the boundaries of the debate." Instead, much like calling someone a heretic in an earlier era, it stifles debate and thereby marks the end of discourse and thus scholarship as many of us have come to know it.

What is particularly concerning is that even Jonathan Brockopp, whose contribution to the *JAAR* roundtable is rather critically-minded

---

16 That she assumes that an approach somehow giving us access to how Muslims *think* and their *ideas* rather than what they *believe* (Grewal 2016: 49) offers a difference of any consequence is itself rather interesting, but not nearly as interesting, I maintain, as her advocacy for a discursive approach that somehow allows us to "engage in the knowledge schemes of Muslim subjects without imposing our own epistemological framework and calling their ways of knowing into question" (57–8; although worrying over imposition is also a theme of Eltantawi's paper on this panel [2015: 63], she seems not to mind asking what our terms modernity and postmodernity "mean" to Nigerians, as if these are commonsense designators of significance to local discourses there) – as if the discursive method was itself somehow transparent and in-step with reality itself. Such advocacy for a consequence-free method should strike readers as rather suspicious.

in many regards (e.g., recognizing just how little material evidence from the early years of Islam we have), also presents us with claims that deserve closer attention. For instance, while observing that "literary accounts of early Islamic history are no longer read as simple mirrors of the past" – a view that suggests a far more complex view of the past than we find in the work of some scholars of religion – he then proceeds to claim that "rather, they reflect the *imaginaire* of the moment in which those accounts were written" (2016: 36). But I'm not sure what gain has been made here – and thus whether this amounts to the shift in the field as Hughes might make it – since in both cases a text is presumed to be a gateway to some unified, originary moment in the past (whether in the mind of an author or the *imaginaire* of a group), a presumption that fails to understand texts as historical artifacts, i.e., as the product of countless possibly disconnected social actors, across generations and in a variety of settings, working for any number of different ends, all of which results, from our point of view in the present, in an item that we, long after them, name and read as a unified thing called a text. By the way, one does not have to buy the entire "Death of the Author" critique to agree with the point just made; for after even just a passing glance at the Barthean or Foucaultian discussion on the author function (but are these the sorts who scholars of religion qua descriptivists even read?) we can at least acknowledge – no? – that texts do not necessarily "reflect" (a term used by Brockopp that's remarkably close to the notion of mirroring that, by the way, we supposedly no longer subscribe to, or so he claims) their time of origins, their author's assumptions about the world, let alone anything about a supposedly coherent group that's behind them.

In yet another example of this tendency to diminish the critical insights that seem at first to be offered, Brockopp later argues that "Islam itself had rather fuzzy boundaries in the early centuries, with Muslims and Christians worshipping at common sites" (2016: 36); contrary to Hughes's discussion (e.g., see ch. 1 of *Muslim Identities*) in which it is clear that modern notions of distinct identities are routinely (and more than likely incorrectly) read back, anachronistically, onto what is only later seen as an emergent period, Brockopp does history by presuming the distinctions we today take for granted, going only so far as to portray them as "fuzzy" back then. For if indeed he is correct when he later argues that "there was a Qu'ran by the late seventh century, and it was a book, but what that book meant and how it was used ... still remain unclear" (37), then on what basis can we presume a coherent group with an *imaginaire* (fuzzy boundaries and all) lurking behind the text?

The problem, of course, is that it is *we* who are building, in his words, the "contextual framework to place what little evidence we possess into a developmental scheme" (Brockopp 2016: 35, 37) – a modern, inevitably anachronistic and always self-serving constructive activity that lacks any experimental control since it is referencing a period for which we have, as he acknowledges, so little historical evidence. So what's to govern our fabrications, other than the contemporary interests that we may happen to have? For we cannot compare our work to an original, to see how accurately we got it. (And thus my problem with scholars who argue that alternative readings are "misinterpretations.") Even when studying contemporary social actors, whose own assessments can most certainly judge our scholarly constructions, this is still a problem, of course (as more careful anthropologists have long told us); for, as noted twice already, we can't afford to overlook that people's claims and answers are to the questions *that we have posed* and were offered in *the situations in which we have put them* (i.e., making interview subjects of them – what Louis Althusser called interpellation) – questions and settings reflective of *our* curiosities and travel grants, and not to be confused with naturally-occurring facts on the ground, as it were. And so into these unavoidable historical and social gaps we have no choice but to inject ourselves (here Brockopp's useful notion of incidental normativity re-enters the discussion, exemplified nicely in the usually unrecognized problem of anachronism in historical writing[17]).

---

17 For instance, consider how we casually name early Islam "a religion" and see it as inherently comparable to those other things we call religions (i.e., Judaism and Christianity), each conceived as itself being internally homogeneous, regardless of acknowledgments that their borders may have been porous.

This is the moment when Hughes's interest in documenting and taking seriously a social formation's inevitably "murky backdrop in which memory and desire, fact and fiction, collide" (2013: 18) offers us a way to moderate the accounts we hear; it is a moment when, inasmuch as we start out by assuming that no anchor can stabilize this murky backdrop, attempts to anchor these otherwise shifting identities can be made evident, allowing us to examine the often overlooked, contingent circumstances, focusing on those moments when alternatives were present and possible (and contested). Studying that anchoring activity itself, i.e., the processes of derivation and how human beings across time have grappled with difference, is what this alternative tradition in the field tries to address – an approach with which I pretty obviously resonate. Unlike Grewal's claim, then, I would argue that it is not an aim that "distracts us from the fact that the object of our study, Islam, is also the source of scholarly disciplines, with norms of study, research and criticism" (2016: 46). On the contrary, her plural nouns need to occupy us – disciplines, norms – thereby inviting us to look for agreements and disagreements, differences and, yes, even contests, in telling the story of how it is that so many today casually talk of this thing called Islam (not to mention Christianity or Shinto, etc., etc.).

To tell such an alternative tale, as is evident from the reception of Hughes's work (data for which can be found in some of the preceding chapters), is to swim upstream, no doubt about it (as the state of the field, at least as represented in that *JAAR* issue, should make plain), but his is an approach that's tough to ignore, both because of the way it takes history (aka contingency) seriously and because of its untiring optimism that at least some readers will be up to the challenge of seeing the end of scholarship as something other than what the people whom we study told us about themselves. To significantly repurpose Gade's generally affirmative response to what I find to be that deeply problematic AAR roundtable (2016: 125), I can borrow and revise her response's closing words to say that it is reassuring for me to know that Hughes, along with a small but dedicated group of scholars, continues to challenge the apparent consensus that all along we have been doing the best job we could when it comes to how we study religion. For if this is the best we can do – and please remember,

Stewart, not I, called most of it shoddy – and if the *JAAR* roundtable represents what most of us think the meaning and purpose of scholarship ought to be (whether on Islam or any other topic in the study of religion), then I have serious concerns for the future of the field.

References

Arvidsson, Stefan. 2006. *Aryan Idols: Indo-European Mythology as Ideology and Science*, trans. Sonia Wichmann. Chicago: University of Chicago Press.

Bazzano, Elliott. 2016. "Normative Readings of the Qur'an: From the Premodern Middle East to the Modern West." *Journal of the American Academy of Religion* 84(1): 74–97. https://doi.org/10.1093/jaarel/lfv103

Brockopp, Jonathan E. 2016. "Islamic Origins and Incidental Normativity." *Journal of the American Academy of Religion* 84(1): 28–43. https://doi.org/10.1093/jaarel/lfv094

Eller, Cynthia. 2016. "Editor's Note." *Journal of the American Academy of Religion* 84(1): 1–2. https://doi.org/10.1093/jaarel/lfw056

Eltantawi, Sarah. 2016. "What Does 'Modernity' and 'Postmodernity' Mean to Northern Nigerians?" *Journal of the American Academy of Religion* 84(1): 60–73. https://doi.org/10.1093/jaarel/lfv096

Gade, Anna M. 2016. "Roundtable on Normativity in Islamic Studies: A Response." *Journal of the American Academy of Religion* 84(1): 113–26. https://doi.org/10.1093/jaarel/lfv121

Grewal, Zareena. 2016. "Destabilizing Orthodoxy, De-territorializing the Anthropology of Islam." *Journal of the American Academy of Religion* 84(1): 44–59. https://doi.org/10.1093/jaarel/lfv095

Hammer, Juliane. 2016a. "Roundtable on Normativity in Islamic Studies: Introduction." *Journal of the American Academy of Religion* 84(1): 25–7. https://doi.org/10.1093/jaarel/lfv123

— 2016b. "To Work for Change: Normativity, Feminism, and Islam." *Journal of the American Academy of Religion* 84(1): 98–112. https://doi.org/10.1093/jaarel/lfv097

Hughes, Aaron W. 2007. *Situating Islam: The Past and Future of an Academic Discipline*. Sheffield, UK: Equinox.

— 2012a. *Abrahamic Religions: On the Uses and Abuses of History*. New York: Oxford University Press. https://doi.org/10.1093/acprof:oso/9780199934645.001.0001

— 2012b. "The Study of Islam Before and After September 11: A Provocation." *Method & Theory in the Study of Religion* 24(4/5): 314–36. https://doi.org/10.1163/15700682-12341234

— 2012c. *Theorizing Islam: Disciplinary Deconstruction and Reconstruction.* Sheffield, UK: Equinox.

— 2013. *Muslim Identities: An Introduction to Islam.* New York: Columbia University Press.

— 2015. *Islam and the Tyranny of Authenticity: An Inquiry into Disciplinary Apologetics and Self-Deception.* Sheffield, UK: Equinox.

Josephson, Jason Ananda. 2012. *The Invention of Religion in Japan.* Chicago: University of Chicago Press. https://doi.org/10.7208/chicago/9780226412351.001.0001

Lewis, Thomas A. 2011. "On the Role of Normativity in Religious Studies," in Robert A. Orsi, ed., *The Cambridge Companion to Religious Studies* (pp. 168–85). New York: Cambridge University Press. https://doi.org/10.1017/CCOL9780521883917.010

Lybarger, Loren D. 2016. "How Far is too Far? Defining Self and Other in Religious Studies and Christian Missiology." *Journal of the American Academy of Religion* 84(1): 127–56.

McCutcheon, Russell T. 1997. *Manufacturing Religion: The Discourse on Sui Generis Religion and the Politics of Nostalgia.* New York: Oxford University Press.

— 2003. *The Discipline of Religion: Structure, Meaning, Rhetoric.* New York: Routledge. https://doi.org/10.4324/9780203451793

— 2005. *Religion and the Domestication of Dissent, or How to Live in a Less than Perfect Nation.* New York: Routledge.

— 2012. "The State of Islamic Studies in the Study of Religion: An Introduction." *Method & Theory in the Study of Religion* 24(4/5): 309–13. https://doi.org/10.1163/15700682-12341239

—, ed. 2015a. *Fabricating Origins.* Sheffield, UK: Equinox Publishers.

— 2015b. *A Modest Proposal on Method: Essaying the Study of Religion.* Leiden: Brill.

Miles, Jack, ed. 2015. *The Norton Anthology of World Religions.* 2 vols. New York: Norton.

Ramey, Steven W. 2015. "Accidental Favorites: The Implicit in the Study of Religion," in Monica Miller, ed., *Claiming Identity in the Study of Religion: Social and Rhetorical Techniques Examined* (pp. 223–37). Sheffield, UK: Equinox Publishers.

Zoloth, Laurie. 2016. "2014 AAR Presidential Address: Interrupting Your Life: An Ethics for the Coming Storm." *Journal of the American Academy of Religion* 84(1): 3–24. https://doi.org/10.1093/jaarel/lfv093

Russell T. McCutcheon is University Research Professor and Chair of the Department of Religious Studies at the University of Alabama. He has written widely on the history of the field and the tools scholars use to define and study religion. His 2005 book, *Religion and the Domestication of Dissent*, specifically focused on the discourse on Islam among contemporary scholars, politicians and the media. Most recent are two collections of his essays, *"Religion" in Theory and in Practice: Demystifying the Field for Burgeoning Academics* (Equinox) and *Fabricating Religion: Fanfare for the Common e.g.* (Walter de Gruyter) (both 2018).

Index

Adorno, Theodor W., 19
Ali, Kecia, 6, 8, 164
Althusser, Louis, 219
American Academy of Religion (AAR), 5, 6, 7, 8, 13, 127–8, 134, 140–1, 157–9, 162, 169–71, 206, 211, 215–16, 220
Anderson, Benedict, 210
Arendt, Hannah, 19, 26, 31
Armstrong, Karen, 134, 159–60
Asad, Talal, 25, 33–4, 38
Aslan, Reza, 159–60
Association for Jewish Studies, 124, 130

Bakhtin, Mikhail, 195
Barthes, Roland, 2, 218
Bauer, Karen, 164
Bayart, Jean-Francois, 210
Bazzano, Elliott, 212, 215
Berg, Herbert, 10
Biale, David, 208
biospolitikos, 26
Bird, Thomas, 131–3
Boko Haram, 4
Bourdieu, Pierre, 210
Bowersock, G.W., 176
Braiterman Zak, 121, 122
Breivik, Andres, 52
Brockopp, Jonathan, 207, 217–19
Brown, Jonathan, 6, 8
Bulletin for the Study of Religion, 1, 8, 9, 10, 15
Butler, Judith, 26

Caeiro, Alexandre, 10, 11, 69
Campus Watch, 3, 56
Carlyle, Thomas, 75

Chabbi, Jacqueline, 82
Christian origins, 12
Cold War, 126
Cook, Michael, 172–4, 209
Cornell, Vincent, 165
Corpus Coranicum, 79
Critical Muslim Studies, 62, 63, 64
Crone, Patricia, 72, 172–5, 183, 209
Crossley, James, 8, 9, 10, 12–13, 102, 125, 138, 208
Culture on the Edge, 4, 9, 13
Cunningham, Lawrence, 208
Curtis, Edward E., 9

decolonization, 47, 64
Denny, Frederick, 39
Derrida, Jacques, 23, 37, 161, 195
Dome of the Rock, 102, 104–5, 107, 115
Donner, Fred, 74, 81, 84, 179
Duke University's Islamic Studies Center Forum, 3

Eliade, Mircea, 24, 212
Elliott, Scott, 32
Enlightenment, 11, 37–8, 46, 60, 69, 72–3, 81
Ernst, Carl, 19, 71, 73, 128, 158, 165–9
Esposito, John, 163
Eurocentrism, 59, 60, 64, 89

Fahd, Toufic, 177
Finnegan, Eleanor, 9
Firestone, Reuven, 179
Foucault, Michel, 25, 33–4, 37–8, 49, 52, 81, 161, 218
Fowden Garth, 176
Freidenreich, David, 6–7

Gadamer, Hans-Georg, 28–9
Gade, Anna, 211, 214, 220
Gasché, Rodolphe, 23, 26–8
Goffman, Erving, 194
Goldziher, Ignaz, 172, 199
Gramsci, Antonio, 49
Grewal, Zareena, 211–12, 215–17, 220

Habermas, Jürgen, 15
Hall, Stuart, 11, 19, 45, 55
Hammer, Juliane, 9, 14, 205, 211–12, 215, 217
Hardt, Michael, 43, 49
Hawting, Gerald, 174
Heidegger, Martin, 26
Heilman, Samuel, 131–3
Hodgson, Marshal, 52, 185
Hoyland, Robert, 103–5
Hughes, Aaron W., 1–14, 19, 43–5, 47–8, 50, 53, 59–61, 64, 98–100, 121, 122, 138–42, 145, 149, 152, 157–9, 161–5, 169–77, 181–8, 194, 199, 206–7, 209–12, 215, 217–18, 220
Hussain, Amir, 32
Hymes, Dell, 195

identity formation, 4
identity politics, 44, 61, 98
Imhoff, Sarah, 8, 9, 10, 12, 121
International Qur'anic Studies Association, 79, 80, 102, 134
interpellation, 31, 219
ISIS, 4
Islamophobia, 48

Jackson, Sherman, 6, 8
Jadaliyya, 1
Jihad Watch, 56
Jones, Robert, 201–3
Josephson, Jason, 210
Journal of the American Academy of Religion, 14, 205–6, 211, 213–15, 217, 220, 221
Journal of Qur'anic Studies, 87

Kant, Immanuel, 37, 38, 81
Kassam, Tazim, 32
Kelsay, John, 10
Kister, M.J., 198
Koselleck, Reinhart, 83

Lewis, Bernard, 134
Lewis, Thomas, 213–14
Lincoln, Bruce, 186, 191, 210
Luxenberg, Christoph, 73, 108, 114, 170
Lyotard, Jean–Francois, 37

Mahmood, Saba, 77, 86
Makdisi, George, 185
Martin, Richard C., 6, 10, 71, 73, 128, 158
Marty, Martin, 199
Marx, Karl, 34, 35, 49, 144, 212
Mas, Ruth, 8, 9, 10, 19
Massignon, Louis, 135, 198
Masuzawa, Tomoko, 62, 70
Mattson, Ingrid, 6, 8
McAuliffe, Jane, 85, 88, 207, 209
McCutcheon, Russell T., 13, 14, 19, 126, 130, 138, 201
Method & Theory in the Study of Religion (MTSR), 10, 19, 206–7, 211
Middle East Forum, 3
Moral Majority, 204
Murphy, Tim, 2, 14
Muslim Identities, 159–60, 182–3, 209, 218
Muslimistan, 44, 56, 58

Negri, Antonio, 43
Neuwirth, Angelika, 79, 85, 87, 89
New Atheism, 140
Newby, Gordon, 176
Nietzsche, Friedrich, 37
Nöldeke, Theodor, 180–1, 199
North American Association for the Study of Religion (NAASR), 148

Oakshott, Michael, 74, 83

Obama, Barack, 54
Orientalism, 11, 12, 44, 45, 47–55, 57–62, 64, 70, 71–2, 77, 89, 91, 100, 128–9,133–4, 140, 198

phronesis, 26
Plato, 26
Planned Parenthood, 201
post-colonialism, 99, 206
post-secular, 69
praxis, 26–8, 145

Qur'anic Studies, 11, 69, 71, 79–86, 88, 90–1, 173, 181

Rabat, Nasser, 169
Rabaté, Jean-Michel, 23, 26
Rahman, Fazlur, 74, 84
Ramadan, Tariq, 163
Ramey, Steven, 207
Reynolds, Gabriel Said, 101
Rippen, Andrew, 10, 78, 81, 84–7, 89
Robinson, Chase, 72
Rodinson, Maxime, 77
Rosen, Lawrence, 197

Safi, Omid, 2, 3, 5–11, 13, 15, 19, 43–5, 47, 53, 59, 60–1, 64, 98–100, 138–40, 160
Saleh, Walid, 164
Said, Edward, 5, 8, 44–5, 48, 50–2, 55, 58, 70–2, 77, 129, 134, 138, 185
Sayyid, Salman, 10, 11, 43
Schalin, Jay, 3, 15
Schmitt, James, 37
Schubel, Vernon, 8, 9
Schweitzer, Albert, 138, 141–2
Scott, David, 33
Scott, James, 194
secularism, 11, 37, 69, 70
Segovia, Carlos A., 10, 12, 98

September 11, 2001 38, 44–5, 69, 71, 76, 79, 81, 86, 90, 139–40
Sezgin, Faut, 171–2, 196
Shahid, Irfan, 176
Sheedy, Matt, 1, 15, 32
Smith, Jonathan Z., 191
Smith, Wilfred Cantwell, 72, 201
Society of Biblical Literature, 102, 147
Stefanidis, Emmanuelle, 10, 11, 69
Stetkevytch, Jaroslav, 177
Stewart, Devin, 9, 10, 13, 157, 201, 205, 221
Stoneham, Carl, 8, 13, 15, 138, 140–2, 145, 149, 152

Tea Party movement, 54–5
theoria, 26–8
Theorizing Islam, 157–8, 160, 171, 180–1, 186, 196
Tite, Philip, 9, 15, 144
Trump, Donald, 201–4

University of Rochester, 3

Van Ess, Josef, 172

Wadud, Amina, 6, 8
Wansbrough, John, 73–4, 173–5, 209
Watt, Montgomery, 75, 83, 177
Weber, Max, 21, 31, 33, 35
Weil, Gustav, 180–1
Weitzman, Steven P., 29–31
Wellhausen, Julius, 177
White, Hayden, 74
Wikipedia, 1, 15
Wissenschaft, 8,12, 123–5, 128, 132–3, 135–6
Wittgenstein, Ludwig, 49, 50
Wright, N.T., 139, 141, 145–6

Zionism, 56, 57

www.ingramcontent.com/pod-product-compliance
Lightning Source LLC
Chambersburg PA
CBHW051056230426
43667CB00013B/2328